$\mathscr{P}$RINCE EDDY AND THE HOMOSEXUAL UNDERWORLD

THEO ARONSON

This edition published in 2013 by:
Thistle Publishing
36 Great Smith Street
London
SW1P 3BU
ISBN13: 978-1-909609-19-8

For
Aedwyn Darroll

$\mathscr{C}$ONTENTS

	Illustrations	*vii*
	Author's Note	*ix*
Prologue:	The Mystery Prince	xi

Part One: CITY OF THE PLAIN

1.	'The lad that's lettered GPO'	3
2.	'Apples of Sodom'	13

Part Two: BORN TO BE KING

3.	Motherdear's Boy	31
4.	'A carefully brought-up boy'	42
5.	The Student Prince	53
6.	The Chocolate Soldier	68

Part Three: JACK THE RIPPER

7.	Royal Jack	103
8.	Ripping for the Prince	112
9.	Kings and Queens	124

Part Four: THE SCANDAL

10. 'My Lord Gomorrah'   139
11. 'The whole terrible affair'   153
12. 'I never mentioned the boy's name'   167

Part Five: DUKE OF CLARENCE
13. 'The greatest position there is'   185
14. The Death and the Legend   203

Epilogue: The Warrior's Tomb   220
            Notes   *222*

$\mathcal{I}$LLUSTRATIONS

1. Prince Albert Victor (Eddy), Duke of Clarence and Avondale
2. Three of the boys involved in the homosexual brothel case
3. The Cleveland Street brothel
4. Charles Hammond, the brothel-keeper
5. Lord Arthur Somerset
6. A male prostitute, in drag
7. The Prince and Princess of Wales with Prince Eddy and Prince George dressed as girls
8. Prince Eddy and Prince George during their visit to Australia
9. The Prince of Wales
10. Alexandra, Princess of Wales
11. The Wales family in the early 1880s
12. Prince Eddy during his first year at Cambridge
13. Jim Stephen, the Prince's Cambridge mentor
14. Prince Eddy at the time of the Jack the Ripper murders
15. The Prince during his tour of India
16. A policeman taking statements from the telegraph boys
17. An artist's impression of a pimp at the time of the Cleveland Street Scandal
18. Five of the boys involved in the brothel case
19. The newly created Duke of Clarence and Avondale
20. Princess Hélène d'Orléans

21. Princess May of Teck

22. An artist's depiction of 'a nation's calamity'

23. Sir Alfred Gilbert's monument to Prince Eddy at Windsor

Plates 1, 8, 9, 10, 11, 12, 14, 19, 21, 22 and 23, Author's Collection; 2, 3, 4, 5, 6, 16, 17 and 18, *The Illustrated Police News*; 7, The Royal Archives © Her Majesty the Queen; 13, from J.K. Stephen, *Lapsus Calami*; 15, J.D. Reese, *The Duke of Clarence and Avondale in Southern India*; 20, Hugo Vickers.

$\mathcal{A}$UTHOR'S NOTE

I have not set out to write a conventional biography of Prince Albert Victor, Duke of Clarence and Avondale. The destruction of all his papers (for reasons which will become apparent on reading this book) would, in any case, have made this impossible. Rather, I have explored the central mystery of his life: his sexual orientation. For the Prince's name has been linked to one of the greatest sexual scandals of the period. The uncovering of a homosexual brothel in London's Cleveland Street led, in turn, to an extraordinary cover-up on the part of the government; a cover-up which is explicable only in the light of the Prince's involvement in the scandal.

At the same time, and in order to put the affair into perspective, I have painted a picture of the active and colourful homosexual underworld during the last decades of the reign of the Prince's grandmother, Queen Victoria.

I am indebted to three main original sources for my material. They are the files of the Director of Public Prosecutions at the Public Record Office, Chancery Lane; the Home Office files at the Public Record Office, Kew; and the Esher papers held at the Archives Centre, Churchill College, Cambridge. I have also been able to consult those two privately printed and circulated studies of the Victorian homosexual underworld held in the British Library: *The Sins of the Cities of the Plain* by Jack Saul and *The*

Intersexes by Edward I. Stevenson, writing as 'Xavier Mayne'. For help, to a greater or lesser extent, I must thank, in alphabetical order, Myrtle V. Cooper of the Archives Department, Metropolitan Police Service; Aedwyn Darroll; Alex Hooper of the Falmouth Art Gallery; R.R. Milne, Sub-Librarian of Trinity College Library, Cambridge; Stephen Mitchell; S.G. Roberts of the Royal Commission on Historical Manuscripts; Barry Rose of the *Criminologist*; Martin Taylor of the Churchill Archives Centre, Churchill College, Cambridge; Hugo Vickers; A. Williams of the Public Record Office; Colin Wilson. I am grateful to the staffs of the Public Record Office at Chancery Lane and Kew, the British Library and the Newspaper Library at Colindale, the Bristol Reference Library, the Bath Reference Library and, most particularly, the Frome Library. Two books that have proved useful are *The Cleveland Street Affair* by Lewis Chester, David Leitch and Colin Simpson, and *The Cleveland Street Scandal* by H. Montgomery Hyde.

As always, my greatest debt is to Brian Roberts for his unfailing interest and support.

$\mathcal{P}$ROLOGUE
THE MYSTERY PRINCE

in November 1970 an article in a relatively obscure British journal unleashed a flood of international speculation. The article concerned the notorious Victorian mass-murderer, 'Jack the Ripper'. Writing in the *Criminologist*, a Dr T.E.A. Stowell claimed to know the Ripper's identity. Although there has never been any shortage of Ripper suspects, what made Stowell's claim especially remarkable was the status of his subject. Without actually giving a name, he supplied enough information to make his candidate's identity abundantly clear. It was none other than Queen Victoria's grandson, Prince Albert Victor, Duke of Clarence and Avondale. As Heir Presumptive to the British throne and future King-Emperor, the Prince had been destined to occupy what the Queen blandly described as 'the greatest position there is'.[1]

The eighty-five-year-old Dr Stowell had been convinced of Prince Albert Victor's guilt for over half a century. He had kept the evidence to himself, he said, 'for fear of involving, as witnesses, some close friends who had still been alive'.[2] But ten years before, in 1960, Stowell had discussed his theory with the writer, Colin Wilson. The two had met, on Stowell's suggestion, after Wilson had written a series of articles on Jack the Ripper. Over lunch, Stowell had told Colin Wilson that he was convinced that Prince Albert Victor – always known in the royal family as Eddy – had been the Ripper. The murders had been committed during fits of insanity brought on by the Prince's syphilis; indeed his death, at the age of twenty-eight in 1892, had been due not, as was generally believed, to pneumonia but to a syphilitic 'softening of the brain'. This information came, Stowell assured Wilson, from his reading of the private papers of Queen Victoria's physician, Sir William Gull.

In his twelve-page article 'Jack the Ripper – A Solution?', published in the *Criminologist* in November 1970, Dr Stowell was less frank than he had been with Colin Wilson. Instead of referring to Prince Albert Victor by name, he called his suspect 'S'. Although Stowell is wrong on several minor points, there can be no doubt that 'S' was Prince Albert Victor.

Stowell's sensational insinuation – that Jack the Ripper had been Queen Victoria's grandson, the great-uncle of Queen Elizabeth II – was eagerly taken up by press, radio and television. But at this point Stowell began to back-track. Interviewed on television, he refused to confirm or deny that the Prince had been the Ripper. On 4 November an entry in *The Times* Diary claimed that Buckingham Palace regarded this 'mischievous calumny' as 'too ridiculous for comment'. It went on to quote evidence from 'a loyalist on the staff of Buckingham Palace' which proved that the Prince had been in Scotland at the time of two of the murders.[3]

Apparently taking fright, Stowell promptly wrote to *The Times* to deny that he had ever implied that Prince Albert Victor was the mass-murderer. He signed his letter as 'a loyalist and a royalist'.[4]

And then, on 8 November 1970 – by one of life's extraordinary twists – Dr Stowell suddenly died. Just over a week had passed since the publication of his theory. Stowell's son, Dr T. Eldon Stowell, interviewed by a clutch of reporters, claimed that all the papers on which his late father had based his extraordinary story had been destroyed immediately after his death. 'I read just enough to make certain that there was nothing of importance,' said Dr Stowell Jr. 'My family decided that this was the right thing to do. I am not prepared to discuss our grounds for doing so.'[5]

By then, however, the story had been taken up by the world's press. It has been estimated that over 3,000 newspapers and magazines carried reports of Stowell's dramatic unmasking of Prince Albert Victor. Suddenly photographs and descriptions of this long-forgotten figure appeared across the globe. The Prince certainly looked suspicious. With his hooded eyes, waxed moustache, elongated face and immaculate clothes, he exuded an odd, mysterious, faintly sinister air. Even allowing for the limitations of late Victorian photography, he had a curiously inanimate look; his gaze was impenetrable.

Although, for a variety of reasons, Stowell's theory was subsequently dismissed, rumours about the intriguing figure of Prince Albert Victor continued to spread. Indeed, they became progressively wilder. He was said to have been slow-witted to the point of imbecility. He had led an exceptionally dissipated life, having indulged in unmentionable vices. He had been homosexual. Secretly married, the Prince had fathered an illegitimate child. If he had not actually been Jack the Ripper, he had been closely connected with the murders. Kept for years under close supervision, Prince Albert Victor had died, not at Sandringham, but in a private mental home, from syphilis. He had been poisoned; his fingers and toes had turned suspiciously black after his death. Some claimed that he had not died in 1892 at all but had lived on, locked away in a castle like some latter-day Man in the Iron Mask, until 1933. The fact that all documentation about his life has been destroyed – that, in the discreet phraseology of the Royal Archives, 'his file has not survived'[6] – merely adds weight to these theories. It renders him even more enigmatic.

Out of this welter of rumour, conjecture, claim and counter-claim about the life of Prince Albert Victor, there emerges one accusation that cannot be dismissed. There is one story that remains unchallenged; one mystery that is left unsolved. This is the Prince's alleged involvement, not in the Ripper murders, but in another Victorian *cause célèbre* – the notorious homosexual brothel case known as the Cleveland Street scandal.

PART ONE
CITY OF THE PLAIN

1. 'THE LAD THAT'S LETTERED GPO'

The Victorians were enthusiastic senders of telegrams: it was such a wonderfully quick and easy way of communicating. 'Telegraphed from lunch till teatime,' reported the ebullient Duchess of Teck, mother of the future Queen Mary, one day in 1880.[1] When Queen Victoria celebrated her Diamond Jubilee, it was suggested that each of her 372 million subjects should send her a telegram of congratulation. Fortunately, the suggestion was never taken up.

Telegraphing was particularly popular among certain homosexuals. This popularity had nothing to do with speed or convenience; it was in the messenger rather than in the message that they were interested. To them, telegraph boys proved a source of irresistible attraction. These cheeky lads in their tight blue uniforms and jauntily angled caps were welcomed – quite literally in some cases – with open arms. To one besotted writer they were 'the aristocracy of the messenger world'; to another, they were 'young modern Mercuries'[2]. Lord Alfred Douglas, Oscar Wilde's companion, was involved with a telegraph boy at Oxford. His namesake, Sholto Douglas, co-translator of a collection of poems on boy-love, coveted a telegraph boy named George Browning. John Gambril Nicholson, one of the leading 'Uranian' poets of the period, claimed that chief among the many 'smart-looking lads' that he admired was 'the lad that's lettered GPO'.[3]

The boys themselves never seemed to mind the frequency with which they were obliged to deliver yet another unnecessary telegram from one gentleman to another. 'For one week the numbers of telegraph and messenger boys who came to the door was simply scandalous,' wrote the well-known illustrator Aubrey Beardsley to a friend.[4] The lads were apparently quite ready to subject themselves to what they called 'spooning' with some heavily bewhiskered 'toff' in his study. This could range from having one's hair ruffled to being masturbated or fellated. There were harder ways, in Victorian London, of earning a couple of shillings.

The hub of this telegraphic activity was the Central Telegraph Office situated in the General Post Office West, an imposing, red-brick, Victorian-Gothic pile in St Martin's-le-Grand in the City of London. So it was altogether appropriate that it should have been here that one of the greatest homosexual scandals of the period had its origins. It all started with the questioning of a fifteen-year-old telegraph messenger boy named Charles Swinscow. On 4 July 1889, young Swinscow was summoned to the office of a senior Post Office official. Here he was questioned by Police Constable Luke Hanks, a retired policeman now attached to the Post Office. There had recently been a theft of a sum of money from the Receiver General's Department, said Hanks; could Swinscow explain how he had been seen with as much as eighteen shillings in his possession? For a boy who earned only a few shillings a week, this was a considerable sum.

'I did not have so much as that,' said the boy, 'but I had fourteen shillings.'

'Where did you get it?' asked Hanks.

'I got it from doing some private work away from the office.'

'For whom?'

'For a gentleman named Hammond.'

'Where does he live?'

'19 Cleveland Street.'

'What did you do for him?'

'Will I get into trouble if I tell you?' asked the lad.

'I cannot say.'

'Must I tell you?'

'Certainly.'

'I will tell you the truth,' said Swinscow. 'I got the money from Mr Hammond for going to bed with gentlemen at his house.'

At this point PC Hanks lost all interest in the theft of money and switched his attention to the far more interesting story which Swinscow had to tell.

Not long after Swinscow had joined the Post Office service he had been approached by a fellow employee, a boy with the appropriate name of Henry Newlove. Newlove had persuaded Swinscow to accompany him into a cubicle in the basement lavatory. The boys had then, as PC Hanks noted in his painstaking police phraseology, 'behaved indecently together'. This indecent behaviour had taken place on several more occasions during the course of the next few days and, at the end of a week, Newlove asked Swinscow if he would like to earn four shillings by going to bed with a gentleman in a house in Cleveland Street. Initially hesitant, Swinscow was talked round and the two boys went to 19 Cleveland Street.

Here the proprietor – the balding, heavily moustached and business-like Charles Hammond – assured young Swinscow that he was delighted that he had been able to come and immediately introduced him to a waiting 'gentleman'. The boy was then taken by the man into the back parlour where there was a bed. 'We both undressed and being quite naked got into bed. He put his person between my legs and an emission took place.' After half an hour they got up and the man gave Swinscow a sovereign. This he handed over to Hammond who gave him back four shillings. Swinscow subsequently visited the house again where he had sex with 'another gentleman'.

Pressed by PC Hanks, Swinscow admitted that he knew of at least two more postal employees who had visited the Cleveland Street house. Hanks sent for the first of these, a seventeen-year-old youth named George Wright. Wright, too, had been recruited by the diligent Newlove. As before, Newlove had inveigled Wright into the basement lavatory where 'more than once, Newlove put his person into me, that is to say behind, only a little way, and something came from him'.

Having been thus satisfactorily broken in, Wright was taken by Newlove to Cleveland Street. Here, he explained to the doggedly recording PC Hanks, 'another gentleman came in whom I should know again, I think a rather foreign-looking chap. I went with the latter into a bedroom, on the same floor and we both undressed and we got into the bed quite naked. He told me to suck him. I did so. He then had a go between my legs and that was all. He gave me half a sovereign which I gave to the landlord who gave me four shillings.'

The industrious Newlove then asked Wright if he knew of 'another nice little boy', younger and shorter than himself, who might be interested in earning four shillings. Wright did indeed. He suggested a friend with another of those wonderfully apposite names, Charles Thickbroom. Thickbroom, too, became a willing partner in Newlove's tireless excursions to the basement lavatory although, as Newlove ruefully admitted to Wright, his attempts to get his 'person into Thickbroom's hinder-parts' proved unsuccessful, no matter how hard or how often he tried. Nevertheless, Thickbroom was duly taken to Cleveland Street. Here, luckily, there was no putting in of persons by the gentlemen; merely 'playing with each other'.

All three boys were very anxious to make clear to PC Hanks that they had been wearing their own clothes at the time of their visits to Cleveland Street. In this way they hoped to prove that, neither literally nor figuratively, had they defiled the uniform of the Royal Mail. Even in the basement lavatory, claimed one of them, he had not actually been *wearing* his uniform: he had taken off his jacket and his trousers had been round his ankles.

Armed with the statements from the three boys (and there were to be three more), PC Hanks sent for their procurer, Newlove. Newlove admitted everything. All four boys were suspended from duty and sent home. When, the following morning, the affair was reported to the Postmaster General, he immediately contacted the Metropolitan Police Commissioner. The Commissioner, in turn, instructed Chief Inspector Frederick Abberline of the CID to take charge of the case. Abberline applied for warrants for the arrest of the proprietor Hammond and his accomplice Newlove on the charge of inciting and procuring 'divers persons to commit the abominable crime of buggery against the peace of Her Majesty the Queen'.

When Inspector Abberline arrived at 19 Cleveland Street the following morning to arrest Charles Hammond, he found the house empty. Hammond, having been warned the day before by Newlove, had lost no time in packing 'a black portmanteau' and clearing out. His parting advice to Newlove was 'to stoutly deny everything'. With Hammond had gone a man dressed as a clergyman. This was his partner, George Veck, who always passed himself off as the Reverend G.D. Veck. Veck was another of that apparently inexhaustible fund of Post Office employees. He had been dismissed from the service for 'improper conduct' with telegraph messengers and was at present living with a seventeen-year-old lad whom he passed off as his son.

Foiled by Hammond's escape, Inspector Abberline hurried round to Newlove's mother's house in Camden Town. Here he arrested Newlove.

'I think it is hard that I should get into trouble while men in high positions are allowed to walk about free,' grumbled Newlove to Abberline as they made their way to the police station.

'What do you mean?' asked the detective.

'Why,' explained Newlove, 'Lord Arthur Somerset goes regularly to the house in Cleveland Street, so does the Earl of Euston and Colonel Jervois.'[5]

With this piece of information, the entire complexion of the enquiry changed. Abberline realized that he had uncovered a potentially explosive scandal. Both the Earl of Euston and Colonel Jervois were prominent figures, while Lord Arthur Somerset was a very important person indeed. The third son of the 8th Duke of Beaufort, he was not only a major in the Royal Horse Guards (The Blues) but also Superintendent of the Stables and Extra Equerry to the Prince of Wales. Thirty-seven years old, 'Podge' Somerset was generally regarded as the very epitome of virile masculinity: an accomplished sportsman, an experienced soldier, an authority on horses and a member of the Prince of Wales's intimate circle. He was, read his pen-portrait in *Vanity Fair*, 'very favourably regarded by the fair sex'.[6] This favourable regard was not, it was now realized, reciprocated.

Indeed, Lord Arthur Somerset's patronage of the Cleveland Street homosexual brothel was to reopen to view a world which the authorities had naïvely imagined they had only just legislated out of existence.

Almost thirty years before, in 1861, the death penalty for buggery had been abolished. It had been in force for over three centuries, having been introduced in 1533, during the reign of King Henry VIII. As the Buggery Act had been largely symbolic – a means by which Henry VIII was able to establish the supremacy of the secular over the ecclesiastical courts – it had seldom been enforced. Nor had it applied only to one man sodomizing another: it had encompassed also the buggering of women or animals. In the main, sodomy was regarded as a sin rather than a crime, and the enforcement of the law varied in accordance with the moral climate of each period. Sexual acts between men, in an age when the poor were often obliged to share beds or when a master felt he had the right to bugger his servant, were common. Sodomy was seen more as a sign of debauchery or, in a gentleman, of a jaded sexual appetite, than as one of homosexuality.

Convictions were difficult to obtain, particularly after 1781 when penetration and the 'emission of seed' had to be proved. Indeed, in the curious belief that this somehow made the act less reprehensible, defendants were always anxious to deny that there had been any emission. 'He forcibly entered my Body about an Inch, as near as I can guess,' testified one earnest witness, 'but in struggling, I threw him off once more, before he had made an Emission, and having thus forced him to withdraw, he emitted in his own Hand, and clapping it on the Tail of my Shirt, said *Now you have it!*'[7] Sentences for acts of buggery, or attempted buggery, ranged from hanging to fines, imprisonment or a spell in the pillory.

The abolition of the death penalty for buggery in 1861 was replaced by penal servitude of between ten years and life. However, this abolition did not introduce a more enlightened attitude towards what were described as 'unnatural practices' – a term covering all sexual acts between men, and not only buggery. For the 1861 act happened to be followed by a spectacular growth of Victorian middle-class puritanism.

A powerful religious revival, laying stress on such things as the sanctity of family life, the virtues of conventional behaviour, the repression of sins of the flesh, even the upholding of Britain's imperial mission, created a climate increasingly hostile to all manifestations of sexual and social unorthodoxy, especially homosexuality.

These attitudes were reinforced by a parallel growth of what the horrified middle classes regarded as upper-class debauchery. That personification of middle-class morality, Queen Victoria, was constantly railing against the depravity of the aristocracy. 'The frivolity, the love of pleasure, self-indulgence and idleness of the Higher Classes' were deplorable, she exclaimed.[8] Prostitution, of all sorts, flourished. To the moral crusaders it was male lust – whether manifesting itself in sex with prostitutes or with other men – that was the prime cause of this lowering of standards. Indeed, to them, homosexuality was synonymous with prostitution: both were products of man's selfish search for sexual gratification.

A series of scandals served to illustrate, only too vividly, the spread of this unbridled sexuality. In 1871 two transvestites, Ernest Boulton and Frederick Parke, always known as Stella and Fanny, were tried on the vague charge of 'conspiracy to commit a felony'. They had been arrested – Stella in a low-cut dress of scarlet satin and Fanny in dark blue trimmed with black lace – outside the Strand Theatre. Their case received enormous publicity. The public was able to be gratifyingly shocked by details of their shameless way of life. There were Stella's love letters to Lord Arthur Pelham Clinton, third son of the Duke of Newcastle, to which Fanny would add messages signed 'your affectionate sister-in-law'. There were the photograph albums of Mr John Stafford Fiske, the American Consul in Edinburgh, in which were pasted photographs of Stella in lavish dresses, including one in which 'she' was posed 'in an attitude of prayer'.[9] The public was able to hear about their dresses, petticoats, hats, chignons, stockings, curling-irons, gloves, boxes of powder and bottles of scent; and about their visits, in full drag on the arms of assorted aristocratic admirers, to theatres, restaurants, race-meetings and even the Oxford and Cambridge boat race.

The fact that their acquittal was greeted by loud cheers (Stella fainted away on hearing it) did nothing to reassure those who saw the case as yet another symptom of society's rapid disintegration.

By the early 1880s, such evidences of moral decay were coming thick and fast. In 1884 Mrs Jeffries, a notorious supplier of prepubescent girls who was proud to number, among her many illustrious clients, King Leopold II of the Belgians, was tried and acquitted. In that same year Dublin Castle, seat of the British Government in Ireland, was the scene of a major homosexual scandal. A homosexual ring which 'for its extent and atrocity, almost staggered belief' was uncovered. 'It included men of all ranks, classes, professions and outlawries, from aristocrats of the highest fashion to outcasts in the most loathsome dens.'[10] The three principal aristocrats were all senior members of the British administration. Together with no less than seven other defendants, they were arrested and tried. Evidence of their 'felonies' – some of it given by unemployed labourers and illiterate navvies – included visits to a male brothel in Golden Lane, near the River Liffey. Sentences varied from acquittal to twenty years' imprisonment. One Dublin wit afterwards suggested that Queen Victoria award the Lord Lieutenant, Earl Spencer, a new title – 'Duke of Sodom and Gomorrah'.

The Dublin trial was followed, the next year, by that of W.T. Stead for criminal abduction. William Thomas Stead was one of the great crusading journalists of the late Victorian age. Bushily bearded and burning-eyed, this son of a Congregational minister brought to his journalism a powerful blend of moral indignation and sensationalism. One of his most celebrated journalistic exposés was the series of astounding articles entitled 'The Maiden Tribute to Modern Babylon' which he wrote for the *Pall Mall Gazette* in 1885. In it he attacked the evils of child prostitution. Girls as young as eight or nine were readily available, and with virgins (or what were passed off as virgins) being highly prized, these young girls were in great demand. The widely held belief that the taking of a girl's virginity could cure venereal disease made them even more sought-after.

Determined to expose this evil, Stead bought a thirteen-year-old girl. His accounts of this transaction, and of the sordid world in which this trade flourished, ran for weeks in the *Pall Mall Gazette*. But instead of being generally applauded, Stead's investigative journalism was deplored by many middle-class puritans. They were apparently far more shocked by the publishing of the articles than by the circumstances which had led to their being written. On the grounds that Stead had not secured the consent of the girl's father when buying her (and regardless of the fact that the incident had been stage-managed and that Stead had no intention of having sex with the girl) he was charged with criminal abduction and sent to jail for two months.

But in circles where it mattered, Stead's crusade had its desired effect. It was welcomed by the agitators for social purity for its attack both on the elderly aristocratic rakes and on the precocious working-class girls whom they patronized. 'On the whole', decided the Reverend Randall Davidson, 'the good outweighs the evil. The wave of moral wrath and indignation which has been evoked will sweep things before it.'[11] Indeed, at a huge demonstration in Hyde Park against these various homosexual and prostitution scandals, speaker after speaker expressed the hope that public figures would set an example in moral purity. These various agitations led, in turn, to the passing of the famous Criminal Law Amendment Bill of 1885.

This Criminal Law Amendment Bill was originally designed 'to make further provision for the protection of women and girls, the suppression of brothels and other purposes'.[12] But after the bill had been given an unopposed second reading, an amendment was introduced by a Radical Member of Parliament, Henry Labouchere. In it he proposed that the issue of homosexuality be addressed as well: that *all* homosexual acts and not only sodomy – whether in private or in public – be made an offence.

Henry Labouchere, who was to play a prominent part in the Cleveland Street scandal, was a maverick figure. Although, like Stead, he was a tireless campaigner against government abuses and injustices, Labouchere had none of Stead's humourless Nonconformist altruism. His touch was altogether lighter, wittier, more satirical. A slightly built man, with 'the graces of a dancing master',[13] rich and well-educated, Labouchere had enjoyed a colourful career. He was never happier than when making mischief; his weekly journal, *Truth*, was forever being sued for libel.

Whether introduced in a provocative spirit or because of a deep-rooted dislike of homosexuality, Labouchere's amendment – the eleventh clause of the Criminal Law Amendment Act – was adopted. It has been argued that because the amendment was adopted, without due consideration, at the end of a long night's sitting, its full implications were not appreciated. True or not, the bill provided that

any male person who, in public or private, commits, or is party to the commission of, or procures or attempts to procure the commission by any male person of any act of gross indecency with another male person, shall be guilty of a misdemeanour, and being convicted thereof shall be liable at the discretion of the court to be imprisoned for any term not exceeding two years, with or without hard labour.[14]

In other words, the amendment criminalized *all* homosexual acts, leaving Britain as one of the few European countries in which even mutual masturbation by adult men in the privacy of their own homes was illegal. France, for instance, had decriminalized homosexual acts between consenting adults almost a century earlier.

The Labouchere amendment, sometimes known as the 'Blackmailer's Charter', led to the growth of hostility towards homosexuals and an increase in prosecutions. It remained on the statute books until 1967. One of the first, and most famous, of these prosecutions concerned the male brothel in Cleveland Street.

2. 'APPLES OF SODOM'

Although the Labouchere amendment of 1885 had made all homosexual acts illegal, it could not, of course, put an end to all homosexual activity; no amount of legislation could do that. But it did encourage the establishment of a more definite homosexual identity. The difference between homosexual acts – casual sex among men, some of whom might be regarded as heterosexual – and a consciously homosexual type, became more pronounced. By coincidence the word homosexual, which had not been coined until 1869 by a Hungarian named Benkert, came into general use in Britain during the 1880s. But it was not the only word to be used. The period saw a rash of bizarre, quasi-scientific descriptions of this newly conscious identity: homogenic love, contrasexuality, similisexualism, Uranism, even the third sex.

In some circles the word 'earnest' was a synonym for homosexual. 'Is he earnest?' became a familiar question. This gave the title of Oscar Wilde's play *The Importance of Being Earnest* not only a double, but a treble, meaning. To the initiated it had all the appeal of an in-joke.

As one in every twenty men is reckoned to be fully homosexual, there were homosexuals of every type in all levels of late Victorian society. Some were serious-minded pioneers in the crusade for an acceptance of their sexual orientation. Inspired by the poetry of the American, Walt Whitman, men like John Addington Symonds, with his dreams of manly companionship, and Edward Carpenter, with his theories of a socialist brotherhood, went so far as to proclaim the higher moral possibilities of homosexuality. More inhibited were literary figures such as the critic and essayist Edmund Gosse and that celebrated apostle of aestheticism,

Walter Pater. Other writers, like Oscar Wilde and a clutch of so-called Uranian poets, reflected an altogether lusher, more exotic world. Poems and articles, written anonymously and published in privately printed magazines, hinted at the ecstasies of illicit love. 'He loves strange sins avidly,' runs the prose translation of one turgid outpouring, in Latin, from a member of this group; 'he gathers strange flowers, fierce with beauty. The more dark his spirit the more radiant his face, false but splendid! The apples of Sodom are here and the very heart of vice and sweet sins ...'[1] Painters who followed the cult ranged from the fashionable Sir Frederick Leighton with his homo-erotic studies of Greek youths to Henry Scott Tuke with his paintings of naked fisherboys splashing in the Cornish seas.

In marked contrast to these quasi-Bohemian personalities were several leading imperial figures. For it was a curious fact that – in an age when the sanctity of family life was claimed to be allied to the civilizing mission of the British Empire, and when homosexuality was regarded as a manifestation of the decadence which had destroyed previous empires – many of the foremost imperialists were not only unmarried but also covert homosexuals. Cecil John Rhodes, the greatest empire builder of the day, was in love with, and willed his immense fortune to, a hearty young man named Neville Pickering. When Pickering died, Rhodes surrounded himself with a court of equally hearty young men. General Gordon, the period's most romantic soldier-martyr, was happiest in the company of boys. That other great military figure, Field Marshal Lord Kitchener, moved in a circle of handsome young officers whom he described as his 'happy band of boys'. He had a couple of favourites – first Frank Maxwell, whom he always called 'the Brat', and then Oswald FitzGerald, his aide-de-camp who, according to Kitchener's official biographer, 'established himself so securely in the affections of his chief that Kitchener never looked elsewhere'.[2]

Lord Baden-Powell, founder of the Boy Scout movement, had a favourite in Kenneth McLaren whom he referred to as 'the Boy' and when, relatively late in life, Baden-Powell felt obliged to get married, it was he, and not his wife, who suffered the headaches whenever sex was being contemplated. Even that great proconsul, Lord Curzon, Viceroy of India, whose suspect boyhood friendship with a master at Eton had led to the master's dismissal, developed the sort of violent antipathy towards homosexuality that is invariably the sign of a repressed homosexual.

As homosexuality was to be found in every section of society – in roistering aristocrats and furtive bank clerks, in tortured clergymen and cheerful navvies, in inhibited schoolteachers and shameless male prostitutes – it was difficult to categorize. Indeed, the great majority of men brought before the courts for homosexual offences in the nineteenth century were husbands and fathers.[3] As a result, and to a degree unusual in Victorian Britain, there was a considerable intermingling of the classes. The idealistic Edward Carpenter fondly imagined that love between men would lead to a breakdown of class divisions. J.A. Symonds cloaked his lust for strapping guardsmen and muscular peasants in a great deal of high-flown talk about a universal brotherhood. 'The blending of Social Strata in masculine love', he declared, 'abolishes class distinctions ... it would do very much to further the advent of the right kind of socialism.'[4]

Sometimes the dreams of such men might come true. Carpenter established a stable relationship with a young artisan called George Merrill. Symonds enjoyed long-standing affairs with first, a nineteen-year-old Swiss sledge-driver and then a Venetian gondolier. Edward FitzGerald, translator of the celebrated *Rubáiyát of Omar Khayyám*, spent much of his life with a giant Norfolk fisherman whom he described as looking 'every inch a King'.[5] E.M. Forster longed 'to love a strong young man of the lower classes and be loved by him and even hurt by him'.[6] 'The greater tolerance of the working class towards sexual deviation' was claimed to be 'in healthy contrast to middle-class inhibition and hypocrisy'.[7]

'There will be nothing surprising in this to those who have seen the humorous generosity, the unquestioning ease with which the unsophisticated young male in any country can respond to the aching introspective need of the intellectual,' wrote Rupert Croft-Cooke, who knew such situations very well. 'Never wavering in his ultimate desire for women, with nothing in the least extraneous in his nature, unspoilt by doubt, having no need to rationalize or probe into motive, or to look for explanation or defence, he can give himself with grace and cheerfulness, even with enthusiasm, and this is enchanting to a more tired and experienced partner. He finds no mystique in this and has no wordy hesitations or self-conscious restraints. There may be an element of sexuality in what he does, or one of gainfulness, but generally it is a bountiful careless instinct which leads often to happy and enduring relationships.'[8]

Idealists tended to be shocked by the cynical approach of men like Oscar Wilde and those members of Queen Victoria's Court, Roden Noel and Lord Ronald Gower, who unashamedly set out to seduce working-class youths for a night's pleasure. Wilde, as Croft-Cooke put it, 'never ceased to believe that he was a pioneer from another class, adventuring into dangerous places'. 'Feasting with panthers' was Wilde's way of describing these pleasurably dangerous excursions into the underworld.[9] Yet, curiously enough, if it was not socialism that drove such men into the arms of working-class youths, their very interest in them was regarded as proof of socialist tendencies. Oscar Wilde's critics were as shocked by his association with the lower classes as they were by the nature of that association. 'What enjoyment was it to you', asked the puzzled prosecuting counsel at the time of his trial, 'to entertain grooms and coachmen?'[10]

One of the chief centres of all this sexual activity was London. Then the world's largest city, the heart of the greatest empire ever known, it had a higher than average population of homosexuals. It was a city of ostentatious wealth and appalling poverty; a situation always conducive to the gratification of sexual lusts. In its foggy, gas-lit streets, noisy with the sound of horse-drawn traffic clashing over the cobbles, the predatory or even the desperate homosexual could usually find whatever he wanted: toffs in top hats, red-tunicked soldiers, bowler-hatted businessmen, whistling errand boys, muscular artisans, flamboyant male prostitutes.

As in any big city, there were recognized places in which to meet or pick up sexual partners. One Victorian guidebook, *The Yokel's Preceptor or More Sprees in London* — while ostensibly deploring the increase in the number of 'monsters in the shape of men, commonly designated *Margeries, Pooffs'* – went on to explain to the visitor exactly where such monsters were to be found. Charing Cross station was one such place; in the windows of several nearby bars were pasted notices warning the public to 'Beware of Sods!' They also congregated 'around the picture shops, and are known by their effeminate air, their fashionable dress etc. When they see what they imagine to be a chance, they place their fingers in a peculiar manner underneath the tails of their coat, and wag them about – their method of giving the office.'[11]

The parks, with their dense, shadowy trees, were favourite places for quick, anonymous encounters. One barrister, famous for securing acquittals for sexual offences in London's parks, complained bitterly that since the lighting in Hyde Park had been improved, he had lost more than £2,000 a year in fees. Public lavatories, too, made perfect locations for impersonal sex: the urinals at Victoria and South Kensington stations were especially notorious. The walls of the cubicles at the Marble Arch lavatories made lively reading: they were full of what Frederick Rolfe, the self-styled Baron Corvo, described as 'storiettes' – graphically written but often imaginary accounts of sexual adventures.

The building, during the latter half of the nineteenth century, of elaborate, iron-work public urinals, resembling the French *vespasienne*, created havens for homosexual activity. 'These small, unobtrusive urinals were, in many ways, the most important meeting places for homosexuals of all and every kind,' remembered one frequent user. 'Always open, usually unattended, and consisting of a small number of stalls, over the sides of which it was quite easy to spy and get a sight of one's neighbour's cock, they were ideally built for the gratification of the voyeur's sexual itch. Many homosexuals spent hours going from one of these places to the next, spying, feeling and indulging in all forms of homosexual pleasure ...

'Frequently there would be several men in these places and they would take turns to keep a watch out against anyone coming in suddenly and disturbing the remaining others while they gratified themselves ... This keeping "a watch out" was often very easy, as there were perforations in the iron walls of the urinal – which allowed the watcher to see anyone coming suddenly on the scene. And in some cases the "watching out" was even easier in the case of there being only one entrance to the place. They were generally so dimly lit that anyone coming in out of the more brightly lighted street was unable to see distinctly for a moment or two exactly what was happening, which would give the actors time to set themselves more or less to rights.'[12] The dense, 'pea-soup' fogs that were so characteristic of late Victorian London, afforded even more effective cover for such activities.

Regent Street, the Haymarket, the area lying between Leicester and Trafalgar squares were all well-known picking-up areas. The arches under the County Fire Office at Piccadilly Circus were especially rewarding. From any of these crowded, well-lit streets, one could, having made contact, slip into a dark alley or lane such as Brydges Place or Dove Mews. Theatres were always fruitful terrain: the Alhambra, the Empire Music Hall, the London Pavilion and the bar of the St James's were all recognized meeting-places. A skating rink in Kensington was very popular. There were numerous pubs and clubs, the most famous bars being the Crown in Charing Cross Road, the Windsor Castle in the Strand and the Packenham in Knightsbridge.

The most celebrated club was undoubtedly the Hundred Guineas Club off Portland Place. This was a lavishly appointed establishment, part-brothel, part-club, where some members and their guests assumed not only women's names but also women's clothes. The sight of those moustachioed and bewhiskered men decked out in the sumptuously swagged and bustled dresses of the 1880s must have been a singular one. Appropriately named – for the subscription was one hundred guineas, well over £3,000 by today's reckoning – the club was managed by the equally appropriately named Mr Inslip. Here, in the long drawing-room, all gilt, plush and potted palms, the gentlemen could lounge on 'French' furniture, sipping champagne as they eyed members of the staff dressed in 'exquisite female attire'.

'For the evening, Fred,' explained Mr Inslip to a couple of new employees, 'your name is Isabel and yours, Mr Saul, is to be Evelyn.'

18

During the first half of the evening, things were very decorous – dancing, hand-holding, small-talk. But at 2 a.m. all the lights were put out; a ruse, claimed one old hand, to prevent any of the members from being disappointed. On no account, the staff were warned, were they to reject *any* advance. But, as it was impossible to see, it hardly mattered. 'Before time was called, about 6 a.m.' claimed one employee, 'I had had six different gentlemen, besides one of those dressed as a girl. We sucked, we frigged [masturbated] and gamahuched, and generally finished off by the orthodox buggery.' He was careful, he went on to explain, to appear at the club on only two evenings a week, 'for fear of getting used up too soon'.[13]

On another occasion, he was invited to a small private party in a house in Grosvenor Square. Present were an earl, three page-boys (one of whom was black) and 'three gentlemen whom the Earl assured us could be found in the pages of Debrett but preferred to be known by their sobriquets – Messrs Wire-In, Cold-Cream and Come-Again'. The evening ended with a playing of the 'Slap-Bum Polka'.[14]

Homosexual prostitution or 'renting' was widespread. In his study, *The Intersexes*, 'Xavier Mayne' – pseudonym of the American researcher, Edward I. Stevenson – claimed that, by the end of the nineteenth century, male prostitution was almost as prevalent as female. These male prostitutes ranged from the casual to the professional. There were young men who were satisfied with the odd expensive present; there were members of the armed forces, labourers, errand boys and stable lads who would occasionally prostitute themselves for a few shillings; and then there were the professionals who, having been known as 'Mollies' in the eighteenth century and 'Marjories' in the early nineteenth century, were by now usually referred to as 'Mary Annes'. When the average wage of an unskilled labourer was £1 a week and when a working man would do anything rather than face the disgrace of applying for public assistance in the 'workhouse', the chance to double one's weekly wage by allowing oneself to be fellated or to sodomize some 'toff', was to be welcomed.

By far the greatest number of part-time renters were soldiers. One had only 'to walk around London, around any English garrison centre, to stroll about Portsmouth, Aldershot, Southampton, Woolwich, large cities of North Britain and of Ireland,' wrote Xavier Mayne, 'to find the soldier prostitute in almost open self-marketing … On any evening, the street corners or the promenades of the big music-halls and the cheap theatres of London and other cities show one the fine flower of the British soldier prostitute, dressed in his best uniform, clean shaven, well groomed and handsome with his Anglo-Saxon pulchritude and vigour, smiling, expectant.'[15]

The increase in the size of the armed forces as the British Empire expanded, allied to low pay and the generally more relaxed attitude of the working class – from which the majority of the private soldiers were drawn – towards homosexuality, encouraged this spectacular growth. In their bright red tunics and pill-box caps, these soldiers proved an irresistible draw for wealthy homosexuals. One could hardly move among certain densely wooded areas of Hyde Park for soliciting guardsmen: 'their weapons', as one ageing queen fondly remembered half a century later, 'in their hands'.[16]

'When a young fellow joins,' explained one NCO, 'someone of us breaks him in and teaches him the trick; but there is little need of that, for it seems to come naturally to almost every young man, so few have escaped the demoralization of schools or crowded homes. We then have no difficulty in passing him on to some gentleman who always pays us liberally for getting a fresh young thing for him. Although of course we all do it for money, we also do it because we really like it, and if gentlemen gave us no money, we should do it all the same. Many of us are married, but that makes no difference [except that] we do not let the gentlemen know it, because married men are not in request.'[17]

Inevitably, snobbery played its part in these sexual activities. 'You can easily imagine it is not so agreeable to spend half an hour with a housemaid,' claimed one guardsman, 'when you have been caressed all night by a nobleman.'[18]

Tobacconist's shops, situated near military barracks, were recognized places of contact. If a customer handed over a ten-shilling note for a box of matches, the shopkeeper would know that what he really wanted was a soldier and would arrange an assignation. A dear old lady by the name of Mrs Truman, who ran a tobacconist's shop beside the cavalry barracks in Albany Street, did a very brisk trade. Indeed, her death affected the supply of soldiers to such an extent that several clubs had to be set up to make good the sudden dearth.

Soliciting by soldiers was often very bold. One night the twenty-four-year-old John Addington Symonds, at that stage still inhibited about his own sexuality, was walking from his club along a passageway between Trafalgar Square and Leicester Square. He was approached by a scarlet-uniformed guardsman. Quite openly, the soldier propositioned him. At first Symonds did not understand what he was suggesting; when he did, he hurried on. But the guardsman followed him, mentioning an address to which they could go. Tempted and horrified at the same time, Symonds fled, leaving the bemused soldier staring after him.

In time, Symonds overcame his inhibitions. Ten years after his flight from the soliciting guardsman, he accompanied a friend to a male brothel near the Regent's Park barracks. Here he spent the afternoon with a brawny young soldier – friendly, open and manly – who treated the episode as though it were the most natural thing in the world, and did not overcharge. After they had had sex, the two men sat happily together, chatting and smoking. The incident encouraged Symonds in his belief that it was quite possible for a homosexual to have a fulfilling sexual and emotional relationship with a heterosexual man.

In fact, these casual encounters often led to more lasting arrangements. 'I know two men in the Blues who are regularly kept by a gentleman,' said one soldier, 'and one has an allowance of two hundred a year for allowing himself to be sucked.'[19]

Edward Leeves, a rich dilettante who divided his time between Britain and Italy, fell passionately in love with a young guardsman in 'the gallant, rollicking, blaggard Blues'.[20] 'I saw you in all your beauty, smiling as your gallant charger reared and pranced ...' wrote Leeves.

'And then in the [sentry] box I spoke to you, and after Parade we met for five minutes and you told me your name.'[21] When, very suddenly, his young lover died, Leeves took up with another of those 'roistering Blues': 'a bold, audacious blackguard such as I like' and whose name, appropriately enough, was Screw.[22] Inevitably, Screw proved as unreliable as any of the breed: he lied, he borrowed money, he never answered letters, he decided to get married. But how stunning he had always looked, sighed Leeves, 'in his White Leathers'.

'Oh! the gallant Blues! Oh! the days that are passed!'[23]

Even bolder than the soldiers were the professional male prostitutes. They varied from fresh-faced boys not long up from the country to rouged and corseted queens well past their prime. Piccadilly and Piccadilly Circus were their favourite soliciting areas. 'Been up the Dilly lately, dear?'[24] their cries would ring out as perfectly respectable heterosexual men hurried by on their way home. Oscar Wilde, in the days before he had fully yielded to his own sexual preferences, once went shopping with his wife at Swan and Edgar's in Piccadilly Circus. 'Something clutched at my heart like ice,' he confessed, on seeing the painted boys lolling about on the pavement.[25]

Xavier Mayne gives a description of a typical encounter between what he calls a 'Uranian' and a male prostitute. 'Before a shop-window, or perhaps at a bench in a park, halts the Uranian. Soon another stroller, loitering in professional alertness, walks towards him – catches his eye expressively and stands or sits near him. The newcomer may be a boy of sixteen or eighteen, or much more an adult, good-looking or plain; likely not really well-dressed; and artificial aids [a padded crotch] improve his physique. He may have a certain *fausse élégance* – cheap jewellery and a gaudy cravat. A conversation is begun. Little by little it slips on towards confidentialities – the discomforts of living and travelling alone, the effects of the evening air, the quiet of the place, the amusements of the town. The talk grows distinctly erotic and the older man becomes surer that he has here one of the profession. Presently the Uranian, certain of his ground and well-enough suited with his interlocutor's physical type, proposes that they take a walk together ... they pause at the nearest latrine, by common consent, if the patron be especially disposed to estimate the physical capital of the other. If satisfied with the *étalage*, he accompanies the vendor to the nearest safe locality – a corner of a deserted thicket in the park, an open field, to an equivocal hotel, to the quarters of his new friend, perhaps to his own lodging ... The encounter over, the client pays the tariff agreed – five or ten shillings. Anon he says good-evening to his acquaintance, who he may or may not care ever to meet again. The incident is closed.'[26]

Sixteen-year-olds were often fully experienced prostitutes. A boy named Wilson, whose 'chestnut hair, dark blue eyes and a set of pearly teeth made him an almost irresistible bait to old gentlemen', once explained his hustling technique. 'Do you think I ever let those old fellows have me?' he scoffed. 'No fear, I know a game worth two of that. You see, I never bring them home with me, and in fact always affect the innocent – don't know where to go; am living with my father and mother at Greenwich or some out of the way part of London, and only came to the West End to look about the shops and see the swells. If a gentleman is very pressing I never consent to anything unless he asks me to accompany him to his house or chambers. Once got home with him I say: "Now sir what present are you going to make me?"

' "Stop a bit my boy 'til we see how you please me," or something very like that is the answer I generally get.

' "No: I'll have it now or I'll raise the house, you old sod. Do you think I'm a greenhorn? I want a fiver. Don't I know too well that little boys only get five or ten shillings after it's all over? But that won't do for me so shell out at once or there'll be a pretty good scandal." '[27]

A youth named George Brown was furious at being offered only £10 by his rich client. 'I could wipe my arse on that!' he protested. 'I mean to have a cool hundred; as I know it's nothing to you, who can swindle more than that any day in the City. Shall I call at your Cornhill Office for it on Monday, or will you give me an IOU?' Although the terrified client scribbled out an IOU, Brown demanded his rings as security until he collected the money the following day.[29]

Others employed even more threatening methods. A renter called Clifton would take clients back to his room 'where by arrangement two or three men are secreted under his bed, and just as they are performing, the men suddenly come out and bounce money out of him by threats.'[30]

From here it was a short step to blackmail. Not without good reason was the Criminal Law Amendment Bill known as the Blackmailer's Charter. Before its passing, social stigma was the worst thing to be feared by those accused of homosexual offences other than buggery; now they faced criminal prosecution. Two particularly successful blackmailers of the time were James Burton and Frederick Atkins. They operated as a team, with the older Burton claiming the teenaged Atkins as his nephew. They were known as Uncle Burton and Freddy.

The back of the circle of the Alhambra Theatre was Freddy's beat. Having made contact with some prosperous-looking, dress-suited gentleman, he would take him back to his rooms in Buckingham Palace Road or, better still, to a hotel room where clients were less likely to make a fuss. Here Freddy and his gentleman friend would be discovered *in flagrante delicto* by Freddy's ostensibly shocked uncle. Uncle Burton would demand a substantial sum of money in exchange for his silence and, having obtained the terrified client's address, would call at his place of work to extort further payment. Once an address was known, blackmail could continue indefinitely.

Even in remote Falmouth in Cornwall, then no more than a small town, a mother and her adolescent son conducted a successful blackmailing business. The boy would pass on the names and addresses of his lovers to his mother who would then arrive at their homes to demand payment for her silence. Her extortions apparently led to at least two suicides and only when one victim was brave enough to take her to court was a stop put to her distasteful practices. But the action ruined the poor victim.

One of London's most notorious prostitutes of the period was Jack Saul. His memoirs, clandestinely printed in a limited subscription edition, were entitled *The Sins of the Cities of the Plain, or the Recollections of a Mary-Anne*. Even allowing for some exaggeration, they give a vivid picture of the Victorian homosexual underworld. The book of memoirs was introduced and edited by a man calling himself 'Mr Cambon'. Cambon had first met Jack Saul, in 1874, in Leicester Square.

'He was dressed in tight-fitting clothes, which set off his Adonis-like figure to the best advantage, especially about what snobs call the fork of his trousers, where evidently he was endowed by nature with a very extraordinary development of male appendage,' wrote Cambon. 'He had small and elegant feet, set off by pretty patent leather boots, a fresh-looking beardless face, with almost feminine features, auburn hair, and sparkling blue eyes which told me that the handsome youth must indeed be one of the Mary-Annes of London ...

'That lump in his trousers had quite a fascinating effect upon me. Was it natural or made up by some artificial means? If real, what a size when excited; how I should like to handle such a manly jewel ...'

Having approached this young Adonis, Cambon suggested that they take a cab to his chambers in Cornwall Mansions, near Baker Street station.

'I see you are evidently a fast young chap and can put me up to a thing or two,' said Cambon.

'Put your thing up, I suppose you mean,' answered Saul, who apparently excelled at this sort of camp *double entendre*.

Emboldened by two bottles of champagne 'of an extra sec brand' and a couple of 'good warm glasses of brandy hot', Cambon suggested that as his guest seemed 'so evidently well hung' he would like to satisfy his curiosity about it. 'Is it real or made up for show?'

'As real as my face, Sir, and a good deal prettier,' quipped Saul, taking out 'a tremendous prick'. 'Did you ever see such a fine tosser in your life?'

Cambon had not. 'He had a priapus nearly ten inches long, very thick, and underhung by a most glorious pair of balls which were surrounded and set off by quite a profusion of light auburn curls. I hate to see balls hang loosely down, or even a fine prick with small or scarcely any stones to it – these half and half tools are an abomination ... "By Jove," I exclaimed.

' "It's my only fortune, sir," Saul replied. "But it really provides for all I want." '

It was not, in fact, Saul's only fortune. His skill, and his preference, was for fellatio and before long he was demonstrating it on Cambon by the light of the blazing coal-fire. Cambon's reaction can only be described as ecstatic.

'After resting awhile, and taking a little more stimulant,' continued Cambon, 'I asked him how he had come to acquire such a decided taste for gamahuching to do it so deliciously as he did.

' "That would be too long a tale to go into now," he replied. "Some other day, if you will make it worth my while, I will give you my whole history."

' "Could you write it out, or give me an outline so that I might put it into the shape of a tale?"

' "Certainly, but it would take me so much time that you would have to make me a present of at least twenty pounds. It would take me three or four weeks several hours a day."

' "I don't mind a fiver a week if you give me a fair lot, say thirty or forty pages of note-paper a week, tolerably well written," I replied.'[31]

So, in the course of the next few weeks Saul provided Cambon with the story of his life as a Mary-Anne; from his schooldays when 'it was sometimes necessary to go in for a general suck all round to give our bottoms a rest', to his adventures among the aristocracy.[32] He once proved to a certain Lord H. that he was not 'too shy or mock-modest' by fellating him in a rocky arbour in the grounds of 'a noble mansion on the banks of the Thames' during the course of a garden party. On another occasion, dressed as a midshipman, he was presented to the Prince of Wales. In the Prince's retinue that day was a member of a German royal family who assured Saul that his fortune would be made if he would consent to visit Berlin and Vienna, where he would be introduced to 'many of the highest personages in Germany'.[33] Dressed in 'charming female costume' he would attend soirées in elegant town houses. He was once sodomized while sitting on the lap of a gentleman playing the piano and singing, 'Don't You Remember Sweet Alice, Ben Bolt'.[34]

Reading Saul's memoirs, one can well believe his assertion that 'the extent to which pederasty is carried on in London between gentlemen and young fellows is little dreamed of by the outside public.'[35]

Many male prostitutes, whether part-time or professional, could take their clients to a so-called *maison de passe*. This was a house which not only supplied sexual partners but in which a client could arrange to meet someone or to which he could bring a casual pick-up. Charles Hammond's house, at 19 Cleveland Street, was a *maison de passe*. There were usually two or three professionals working there but – much to their annoyance – Hammond would often recruit complete amateurs, such as the ring of telegraph boys which was uncovered in the summer of 1889. The client would pay his sovereign direct to one of the boys, who would then hand it over to Hammond. Hammond would give him four shillings and keep sixteen for himself. As £1 in the 1880s was equal to £35 today, these were not inconsiderable sums. In half an hour of not unpleasurable activity, a boy could earn at least twice the equivalent of a week's wages. On a good night, prostitutes like Saul could make £8: almost £300 today.

Lord Arthur Somerset – whom Newlove, that diligent seducer and procurer of his fellow Post Office employees, revealed as a frequent visitor to the Cleveland Street house – appears to have made full use of all its facilities. He had sex with telegraph boys and he would arrange to meet chance pick-ups, such as soldiers, at the address. Within a couple of days of Newlove's accusation, Lord Arthur Somerset was seen meeting a soldier outside the now empty house – Hammond and the self-styled Reverend Veck having fled – and a few days after this he was again positively identified by a couple of the telegraph boys.

And yet, to the mystification of the police, no warrant was issued for Somerset's arrest. Not even when the authorities finally decided that proceedings should be instituted against him, was any move made. There seemed to be an inexplicable reluctance on the part of certain government departments to act.

What was the reason for this delay? Were the authorities giving Somerset time to get out of the country? And, if so, why? The answer was to be found in a claim made by Lord Arthur's solicitor – the young Arthur Newton. Newton warned Hamilton Cuffe, the Assistant Public Prosecutor, who hurriedly passed the warning on to his chief, Sir Augustus Stephenson, that if Lord Arthur Somerset were prosecuted, 'a very distinguished person' would become involved.[36] In his report to his chief, Cuffe used the initials of this person only but they were enough to cause consternation in the upper echelons of the administration. To hold Cuffe's letter, with its heavy scoring beside the initials, in one's hands today, is to appreciate the alarm with which it was passed, in strictest confidence, from one departmental head to another until it reached the Prime Minister, Lord Salisbury, himself.

For the initials – PAV – stood for Prince Albert Victor who, as Queen Victoria's grandson and the eldest son of the Prince of Wales, was Heir Presumptive to the British throne. True or not, the rumour that a future King had been a visitor to the Cleveland Street house would mean a scandal of monumental proportions.

To understand how the name of Prince Albert Victor could possibly have been mentioned in connection with a homosexual brothel, one needs to go back and follow – from the time of his birth twenty-five years before – the curious career of this young Prince.

PART TWO

BORN TO BE KING

3. MOTHERDEAR'S BOY

If, as one theory suggests, the first-or last-born son of a preoccupied father and a possessive mother is very likely to be born homosexual, then Prince Albert Victor could serve as a classic example. Born on 8 January 1864, he was the eldest son of Albert Edward, Prince of Wales who, in turn, was Queen Victoria's eldest son and Heir Apparent to the British throne. His mother was Princess Alexandra, daughter of King Christian IX of Denmark.

Seldom can two parents have fulfilled the prerequisites of the theory so comprehensively. The Prince of Wales was one of the most preoccupied men of the age, his chief preoccupation being the pursuit of pleasure. Restless, easily bored, lacking in application, denied any meaningful employment by Queen Victoria, the Prince of Wales lived in what his despairing mother called 'a whirl of amusements'.[1] The high-minded if heavy-handed efforts of the Queen and Prince Albert to mould their eldest son into an intellectual and moral paragon had been completely wasted. The Prince of Wales emerged from his years of force-fed education as an unashamed hedonist. Even before his marriage, at the early age of twenty-one, he showed signs of the unremitting search for distraction that was to characterize his entire life.

Of all these distractions, the one to which the Prince of Wales applied himself with the most zest was fornication. Indeed, it was in the hope that his budding sexuality might be curbed that his marriage had been hurried on. The Prince's affair with an actress had so shocked his upright father, Prince Albert, that it had led, in Queen Victoria's distraught imagination, directly to her husband's premature death. Having been told 'the disgusting details' of her son's 'fall', the widowed Queen admitted to her eldest daughter Victoria, Crown Princess of Prussia, that 'I never can or shall look at him without a shudder.'[2] An early marriage was essential to halt her son's drift into debauchery.

'Marry early he must ...' agreed the serious-minded Crown Princess in a letter to her mother. 'The chances are, if he married a nice wife that he likes, she will keep him straight; and, as he is too weak to keep from sin for virtue's sake, he will only keep out of it from other motives, and surely a wife will be the strongest.'[3]

It was a vain hope. Denied enough time for the sowing of his wild oats before marriage, the Prince of Wales simply sowed them after. His brief honeymoon over, he plunged himself, with even more enthusiasm, not only into his frenetic social activities but also into the gratification of his sexual appetite.

That his eighteen-year-old bride should be affected by all this was inevitable. Princess Alexandra of Schleswig-Holstein-Sonderburg-Glucksburg had been raised in relative obscurity and simplicity. Her outstanding beauty rather than her dynastic importance had been the chief reason for her choice as a suitable wife for the future King of Great Britain. In spite of her bandbox elegance, Princess Alexandra retained something of the domesticity and provincialism of the Danish court. Home and family would always be at the centre of her world. Although ready enough, in the early days of her marriage, to accompany her husband on his social round, she could never really keep up with him. She was simply not sophisticated enough for his worldly milieu. By no stretch of the imagination an intellectual, the Prince of Wales nevertheless enjoyed the company of quick-witted women. His wife soon proved herself to be too artless and childlike for his taste.

Drawing them still further apart was her increasing deafness. From her mother, Queen Louise of Denmark, the Princess had inherited a form of deafness known as otosclerosis. It was to be inherited, in turn, by her eldest son. As the years went by, so the Princess found it more and more difficult to follow conversation. This not only cut her off from the sparkling company in which her husband delighted but from her husband himself.

Nor was Princess Alexandra, for all her grace and beauty, sensual or voluptuous enough for the Prince of Wales. Lady Antrim, who knew her well, suspected that she was sexually cold. The Prince might have been a more faithful husband if the Princess had been a more loving wife, Lady Antrim once claimed. The Prince's infidelities ('I often think her lot is no easy one,' wrote Queen Victoria in the year after the couple's marriage, for although the Princess was fond of her husband, she was 'not blind'[4]) had the effect of narrowing Princess Alexandra's horizons yet further. She began to cling, ever more tenaciously, to those whom she knew best: a small circle of companions, her warm-hearted Danish family and above all, her children. She clung, most tenaciously of all, to her first-born son, Prince Albert Victor.

There is only one recorded occasion on which Prince Albert Victor, notorious for his dilatoriness, was not merely on time but actually early: this was for his birth. Due to be born in March 1864, a year after his parents' marriage, he arrived two months premature, on 8 January.

During the first few months of the marriage, Queen Victoria had despaired of the couple ever having a child. In her opinion, the rackety life which the Prince of Wales was forcing his wife to lead was seriously undermining her health. 'I fear Bertie [the Prince of Wales] and she will soon be nothing but two puppets running about for show all day and night,'[5] complained the Queen; Alix [the Princess of Wales] was 'looking so sallow and losing her *fraîcheur*.[6]

'We are all seriously alarmed about her,' she confided to the Crown Princess of Prussia in June 1863, 'for although Bertie writes and says he is so anxious to take care of her, he goes on going out every night till she will become a skeleton.' Hopes of her becoming a mother, sighed the Queen, 'there cannot be!!'[7]

Within a few weeks of writing this letter, the Queen was proved wrong. By the end of June the Princess was pregnant. According to one witness who saw Princess Alexandra that summer, she 'showed her condition very little … she seems perfectly well, has not an ailment of any kind or sort to complain of and has a very good fresh colour.'[8]

But all was not as well as it appeared. Throughout her pregnancy, the Princess of Wales was in a highly emotional state. The reasons for this were political. Prussia, setting out on its road of national aggrandizement, laid claim to the Danish duchies of Schleswig-Holstein. In December 1863, the sixth month of the Princess's pregnancy, war broke out between Prussia and Denmark. The Princess, whose view of politics was always intensely personal, was appalled by the Prussian threat to her father's kingdom. It was a threat which ended, a few months later, by the loss of half his territory to Prussia. Nor were Princess Alexandra's feelings of anguish helped by the fact that the sympathies of her husband's family – the German-related British royal family – were almost entirely on the Prussian side. The Crown Princess of Prussia was her husband's sister. The Prince of Wales was supportive but nothing could alleviate Princess Alexandra's feelings of insecurity and isolation. This all had a significant effect on her pregnancy.

Christmas 1863 was spent with Queen Victoria at Osborne House on the Isle of Wight. The occasion was anything but convivial. 'Christmas was as sad as possible,' reported the Queen to the Crown Princess. The death of the Prince Consort, two years before, 'has left your old home desolate and wretched and broken your mother's heart and health'.[9] Matters were not helped by the fact that, try as they might, the Queen and Princess Alexandra could not quite hide their opposing political sympathies in the Prusso-Danish conflict. Alix, reported the Queen, 'is very unhappy about her poor father and cries much'.[10]

One can appreciate why the Prince and Princess of Wales were so delighted to get away from Osborne to Frogmore House at Windsor. Here, free from the Queen's lamenting presence, Princess Alexandra could enjoy the sort of unsophisticated entertainments she preferred: giving a children's party, listening to the brass band, watching the skaters playing ice-hockey on the frozen lake.

On 8 January 1864 she insisted on being driven, wrapped in sables and seated in a sledge-chair, to nearby Virginia Water to join the Prince's skating party for lunch. She did not return to Frogmore until dusk. Within half an hour of her arrival home her labour pains started. Her lady-in-waiting, Lady Macclesfield, having given birth to no less than thirteen children of her own, remained understandably calm. With no royal doctors within reach, she sent for Dr Brown, the local Windsor doctor (this happy accident earned him a knighthood), to Caleys, the local draper, for some flannel, and raided a jewellery box for some wadding. 'As long as I see your face,' the Princess assured the competent Lady Macclesfield, 'I am happy.'[11]

Just before nine o'clock that evening the Princess gave birth to a two-months' premature boy weighing only three and three-quarter pounds. But he was strong and healthy. 'The dear little baby ... has a very pretty, well-shaped, round head, with very good features, a nice forehead, a very marked nose, beautiful little ears and pretty little hands,' reported the Queen, who had come hurrying over from Osborne.[12]

One of the Queen's chief concerns was the matter of the baby's names. She decided that he was to be called Albert Victor, after his paternal grandparents, Albert and Victoria. The first the parents heard of this decision was when the Prince of Wales's little sister, the six-year-old Princess Beatrice, happened to mention it to Lady Macclesfield. The Prince was understandably annoyed. To his protestations, the Queen blandly answered that the naming of the Heir Presumptive was a dynastic rather than a personal matter. It was her intention for all future British monarchs to bear the name Albert. Just as she wished the Prince of Wales to be one day known as King Albert I, so she wanted his new-born son to become King Albert II.

Accordingly, the child was christened Albert Victor Christian Edward: Christian being the name of Princess Alexandra's father, King Christian IX of Denmark, and Edward that of the Queen's late father Edward, Duke of Kent. In view of the fact that he had been born so soon after the Princess's return from a skating party, Society wags dubbed him a 'N-ice baby' or 'Prince All-but-on-the-ice'. But to everyone in the family, other than Queen Victoria – and eventually, even to her – the boy was to be known as 'Eddy'. He liked to be known, officially, as Prince Edward.

The christening ceremony was held in the private chapel at Buckingham Palace on 10 March 1864, the first anniversary of the Wales's wedding day. Wearing what she called her 'poor sad dress'[13] and 'a sort of Mary Stuart cap decorated with diamonds',[14] Queen Victoria behaved, says the watching Henry Greville, gentleman usher at court, with her 'usual composure'. To her daughter, the Crown Princess, the Queen gave her customary doleful account of the occasion but, according to Greville, she laughed heartily when 'the Royal baby began howling, which it did lustily throughout the service'.

'I am told this is considered to be a lucky omen,' continued Greville. 'If so, the Prince should be the most fortunate of men.'[15]

An even more optimistic wish was made by the Crown Princess. She hoped that the baby would grow up to be 'dear Papa's own grandson in all that is good and great'.[16]

Prince Eddy was raised in two homes: Marlborough House in London and Sandringham House in Norfolk. Marlborough House, facing on to the Mall, was the Prince of Wales's London home for almost forty years, from the time of his marriage until his accession to the throne, as King Edward VII, in 1901. He became so closely associated with it that his circle of rich, raffish, pleasure-loving friends were known as the Marlborough House set. It was one of the great social centres of Victorian London.

To an even greater extent and for an even longer period – from before his marriage until his death in 1910 – Sandringham House reflected the Prince of Wales's way of life. That it was set in flat, featureless countryside, rebuilt in a hideous neo-Elizabethan style and furnished in the worst contemporary taste, bothered the frankly philistine Prince not at all. He felt more at home here than anywhere else. His Sandringham house parties, with their kaleidoscopic guest lists and day-long shoots were a source of immense pleasure to him.

Princess Alexandra, too, was devoted to Sandringham. The marshy surroundings, invariably scoured by the salt wind off the Wash, reminded her of her native Denmark. Indeed, within both Sandringham House and Marlborough House, the Princess was able to recreate something of the flavour of her Danish girlhood. Her private apartments mirrored her taste for a homely, domestic life. Little islands of intimacy were formed by the arrangement of screens and curtains and banks of flowering plants. These were crowded with small sofas, love-seats and pouffes. At every turn stood yet another what-not or occasional table loaded with silver-framed family photographs and assorted bric-à-brac. 'Cosy' was a word of the highest praise in the Princess of Wales's vocabulary. These rooms perfectly encapsulated the warm, affectionate, slightly cloying atmosphere in which Prince Eddy spent much of his early years.

The little boy, wrote Queen Victoria when he was a year old, was 'a perfect bijou – very fairy-like but quite healthy, very wise-looking and good. He lets all the family carry him and play with him – and Alix likes him to be accustomed to it. He is very placid, almost melancholy-looking sometimes. What is not pretty is his very narrow chest (rather pigeon-chested) which is like Alix's build and that of her family … He is decisively like her; everyone is struck by it.'[17]

By this time Princess Alexandra was again pregnant and on 3 June 1865 she gave birth to a second son. Moving fast, the parents denied Queen Victoria the opportunity of once again choosing the baby's name. To her considerable disappointment, they decided on George as the first name ('as we like the name and it is an English one') and Frederick – a Danish royal name – as a second. Thwarted, the Queen had to be content with insisting that 'of course, you will add *Albert* at the end'.[18]

During the following six years, Princess Alexandra gave birth to four more children: three girls, and a boy who lived a few hours only. Louise was born in 1867, Victoria in 1868 and Maud in 1869. The birth of Princess Louise, the first of the three girls, was complicated by a severe attack of rheumatic fever and for weeks Princess Alexandra was confined to bed in great pain. The attack left her with a permanent limp. So gracefully, though, did the Princess cope with her stiff knee that in time Society women began to imitate 'the Alexandra limp'. A more serious consequence was the worsening of her deafness. In time, it was to be total.

Princess Alexandra's prolonged illness accelerated the steady drift apart of husband and wife. Incapable of sitting still for hours on end, wanting always to be surrounded by amusing people, too immature to face up to anything painful or unpleasant, the Prince of Wales, still in his twenties, avoided his wife's sickroom as much as possible. He could hardly wait to get away to more congenial company. That such company was often female was only too apparent. The Princess would have heard of his involvement with 'various Russian beauties' when he was in St Petersburg just before her illness, and of his suppers with 'female Paris notorieties' during the course of it.[19] She must certainly have suspected the worst when he stayed out night after night, often not coming home until three in the morning.

Although the Prince and Princess of Wales were to remain fond enough of each other and he would always treat her with great respect and courtesy, their relationship was never to be particularly close or loving.

On the children, and particularly on Prince Eddy, this estrangement between their parents would have had a pronounced effect. The young princes and princesses spent far more time with their mother than was usual in upper-class Victorian households and the Prince's neglect of his wife tended to make her even more possessive. This is not to claim that the Prince of Wales was in any way unkind to his children; on the contrary, he was a very indulgent father. Determined that his own children should not be subjected to the sort of merciless discipline which had blighted his own youth, he favoured as free and easy an upbringing as possible.

'If children are too strictly or perhaps too severely treated,' he once wrote to his mother, 'they get shy and only fear those whom they ought to love.' He was not, however, prepared to spend too much time in their company. A child, he claimed, 'is always best looked after under its mother's eye'.[20] But whenever he could spare the time from his relentless social round, the Prince of Wales revealed himself to his children as a sympathetic, jocular, uncensorious figure.

Their mother they adored. The Princess of Wales no more encouraged her children to engage or expand their intellects than did their father. With no interest in reading and with her deafness cutting her off from intelligent or enlightening conversation, she retained the mind of an adolescent. To her five children, Princess Alexandra seemed hardly more grown-up than themselves. They called her 'darling Motherdear': a gay, spontaneous, impractical, unpunctual creature, ready enough to toboggan down the stairs on silver trays or to crouch behind sofas in a game of hide-and-seek. 'We are to have blind man's buff, tapping hands, snapdragon etc,' wrote one long-suffering guest. 'The Princess is as wild as she can be and delights in games.'[21] She once dressed one of her nephews in the crinoline and bonnet which Queen Victoria had worn during her state visit to Paris in 1855 and solemnly led him into the sickroom of her equally fun-loving sister Dagmar, Empress of All the Russias. The bizarre sight is said to have considerably hastened the invalid's recovery.

One result of this undisciplined upbringing was that the Wales children ran very wild indeed. 'A fearful romp with the little Princes,' reported Annie de Rothschild in December 1869; 'we taught them blind man's buff, and ran races with them. The eldest is a beautiful child, the image of the Princess, the second has a jolly little face and looks the cleverest. The Princess said to me: "They are dreadfully wild, but I was just as bad." '[22]

Queen Victoria was not nearly as tolerant. 'They are such ill-bred, ill-trained children I can't fancy them at all,' she once complained. They were as 'wild as hawks'. Lady Geraldine Somerset described the three Wales princesses as 'rampaging little girls'.[23] At other times the Queen would maintain that the over-active social life which the Prince of Wales was obliging his wife to lead was making the children 'puny and pale'; 'poor frail little *fairies*', she called them.[24] Of one aspect only of the Princess's upbringing of her children did Queen Victoria approve. Her daughter-in-law insisted on 'great simplicity and an absence of all pride, and in that respect she has my fullest support'.[25]

With each passing year Prince Eddy revealed himself, ever more markedly, as the odd-one-out in this rumbustious Wales brood. His nurse, Mary Blackburn, testified to his 'gentleness of heart', and another observer claims that his 'habit of forgiveness, his instinctive desire to be forgiven, had their origins in the affectionate disposition which was the most beautiful point in the Prince's character'.[26] By the age of seven, in 1871, he was a beautiful boy but with a dreamy, wistful, curiously vulnerable expression and a decidedly lethargic manner. That the Prince of Wales was disappointed in his sensitive eldest son was becoming increasingly apparent.

In his authorized life of Prince Eddy's younger brother George, afterwards King George V, Sir George Arthur claims that the Prince of Wales's 'own robust constitution and tireless energy contrasted sharply with the delicacy alike of physique and demeanour, the shrinking from anything approaching the boisterous, which marked his elder son and might at times act as something of an irritant: the love of fun and frolic, the eagerness and *élan* with which the younger [Prince George] was so fully endued, were dear in his father's eyes and served to forge a bond between them from which Prince Eddy – the idol from his birth of his mother – could not but be a little withdrawn.'[27]

This merely led to the Princess of Wales becoming even more protective of her eldest son. The only occasions on which she is known to have spoken sharply to Prince George was when he bickered with his elder brother. 'Above all,' she once admonished, *'don't ever quarrel* with your brother.' And on another occasion she wrote that 'in particular, do not quarrel with or irritate your brother.'[28]

During these early years a bond was formed between Princess Alexandra and Prince Eddy that was to be broken only by his death. 'A fearless, open-hearted converse grew up between the mother and her elder son from childhood, and which nothing afterwards ever came to spoil,' claims one observer. 'Nothing that gave pleasure to him ever seemed too insignificant to be communicated to her. The mother and the sisters seemed ever to recur again and again in his thoughts; not only in his boyhood, but in his youth and manhood was this constantly the case, and all who were intimate with him, either while he was in the navy, or at college, or in the army, have alike remarked how often he would revert artlessly and almost unconsciously, if only by a passing reference, to the one topic that seemed ever uppermost in his mind.'[29]

Time and again, Prince Eddy would tell friends of his 'devotion' to his sympathetic and elegant mother.[30]

4. 'A CAREFULLY BROUGHT-UP BOY'

In the year 1871, when Prince Eddy was seven and Prince George almost six, the Prince and Princess of Wales decided that their formal education must begin. The parents' first choice as tutor was, in the light of his future career, a singular one. For it was Edward Carpenter – later to develop into that ardent socialist and campaigner for homo-sexual recognition. But in 1871, Carpenter was a young clergyman and Cambridge graduate. He was invited to spend a couple of days at Windsor Castle to be inspected by Queen Victoria. Here he professed himself delighted by the 'gracious way' in which he was treated by Princess Alexandra.[1] But he refused the position. Already, apparently, Carpenter was undergoing some sort of identity crisis: not long after the Windsor interview he suffered a nervous breakdown and left the ministry. Instead of spending his life among the highest in the land, Carpenter made the decision that 'I would and must somehow go and make my life with the mass of the people and the manual workers.'[2]

The rest of Carpenter's long career was devoted to those two causes which would have rendered him, in the eyes of the Prince of Wales, a highly inappropriate choice as tutor to his sons: socialism and homo-sexuality. Carpenter developed into a leading exponent of the 'New Thought' – a vegetable-growing, sandal-making proclaimer of 'William Morris Socialism, Hindu mysticism, neo-paganism and sexual reform'.[3] His sexual tastes were for 'the thick-thighed hot coarse-fleshed young bricklayer with a strap around his waist' and for 'the grimy and oil-besmeared figure of a stoker'.[4] What *would* Queen Victoria have said about that?

Instead, the post of tutor went to the thirty-two-year-old Reverend John Neale Dalton. As a curate to Canon Prothero, rector of Whippingham near Osborne House, the young clergyman had caught the eye, and won the approval, of Queen Victoria.

Dalton was everything the Queen could have wished for: unmarried, well-educated, conscientious and orderly. His pupils' days were divided into neat compartments, from the time that they rose at seven in the morning until they were put to bed at eight in the evening. He strongly disapproved of the interruption of lessons by the princes' convivial father and scatterbrained mother and never hesitated to air this disapproval in his booming voice. Still less did he approve of the parents' restless, luxurious, frivolous way of life.

But Dalton was not quite as censorious as he appeared. Even he, who could be so ponderous, was not above employing the sort of extravagantly sentimental language to which the Princess of Wales had accustomed her sons. 'I thought much of my darling little Georgie,' he once wrote to Prince George, who was by then eighteen years old and serving in the Navy, and he always signed his letters to 'dearest boy with much love'.[5] After Prince Eddy's death, Dalton spoke lyrically of 'the infinite sweetness of nature' shown by his otherwise unrewarding pupil.[6]

There was, indeed, something equivocal about Dalton's sexual orientation. His closest friend was none other than Edward Carpenter. The two men had been students together at Cambridge and their relationship has been described as one of 'the greatest intimacy, affection and concern'.[7] They remained close friends throughout their lives in spite of Carpenter's openly homosexual way of living. Dalton apparently read 'all' Carpenter's increasingly outspoken books on social and sexual subjects. 'Though our paths in life have been divergent ...' wrote Dalton to Carpenter in 1920, 'yet still I can't help thinking that our outlook on life and its problems is not so wholly dissimilar as one might imagine it would be.' Carpenter's tireless campaigning for some sort of socialist-homosexual brotherhood had left, admitted Dalton, 'an enduring influence on my mental and moral outlook'.[8]

The friends would often visit one another. Towards the end of his life Carpenter one day unearthed some photographs of Prince Eddy and Prince George and of the two princes with Princess Alexandra. They had given him the photographs, on different occasions, during his visits to their tutor.

The Reverend Dalton was to remain with both princes for eleven years and with Prince Eddy for three more. Although the lively Prince George responded well enough to Dalton's tutoring, Prince Eddy did not. Try as he might, the tutor was seldom able to catch, and certainly never to hold, Prince Eddy's attention. The boy was a dreamer, sadly deficient, as the despairing Dalton reported, 'in any habits of prompti-tude and method, of manliness and self-reliance'. He lacked all 'physical and mental tone'. Only the company of the younger and brighter Prince George encouraged Prince Eddy to work at all. 'Difficult as the educa-tion of [Prince Eddy] is now,' claimed Dalton, 'it would be doubly or trebly so' without Prince George as 'his mainstay and chief incentive to exertion'.[9]

This was why when, in 1877, the twelve-year-old Prince George was due to start a naval career by joining the training ship *Britannia* as a cadet, it was decided that Prince Eddy must accompany him. It would be the only way, Dalton assured Queen Victoria, of improving 'His Royal Highness's moral, mental and physical development'. The Queen was not so sure. The future positions of the two princes, she explained to Dalton, 'will be totally *different* and it is not intended that they should *both* enter the navy … The very rough sort of life to which boys are exposed on board ship is the very thing not calculated to make a refined and amiable Prince, who in after years (if God spares him) is to ascend the throne.' What Queen Victoria was hoping for was another man like her late husband, the Prince Consort, not another like her son, the Prince of Wales.

Having – with customary good sense – warned against the feelings of narrow national superiority which a naval career might encourage in Prince Eddy, the Queen touched on a more sensitive issue. 'I have a great fear', she confided, 'of young and carefully brought up Boys mixing with older Boys and indeed with any Boys in general, for the mischief done by bad Boys and the things they may hear and learn from them cannot be over-rated.'[10] The late Prince Consort had always been convinced that boys, left unsupervised, would 'talk lewdly'.[11] The gentle, easily influenced Prince Eddy would be safer, she argued, attending a school such as Wellington College, where he could live, with his tutor, in a house nearby.

One cannot know exactly what 'mischief' Queen Victoria had in mind but she undoubtedly shared the contemporary obsession with the imagined dangers of masturbation. Upper-and middle-class Victorian parents believed that 'the sacred beauty of male virginity' had to be preserved, as a duty to God, for as long as possible.[12] Many a schoolmaster spent a suspiciously long time lecturing his charges on the dire effects of 'self-abuse' and listened, perhaps a shade too avidly, to their blushing confessions. Even doctors, who should have known better, maintained that the self-induced loss of semen weakened the body, enfeebled the brain and often led to madness.

In a sermon, not to schoolboys but to undergraduates at Oxford, the saintly Dr Pusey once offered a 'Remedy for Sins of the Body'. Masturbation, he warned, could have the most dreadful consequences. 'I have known of manifold early death; I have seen the fineness of intellect injured; powers of reasoning, memory impaired; nay, insanity oftentime, idiocy; every form of decay of mind and body; consumption too often, torturing death, even of a strong frame.

'Lesser degrees of punishment were God's warning voice: at first bodily growth checked, eyesight perhaps distressed or impaired; that fine, beautiful delicate system which carries sensation through the whole human frame, in whatever degree harmed, and for the most part, in that degree irreparably.'

The only thing to do with one's straying hands, advised the good prelate, was 'to clasp them together, and pray earnestly to God for help'. He had known one young man who 'under an almost supernatural power of temptation' had prayed for seven days and six nights and 'at the end, the temptation left him as though it had never been'.[13]

By the mid-nineteenth century, it was seriously believed that the 'secret sin' of masturbation led directly to the 'dual vice' of homosexuality. 'The secret sin which has been learned at a private school, imported to a public school, and there taught to the youngest boys,' claimed one authority, 'will inevitably produce the more fashionable vices of the larger society.'[14] In other words, if masturbation could be stamped out early, homosexuality would almost certainly disappear.

But overcoming her reservations about these and other matters, Queen Victoria eventually allowed herself to be persuaded that both princes should be sent to *Britannia*. They would remain, however, in the care of Mr Dalton. Their mother, the Princess of Wales, in writing to thank the tutor for 'all the devotion you have shown to our boys and for the unending trouble and interest you have taken in their education', stressed various points in connection with their future upbringing. They were all eminently sensible. The tutor must 'pay great attention to their being obedient and obeying the moment they are told. Also let them be civil to everybody, high and low, and not get grand now they are by themselves, and please take particular care they are not toadied by any of those around them.'[15]

Their leaving broke her heart, and theirs. 'It was a great wrench ...' wrote Princess Alexandra to the Queen, 'poor little boys, they cried so bitterly.'[16]

In September 1877, the thirteen-year-old Prince Eddy and the twelve-year-old Prince George joined the training ship *Britannia*, anchored in the River Dart, in Devon. Except that they had a cabin to themselves and that they were watched over by Mr Dalton, they were treated much as any other of the two hundred cadets. According to Prince George, in later life, they were treated a good deal worse. 'It was a pretty tough place,' he remembered, 'and, so far from making any allowances for our disadvantages, the other boys made a point of taking it out of us on the grounds that they'd never be able to do it later on.'[17]

In one respect, the *Britannia* experiment failed dismally. Although it served as an excellent first step on Prince George's naval career, it did nothing for Prince Eddy. In fact, his standard of intelligence was so low that he was unable to keep up with even the weakest cadets. By December 1878 there was talk of removing him altogether. But while professing herself *'dreadfully* distressed about poor Eddy's progress', Princess Alexandra would not hear of his being shifted from *Britannia* in order to be *'educated at home alone'*.[18] So he remained. A few months later, in a gloomy report to the Prince of Wales, Dalton complained that Prince Eddy was unable 'to fix his attention, to any given subject for more than a few minutes consecutively', and that 'he fails, not in one or two subjects, but in all'.[19]

'It is to *physical* causes', the desperate Dalton decided, 'that one must look for an explanation of the abnormally dormant condition of his mental powers.'[20]

Perhaps he was right. A recently propounded theory claims that children born prematurely are invariably less mentally alert than those born after a full term. A third of such children have learning difficulties and an educational level well below the average. They suffer from what is termed 'neuro-developmental impairments'.[21] Prince Eddy was a full two months premature. This handicap could have been aggravated by yet another physical failing; it has been suggested that he suffered from *petit mal*, a minor form of epilepsy which affects children and adolescents and is especially prevalent during puberty. Seizures can occur many times a day and manifest themselves by such things as vacancy of facial expression, momentary loss of awareness and a drooping of the eyelids. Although the affliction usually, but not always, disappears in adulthood, it can by then have seriously disrupted the sufferer's education.

Another physical cause could have been the Prince's slight deafness. Queen Victoria's private secretary, Sir Henry Ponsonby, noticed this during one of Prince Eddy's visits to Balmoral. It has been claimed that the Prince, like his mother, always tilted his head forward and sideways when carrying on a conversation. This deafness was something to which Princess Alexandra, conscious of the fact that it was from her that he had inherited it, would not have wished to draw too much attention. In any case, the family all hoped that the Prince's torpid condition was temporary. They comforted themselves with the usual excuses: he was shooting up too fast, he was just absent-minded, he would grow out of it.

The end of Prince Eddy's two-year stint on *Britannia* simply reopened the question of what was to be done with him. Dalton could only suggest more of the same. Instead of going to a public school as had originally been planned, he should go to sea. When Prince George joined HMS *Bacchante* for a series of cruises, Prince Eddy should be allowed to accompany him. Not only would he benefit from the continued company of his livelier younger brother but by being surrounded by a hand-picked company of sub-lieutenants, midshipmen and cadets of 'irreproachable character', he would be shielded against the 'evil associations' so characteristic of public school life.[22]

After months of discussion, involving the Queen, the Prince and Princess of Wales, the Prime Minister, their respective private secretaries, the First Lord of the Admiralty and the Captain of the *Bacchante*, the matter was decided. The two princes, still accompanied by the long-suffering Mr Dalton and their personal attendant Charles Fuller, would set sail on the *Bacchante* in September 1879.

Among the galaxy of royal relations and family friends who boarded the *Bacchante* as it lay off Cowes for Regatta Week, prior to setting sail, was the Prince of Wales's current mistress, Lillie Langtry. From Bensons, the jewellers in Cowes, she bought the fifteen-year-old Prince Eddy a little trinket. He immediately attached it to his watch chain. 'I had to take off my grandmother's [Queen Victoria's] locket to make room for it,' he told the gratified Mrs Langtry.[23]

The two princes spent almost three years aboard the *Bacchante*. Their first cruise took them to the Mediterranean and the West Indies; their second to Ireland and Spain. Their third, and longest, took them to South America, South Africa, Australia, Japan, China, Singapore and Egypt. These cruises were broken by short visits ashore and longer holidays at home.

While Prince George was treated in almost all respects like other midshipmen on board, Prince Eddy, who was not destined to become a naval officer, was kept to his books. The brothers shared a cabin, ate with the other midshipmen and cadets and were accorded no special privileges. Ashore, it was a different matter. Although Queen Victoria had stipulated that they were to be granted no royal honours whatsoever, there were times when it would have been churlish to refuse such treatment. In Cape Town, for instance, they were accommodated in Government House (whose interior doors were decorated with 'daintily executed flower paintings' by the previous Governor's spinster daughters[24] and in Alexandria they were rowed back to the *Bacchante* in 'two tremendous state barges, in one of which there was a great blue velvet and gold sofa, beneath a heavy silk canopy, in a thoroughly oriental style'.[25]

But more often than not, their trips ashore were turned, by the conscientious Mr Dalton, into sightseeing marathons. On neither of the princes did this cultural force-feeding have any noticeable effect. They remained insular, uninterested, unenthusiastic.

Anyone hoping to follow Prince Eddy's mental and psychological progress during these years at sea will get no help from Dalton's account of the voyage. His 1,500-page, two-volume work entitled *The Cruise of HMS Bacchante 1879–1882* is as impersonal a study as one could hope to find. The scrappy and ill-spelt diaries kept by the two princes were converted by their tutor into a mammoth, learned and sanctimonious tome, crammed with Latin quotations, moral maxims and radical opinions. Of the apathetic Prince Eddy and the alert Prince George there is no trace in these professorial pages; one would assume, from their apparent grasp of philosophy and mastery of statistics, that they were young men of exceptional erudition.

One example will do. Prince George's typically unadorned diary entry to the effect that in South Africa 'we passed an ostridge farm and saw many ostridges [*sic*]' is transformed by Dalton into four densely printed pages on the genus *Struthio*, including a detailed analysis of the practicalities and finances of ostrich farming.[26]

Can one of these intellectual paragons be the same Prince Eddy about whom Dalton is writing to complain to the Prince of Wales in May

1880? He 'sits listless and vacant, and … wastes as much time in doing nothing, as he ever wasted.' This 'weakness of brain, this feebleness and lack of power to grasp almost anything put before him, is manifested also in the hours of recreation and social intercourse'.[27]

But now and then it is possible to catch a rather more sympathetic glimpse of Prince Eddy. Lord Napier, the Governor of Gibraltar, who met the princes in 1879, reported: 'the eldest is better suited to his situation – he is shy and not demonstrative, but he does the right things as a young gentleman in a quiet way. It is well that he should be more reticent and reflective than the younger boy.'[28] Although one cannot help suspecting that the Governor was misreading Prince Eddy's lethargy for reflectiveness, it is significant that the young man could give this impression. The fact that he was called upon to speak – or at least to read speeches – in public, and that he is reported as having acquitted himself very well, indicates that he could appear to be quite normal. The few of his youthful letters to survive show that he was able to express himself in a natural and articulate fashion.

Ashore, when not being marched around historic sights by Mr Dalton, he behaved much as any other young prince would have done. He attended balls and banquets, he played cricket, he shot game, he went down mines and up mountains. In Tokyo, both he and his brother were tattooed. They arrived home with elaborate red and blue dragons writhing down their forearms. A press report – that they had had their *noses* tattooed – brought angry letters from the Queen and the Prince of Wales and a characteristically amused one from Princess Alexandra. 'What an *object* you must look, and won't everybody stare at the ridiculous boy with an anchor on his nose? Why on earth not have put it somewhere else?' she wrote.[29] But Dalton was able to reassure the boys' father, a shade testily, that their noses had merely been powdered by the yellow pollen of the lilies they had been sniffing in the Botanical Gardens in Barbados.

It was, however, with the princes' moral welfare that Queen Victoria was more seriously concerned. She was forever reminding her eldest son of the need to protect both princes from contamination by the 'fast' society in which he delighted. His greatest wish, the Prince of Wales reassured her, was to keep his sons 'simple, pure and childlike for as long as possible'. They were in no danger at all, he wrote on another occasion: 'they are so simple and innocent, and those they have come in contact with have such tact with them, that they are not likely to do them any harm.'[30]

In this context, 'innocent' can only have a sexual connotation and Dalton certainly saw to it that his charges were kept sexually uncorrupted. But it is difficult to believe that, in a three-year-long series of cruises at sea, Prince Eddy, no matter how carefully chaperoned, did not experience, or at least hear about, the obscenities and ribaldries of shipboard life. Months at sea were made more tolerable by the traditional naval solaces of 'rum, bum and baccy'. And among initiatory rites was the stripping naked of the initiate, the caning of his buttocks and the filling of his rectum with soap.

'I have been stationed, as you know, in two or three ships,' wrote a British naval officer to Xavier Mayne, 'and I think they have been thoroughly representative of the best sort of British seamen. On the D—— homosexuality was rife, and one could see with his own eyes how it was going on between officers ...

'To my knowledge sodomy is a regular thing on ships that go on long cruises. In the war-ships I should say that the sailor often preferred it. In the circumstances I have described the intimacy was spoken of slyly. The friendships between men, in all grades of service at sea, tend to be much closer, more sentimental than when ashore. Everything makes for confidentiality, one is shut away from the world, and so much in pairs with his friends, in watches, and so on. Of course, when the forecastle men come ashore they are keen after the girls, but sometimes the interest quite disappears, I am told.'

In the Navy the term for buggery was, graphically, 'a feed of arse' or just 'a feed'.[31]

Dalton, who was regarded as something of a pretentious prig by those officers who were obliged to mess with him, seems to have been fully alive to the dangers of such sexually charged shipboard relationships. Although he encouraged his charges to be friendly and approachable towards their fellows, he discouraged 'any close familiarity, any partial preferences, any selective fraternization'.[32] When one all-too-familiar naval type, a senior midshipman by the name of Munro, with 'his almost feminine ways and silly over-deference to [the princes] induced them to take liberties with him', the alarmed Dalton ensured that he was removed from the *Bacchante*, on grounds of health, after the first cruise.[33]

Three days after returning home from their final voyage, on 8 August 1882, the two princes, having been instructed by Mr Dalton, were confirmed by Archbishop Tate in the presence of Queen Victoria at Whippingham Church, near Osborne. Prince Eddy was then eighteen, Prince George seventeen. 'God grant that you, Sirs,' intoned the Archbishop to the two kneeling boys, 'may show the world what Christian Princes ought to be.'[34]

It was as well, perhaps, that as far as one of these Christian Princes was concerned, the Archbishop died before the year was out.

5. THE STUDENT PRINCE

In January 1883, Prince Eddy turned nineteen. Although, according to Queen Victoria, he was by now taller than his father, he was still 'very slight'.[1] Facially, he resembled both parents: he had his mother's long, narrow head and his father's heavy-lidded eyes and sensuous mouth. His air remained vague, abstracted. Yet he was capable of creating a good impression. Sir Henry Ponsonby, never one to be bowled over by the mere fact of royal birth, noted – privately – that Prince Eddy 'is pleasing, talks well, and will be popular when he gets more at his ease'.[2] This is hardly the description of some inarticulate moron.

His nineteenth birthday found Prince Eddy, together with Prince George, at the Hotel Beau Rivage in Lausanne. The two of them had been sent there to learn French. With them was the inevitable Mr Dalton and a bushily bearded Frenchman by the name of Monsieur Hua. As far as Prince Eddy was concerned, the six-month-long Beau Rivage experiment turned out to be no more successful than the periods spent aboard the *Britannia* and the *Bacchante*. It brought forth the usual stream of complaints on the part of Mr Dalton and the usual cries of despair on the part of Princess Alexandra.

'It is indeed a bitter disappointment that … he should have relapsed into his old habits of indolence and inattention,' she wrote in March 1883. 'It does indeed seem strange that at his age he does not yet see the great importance of exerting himself to the utmost, and lets his precious time slip by which can never be recalled.'[3]

Back home, the two princes were finally parted. While Prince George (who had learned almost as little French as his brother) went off to continue his career in the Navy, Prince Eddy remained at Sandringham to be prepared for the next stage of his. He was to go up to Trinity College, Cambridge. Prince Eddy felt the parting keenly. 'So we are at last separated for the first time,' he wrote in June 1883, 'and I can't tell you *how* strange it seems to be without you and how much I miss you in everything *all day long!*[4]

Prince George's departure left Prince Eddy stranded in a family circle that was almost entirely feminine. With his father, who was seldom home, he had very little rapport. The Prince of Wales was too extrovert, too impatient, too quick-tempered a man to make allowances for his son's sensitive nature. 'I hear the Prince of Wales snubbed Prince Eddy uncommonly,' reported Ponsonby on one occasion.[5] And when he was not snubbing him, he was subjecting him to the sort of banter – or what one of his cousins calls 'odious chaffing' – which is guaranteed to make a self-conscious person even more so.[6] Margot Asquith thought that Prince Eddy had been made a more 'backward, timid boy' because of his father's 'perpetual teasing – a form of ill-judged chaff'.[7] And some years later, at Cambridge, Prince Eddy confessed to a friend that he was 'rather afraid of his father, and aware that he was not quite up to what his father expected of him'.[8]

From his mother and three younger sisters, however, Prince Eddy received nothing but adoration. Within the cluttered drawing-rooms of Marlborough House and Sandringham, crammed with portraits, photographs and busts of the Princess and her daughters, the women of the Wales household created what has been described as a mutual admiration society. They lived in a self-contained, whimsical, almost make-believe world. So young-looking and immature herself, the Princess of Wales was determined to keep her daughters as childlike as possible for as long as possible. The three princesses – Louise, Victoria and Maud – even looked like their mother but without her marvellous beauty. Always identically dressed, they were pale and narrow-skulled with protruding eyes and fashionably crimped hair. Diffident in public and boisterous in private, they enjoyed their girlish games and played their practical jokes well into adulthood. They all enjoyed the same happy-go-lucky system of education. Even their conversation had a similarity. They always talked, claimed one of their cousins, about people as 'the dear little thing' or 'the poor little man'. They 'spoke in a minor key, *en sourdine*. It gave a special quality to all talks with them, and gave me a strange sensation, as though life would have been very beautiful if it had not been so sad.' The three of them were often referred to as 'the whispering Wales girls'.[9] Their rooms were like those of little children: packed with an accumulation of tiny, pretty, dainty but far from aesthetic *objets* – miniatures, shells, little vases, diminutive paintings, tiny china ornaments.

That Prince Eddy should find this undemanding and uncritical atmosphere congenial is understandable. Within it, his lackadaisical air was hardly noticeable. 'There was one noteworthy feature in his character,' wrote someone who knew him well, repeating a frequently made observation, 'and this was his affection for his mother and sisters. He continually turned the conversation to them. They were evidently much in his thoughts. He quoted what they had said and spoke of what they were doing.'

He was, says his tutor, very much his mother's son. 'The fact cannot fail to have impressed itself upon anyone who was ever brought into personal contact with him and with the Princess of Wales. Such, for instance, was the gentle amiability of demeanour, the modesty, almost akin to bashfulness, the slight involuntary action of the head while conversing, the turn of phrase and expression in which his thoughts found readiest utterance.' Whenever the two of them walked together, the Prince 'would draw his arm through his mother's, press it close to his, and brighten up altogether'.[10]

Another feminine presence in the Prince's life was, of course, his grandmother, Queen Victoria. Never the ogre of popular legend, the Queen was especially indulgent towards Prince Eddy. She considered his manners charming, his consideration for servants admirable and his lethargy soothing. She was delighted to see that, thus far, he was showing no signs of emulating his father's restless and licentious way of life. In the summer of 1883, Prince Eddy was summoned to Balmoral to be invested with the Garter. His undemanding presence in no way disrupted the Queen's secluded and strictly ordered routine.

He appears to have found her equally sympathetic. 'I am delighted to see Eddy looking so well and having enjoyed his visit to you in Scotland so much,' wrote Princess Alexandra to Queen Victoria on the Prince's return to Sandringham. 'I am so glad you seem to have understood his disposition, which is really an excellent one, and he is a very good boy at heart though perhaps he is a little slow and dawdly which I always attribute to his having grown so fast. I am delighted you gave him such good advice and the very points you mention are those which I always try to impress upon him, and I am particularly glad you did not allude to any of the other subjects you intended speaking about, such as races, clubs etc. as he really has no inclination that way and it might only have put them into his head …'[11]

Prince Eddy's immersion in his mother's syrupy world was interrupted by the necessity of preparing him for university. For, as James Edmund Vincent, in his obsequious and officially sanctioned memoir of the Prince puts it, 'it had been decided that Cambridge should be honoured with a share in the training of him who stood next to his father in succession to the throne.'[12] As even the unexacting standards expected of a prince up at Cambridge would have been beyond Prince Eddy, he was subjected to a further course of concentrated study. He was removed to the 'Bachelors' Cottage' on the Sandringham estate where, in the company of the ubiquitous Mr Dalton and four actual or prospective undergraduates, he was to be indoctrinated into university ways.

To replace Prince George's steadying and encouraging influence, it was decided that some suitable young man should be appointed as part-tutor, part-companion. The choice for this important post was the twenty-four-year-old James Kenneth Stephen. In the course of a dinner-table conversation during one of the Prince of Wales's flying visits to Sandringham, he and young Stephen discussed Prince Eddy's educational regime. The Prince of Wales was apparently impressed by Stephen's character and abilities.

But he had been ill-advised. As a mentor for the malleable, sexually equivocal Prince Eddy, Jim Stephen could hardly have been a more unfortunate choice.

On the face of it, Jim Stephen was the *beau idéal* of the High Victorian scholar-sportsman. He was a member of a distinguished family which, in the course of the preceding century and through its own efforts, had risen to academic, legal and social prominence. His father was a judge, Sir James Fitzjames Stephen; his grandfather, Sir James Stephen, had been a leading Colonial Under-Secretary. Jim Stephen has been described as 'classically beautiful', and he was certainly handsome in a clear-eyed, firm-jawed, indubitably masculine fashion. When the part of 'Ajax' in a Greek play was being cast, Stephen with his 'massive frame and striking face' was the obvious choice. As a footballer, he was said to be famous. 'A hearty man was this, and a vigorous,' writes Vincent, who met him at Cambridge, 'warm-hearted, large in mind, versatile in taste, intensely human.'

He was also an accomplished scholar. He had won scholarships and prizes at Eton and Cambridge; he had been president of the Cambridge Union in 1882, where his oratory was 'outstanding'. But, continues Vincent, Stephen was 'no mere bookworm, but a man with a natural bent towards dainty and exquisite language in prose and verse'. His literary tastes have been described as 'elegant and refined'. Harry Wilson, another member of the Prince's little court at Bachelors' Cottage, claims that no better choice as tutor could have been made. 'For Mr Stephen, to an extraordinarily brilliant and subtle intellect, united a geniality of disposition that made him, to those who knew him well, one of the most lovable of men.'[13] He charmed, says Vincent, 'every man he met'.[14]

But the picture was not quite as rosy as it seemed. The Stephen family was emotionally unstable. The bland phrase 'severe illness, caused by overwork', which was applied to several members of the family, was a euphemism for mental derangement. It was certainly the cause of the premature retirement of Jim Stephen's father from the Bench. This 'curse of the Stephens' even extended to Jim's cousin, Virginia Woolf, who, after protracted periods of mental disturbance, took her own life in 1941. A few years after first meeting Prince Eddy, Stephen began to show signs of serious mental instability himself and his behaviour became increasingly erratic. He died on 3 February 1892 in a lunatic asylum, at the age of thirty-three, having refused to take food or drink for twenty days; just twenty days after he had been told of the sudden death of his one-time charge, Prince Eddy.

There can be little doubt that Jim Stephen, in the course of the period that he was so closely associated with Prince Eddy – first at Sandringham and then at Cambridge – gradually became drawn to him. On first taking up his duties at Bachelors' Cottage, he described the Prince as 'a good-natured, unaffected youth',[15] and to Dalton – who needed no telling – complained that 'he hardly knows the meaning of the words *to read*.' Stephen doubted that his pupil would 'derive much benefit from attending lectures at Cambridge'.[16]

But Stephen came from a socially ambitious family. Put in the unique position of having to befriend and mould the future King-Emperor, he developed proprietorial feelings towards him. He resented anyone else trying to influence, or to win the confidence of, the young man. Given his good looks and overwhelming charm, it did not take Stephen long to gain the trust of the simple Prince Eddy.

And then Stephen, for all the apparent heterosexuality of his appearance and manner, was what the Victorians called a 'woman-hater'. To him, moreover, the phrase could be applied in its literal meaning. One needs to read only one of his many poems to appreciate the depth of Stephen's irrational detestation of women.

> If all the harm that women have done
> Were put in a bundle and rolled into one,
> Earth would not hold it,
> The sky could not enfold it,
> It could not be lighted nor warmed by the sun;
> Such masses of evil
> Would puzzle the devil
> And keep him in fuel while Time's wheels run.

On the other hand, runs the second stanza of this curious poem, if all the harm that was done by men were 'doubled and doubled and doubled again', it would still not provide enough fuel for even 'a tenth of a year'.[17]

It is hardly surprising, then, that the socially aspiring and neurotically woman-hating Stephen should feel attracted to this kindly, affectionate and curiously sensuous young prince. He was not the first, nor the last, person, in whom Prince Eddy brought out strongly protective instincts. That the relationship between the two young men was ever overtly homosexual is open to question. But homosexual or not, an intimacy – 'jealously possessive on Stephen's side and lazily tolerant on Prince Eddy's' – developed between them during those high summer days at Sandringham.[18]

In mid-October 1883 Prince Eddy, still in the care of Jim Stephen and accompanied by Dalton and the rest of the Bachelors' Cottage coterie, went up to Trinity College, Cambridge. He was to remain there for eighteen months.

Unlike his father, who had been accommodated in a private house three miles out of town during his singularly unproductive spell at Cambridge, Prince Eddy had rooms in college. There was less reason, it was decided, to protect the son from the more rakish elements of undergraduate life. Prince Eddy was allotted two sets of rooms – known at Cambridge as 'attics' – on the top floor of Nevile's Court. Although comfortably furnished, the Prince's rooms were not noticeably different from those of the other undergraduates. Dalton's rooms were said to have had much more character, 'ornamented as they were with many mementoes of the cruise of the *Bacchante*'.[19] Indeed, Dalton made use of this period at Cambridge to work on his exhaustive account of the voyage of the *Bacchante*. He was quite content, it seems, to leave Prince Eddy in the hands of Jim Stephen.

Nevile's Court, reads one honeyed account of the Prince's stay there, 'is the chosen abode of dons and scholars, and seldom re-echoes the sound of undergraduate revelry, presenting in this respect a strong contrast to the adjacent New Court ...'[20] This same air of tranquillity characterizes the whole of Prince Eddy's Cambridge career. Try as he might, the Prince's official biographer James Edmund Vincent can praise him in negative terms only. The Prince is 'naturally simple and docile'; he is 'quiet and moderately industrious'; he gives his tutors 'as little trouble as possible'. If one of his friends happens to be speaking, he will attend the Cambridge Union as 'a silent member'. At concerts he is 'a constant listener'. He 'patronizes performances' of the Amateur Dramatic Society.[21] It is just as well, one feels, that the Prince enjoyed 'the privilege of escaping university examinations, a privilege properly accorded to his high rank'.[22]

Anecdotes about his naïvety were legion. When, on his arrival at Cambridge, Dr Thompson, Master of Trinity, took him on a tour of the paintings, which included a recent one of the Master himself, Prince Eddy politely remarked, 'Another old master, I suppose?'[23]

The Prince seems to have been even less of a sportsman than he was a scholar. Vincent, ploughing manfully on, admits that 'in the athletic world the Prince was no very prominent person.' He played neither cricket nor football. An initial interest in rowing soon dwindled and such riding as he did was 'in a quiet way'. He did try his hand at lacrosse and lawn tennis ('HRH plays better than he did' is the best that can be dredged up by way of a comment on his game) and it is with almost palpable relief that his biographer claims that the Prince played hockey 'often and well'. His favourite outdoor occupation appears to have been spending 'a pleasant summer evening with a friend upon the water among the beautiful surroundings of the "Backs" '. It was the friend, however, who handled the punt.[24]

It was indoors, and chiefly at what Vincent describes as 'the modest little dinner parties which bring men, whether princes or commoners, into closer intimacy', that Prince Eddy seems to have taken the greatest pleasure.[25] Under the watchful eye of Jim Stephen, the Prince – known to his companions as 'the Pragger' – was allowed to extend his circle. Hating women as he did, Stephen would have discouraged any friendships, however innocent, with the girls whom his charge would have met at dances or tennis parties. Not, of course, that women would have been allowed into the undergraduates' quarters. Prince Eddy's name was certainly never linked, in the way that his father's had been during his university days, with that of any woman.

The Prince's demeanour, at these 'modest little dinner parties', was so self-effacing that his companions often forgot his exalted rank. Once, when his host was having trouble uncorking a bottle of soda water and the Prince offered some rather obvious advice, the host petulantly exclaimed, 'Go and teach your grandmother to suck eggs!' Only after saying it did he remember who the Prince's grandmother was.[26] The Prince of Wales, at any age, would have been furious; the good-natured Prince Eddy was highly amused.

A study of the personalities in whose company Prince Eddy spent many of these intimate evenings is revealing. Some of them were simply fellow undergraduates but of the poetry-writing, whist-playing, amateur-acting variety; others were overt or covert homosexuals, followers of the somewhat self-conscious cult of 'Greek love'. This particular form of love was widespread in schools and universities during the second half of the nineteenth century, cultivated as part of the newly fashionable Aesthetic Movement. With its literary roots in two of Plato's Dialogues, this Platonic love – the affection of one man for another unsullied by sex – was regarded as the highest possible form of love. No relationship between a man and a woman, inseparable from lust and procreation, could match the purity and disinterestedness of the love between two men. Just as the Spartan warriors had had their cadets and medieval knights their pages, so could the heroes of the playing field establish innocent friendships with younger students. The resulting idealized companionships were often intense and romantic, manifesting themselves in reams of passionate verse and torrid prose.

But they were not always innocent; any more, in fact, than love between men in ancient Greece had been innocent. The Greeks were decidedly bisexual. Marriage was for the procreation of children and for the ensuring of a well-managed home. The marriage having been consummated, the husband would return to his younger male lover for both sexual gratification and intellectual companionship. This presented the ideal for John Addington Symonds and other sexually tormented intellectuals. They looked to Greek civilization to bear out their contention that homosexuality was simply 'part of the accepted way of life, part of an organic whole'.[27]

That the majority of undergraduates who practised Greek love concerned themselves with the finer philosophical points of the theory is doubtful. It was all too easy for two young men expressing undying love for each other on paper, to feel tempted to express it between the sheets. Greek love also gave practising homosexuals the perfect framework in which to conduct their less cerebral affairs. Occasionally the cult would be rocked by an open scandal, as when one of its chief proponents, the painter Simeon Solomon, was discovered by the police, fellating a man called Roberts in a public lavatory.

Even without the cloak of love, whether of the Greek variety or not, students engaged in sexual activity. Raymond Asquith, writing to a friend from his college at about this time, gleefully reported on a mass meeting at which the students were lectured on 'the disadvantages' of sodomy. 'He spoke in hushed accents of the abominable crime and exhorted us with passionate fervour to prefer every known form of prostitution and bestiality to the sin of Sodom. He told us that the Headmasters, in league with the Government, were proposing to increase the legal penalty from two to fourteen years; whereat a perceptible shudder ran through the audience, of whom some 85 per cent – by the lowest estimate – were liable for incarceration on that charge.'[28]

It is significant that the philosophy of 'Greek love' was known as 'the Higher Sodomy' by the semi-secret Cambridge society called the Apostles. More significant still, almost all the members of Prince Eddy's university circle were Apostles. The group had been started in 1820 as the Cambridge Conversazione Society: a serious-minded debating society concerned with religious matters. During the following sixty years, however, the Apostles had developed into a more sophisticated, esoteric and quasi-mystical organization, centred on Trinity College and with a pronounced homosexual bias. Although Jim Stephen had by now retired from the Apostles and was known as an Angel – a life member no longer obliged to attend all the meetings – the Prince's other companions were all members.

Prince Eddy's closest friend at Trinity was an Apostle: this was the brilliant Henry Francis Wilson – always known as Harry – who had been one of the Bachelors' Cottage group at Sandringham in the summer of 1883. Wilson shared rooms with Jim Stephen's brother, Henry Lushington Stephen, another Harry. Harry Stephen who, like his brother Jim, was exceptionally good-looking, claimed Wilson as his 'most intimate friend' and in Harry Wilson's diary, now in Trinity College Library, is scrawled, opposite a mention of Harry Stephen, the words, 'I love him, I love him.'[29] It was generally believed that, had Prince Eddy not died in 1892, Harry Wilson would have become his private secretary.

A frequent visitor to Prince Eddy's rooms was Arthur Benson, one of the sons of the Archbishop of Canterbury, later better known as the writer A.C. Benson, Master of Magdalene. In his discreet diaries A.C. Benson claimed that Prince Eddy 'was always good-naturedly pleased to see one, and Dalton showed me much fatherly kindness'.[30] Dalton's kindness was not quite as fatherly as Benson claims. To Dalton, young Benson, who was homosexual, was 'an object of adoration'.[31]

A name on Prince Eddy's intimate dinner party lists is 'Ronald'. This was Lord Ronald Sutherland Gower, a younger son of the second Duke of Sutherland and a Trustee of the National Gallery. The flamboyant Gower, almost twenty years older than the Prince, made very little secret of his sexual tastes. His approach to sex was cheerfully unsentimental; he had a preference for working-class men, or 'rough trade'. (It was of Gower, who had taken up with an objectionable young man named Frank Hird, that Oscar Wilde once said: 'Gower may be seen but not Hird.'[32] Gower was generally believed to have been Oscar Wilde's model for the decadent and cynical Lord Henry Wotton in *The Picture of Dorian Gray*.)

Equally uninhibited about his sexual preferences was the celebrated Oscar Browning, a Fellow of King's College. Sacked as a master from Eton because of his suspect friendship with a pupil, the good-looking George Curzon, afterwards Viceroy of India, Browning – or O.B. as he was usually called – was a relentless pursuer of young roughs. His rooms at Cambridge were invariably filled with soldiers and sailors, stable lads and artisans. Few nights were spent without a muscular companion beside him, 'in case he was seized by sudden illness'.[33] In those more innocent days, O.B.'s addiction to working-class boys was put down to his kindness of heart and eccentricity of character.

Browning, in whom snobbery went hand in hand with sodomy, chased royal titles as eagerly as he did rough trade. His remark, after being presented to the Emperor Franz Josef of Austria, that 'he was the nicest Emperor I ever met', became a famous O.B. catchphrase.[34] He was particularly delighted when Queen Victoria's hearty sailor son, Prince Alfred, Duke of Edinburgh, in thanking him for the gift of a book, assured O.B. that he retained the most pleasant memories of the times the two of them had spent together in the Turkish baths.

Browning was introduced to Prince Eddy by Jim Stephen. Bitterly envious of Stephen's catch, O.B. always claimed that the plum appointment of tutor to Prince Eddy had gone to Stephen by default: Browning had merely happened to be out on the day that the 'official arranging the matter' had called to see him about it.[35] He made up for this mischance, however, by inviting the Prince to his rooms as often as possible. 'O.B.'s rooms', as one undergraduate blandly puts it, 'were a trysting-ground for all the celebrities and oddities of the university.'[36] He even, this plumpest, least athletic of men, took to playing hockey – the only game Prince Eddy enjoyed – 'for the sole purpose of being near to him and receiving a princely whack on the shins'.[37] For Christmas 1884, O.B. gave the Prince a silver cigarette case.

Browning's rooms were furnished in the most *outré* manner: Turkey carpets, Morris wallpapers, 'bits of statuary picked up for a song in Italy; choice line engravings; dainty bronzes'.[38] His Sunday evenings, which were often attended by Prince Eddy, were renowned for their unconventional mixture of guests. 'In an armchair', wrote one discomforted undergraduate attending for the first time, 'an elderly peer, who had evidently enjoyed the College wine in the Common room, was slowly expounding politics, with the help of a cigar, to a circle of squatting young men; standing by the fire a Tommy in scarlet uniform was shaking into the flames the spittle from the clarinet he had just ceased playing; here and there, seated on the floor, were pairs of friends conversing earnestly in low tones as oblivious as lovers to their surroundings … Presently the piano began in the room beyond, and we went in to watch our host trolling out *Voi che sapete* with immense gusto. At the close of his performance, the clarinet player gave him a spanking …'[39]

The pride of Oscar Browning's apartment was his recently installed bathroom. On one occasion, as he was showing it off to Prince Eddy, one of the more knowing undergraduates crept up to the door and locked the couple in. What the two of them did in the course of an 'imprisonment which lasted quite a long time' no one knew. Perhaps O.B. subjected the Prince to one of his famous masturbation lectures. The discussion of this 'delicate subject' was one into which Browning was known to plunge himself on the slightest excuse. But whatever happened, 'the Pragger took the joke in good part'.[40]

On whether Prince Eddy experienced his first sexual encounters while at Cambridge one can only speculate. It seems likely – given his easy-going nature, the predatory habits of some of his associates, the tastes of most of the Apostles and the lustful, cloistered, all-male atmosphere of the College itself – that he did. What were afterwards darkly referred to as his 'dissipations' must have started somewhere. This is not to claim that the Prince was exclusively homosexual; simply that, in common with many another randy twenty-year-old he would probably have responded favourably to any sexual advance.

There must have been some reason why the magazine *Punch* considered it appropriate to publish a page of cartoons depicting a typical day in the Prince's Cambridge life. In one he is shown playing hockey in a particularly dainty fashion; 'Oh don't hurt him!' exclaims one undergraduate from the sidelines. In another, two undergraduates gaze admiringly at him as he brushes his hair. 'Isn't it beautiful?' exclaims one. 'Too lovely to look at,' answers the other.[41]

Prince Eddy celebrated his twenty-first birthday on 8 January 1885. 'It seems quite like a dream, and but so short a while ago,' wrote Queen

Victoria, 'that I hurried across from Osborne to Windsor, or rather Frogmore, to find that poor little bit of a thing, wrapped in cotton! May God bless him and may he remain good and unspoilt, as he is!'[42]

Her opinion was echoed by those of the Prince's Cambridge friends who had been invited to Sandringham for the coming-of-age celebrations. They were delighted to find him – amid all the grandeur of this royal occasion – 'as quiet, as kindly, and as simple as if he had been in his rooms, or theirs, at Trinity'.[43] Lady Geraldine Somerset, lady-in-waiting to the old Duchess of Cambridge, Queen Victoria's aunt, could also report that Prince Eddy was '*charming*, as nice a youth as could be, simple, unaffected, unspoiled, affectionate'. But his ignorance, she sighed, was lamentable. 'What on earth', she continues unfairly, 'stupid Dalton has been about all these years! He has taught him *nothing*!'[44]

The Prime Minister, W.E. Gladstone, having written to the Prince to congratulate him on his birthday, asked permission to publish his reply. 'On reading it over again this afternoon,' claimed Gladstone's secretary, 'I found part of it admitted of no possible grammatical construction; so I took it to Marlborough House and got the Prince of Wales to agree to my suggested alterations and then sent copies of it round to the papers.'[45]

But lamentably ignorant or not, the Prince was from now on obliged to play a more prominent role on the royal stage. In March that year he accompanied the Prince of Wales on a state visit to Berlin for the eighty-eighth birthday celebrations of Kaiser Wilhelm I. Here he disgraced himself by letting his dinner-table companion, the sharp-tongued Princess Catherine Radziwill, involve him in her ridiculing of the elderly guest sitting opposite. The butt of their giggling was the Grand Duke of Saxe-Weimar – the German Empress's brother.

A few weeks later he accompanied both parents on a tour of Ireland where, in Cork, they were given an extremely hostile reception. The streets, reported the Prince of Wales's equerry to Queen Victoria, 'were filled with sullen faces – hideous, dirty, cruel countenances, hissing and grimacing into one's very face, waving *black* flags and *black* kerchiefs – a nightmare! The royal carriage was pelted with rotten vegetables.'[46] This manifestation of anti-English hatred was gushingly interpreted, by the *Daily Telegraph*, as 'Royal Visit to Cork, Enthusiastic Reception in the City'.[47]

From this sobering experience, Prince Eddy returned to Cambridge for the last weeks of his second and final year. James Stuart, a Fellow of Trinity and a member of Parliament who had rooms on the same staircase at Nevile's Court, has an interesting anecdote about the Prince at this time. 'Though somewhat stiff and slow in his manner, he had yet a keen perception of what was necessary to put people at their ease ...' wrote Stuart. 'When I stood for the undivided borough of Hackney in 1884, I pledged myself to vote against any further increase of grant to the royal family, and in particular against the grant which was then mooted to the Prince himself on coming of age. When I returned to Cambridge after my election, the Prince came into my room – exactly as before – and I noticed how, with a little awkwardness, and yet with such evident good feeling, he strove to let me see that my pledge, to which he somewhat slyly alluded, made no difference to his friendliness.'[48]

Prince Eddy's final year ended with a series of brilliant May Week celebrations. One of his friends has left a lyrical account of the last occasion on which the Prince and his male coterie savoured the particular pleasures of university life. Having danced until dawn at a ball at St John's Lodge, the little group of undergraduates strolled back to Trinity. 'When we reached the Great Court,' he writes, 'the charm of the fresh summer morning made the thought of bed impossible. It struck someone that it would be a good idea to turn into the Bowling Green and have a final cigar before we separated. In a day or two we should all be going down, some of us for the last time, and it seemed a pity not to see the thing out to the end. How clearly I recall the very sounds and scents of that delicious June day – the gay squealing of the swifts as they circled round the old towers, and the moist odours of the shaven turf at our feet. It was as though the quintessence of our happy life at Cambridge had been distilled into a golden cup and offered as a final draught to our regretful lips.'[49]

6. THE CHOCOLATE SOLDIER

In the summer of 1885 Prince Eddy performed his first important public functions. He was created Master of the Bench of the Middle Temple at which, in the ancient Middle Temple phrase, he was 'called to the Degree of the Utter Bar'. On 29 June he accepted the freedom of the City of London at an impressive ceremony at Guildhall. His own performance was less than impressive. 'He read his speech', noted one member of his audience, 'and we could not hear a word of it, and the poor fellow seemed very nervous. The Prince of Wales looked annoyed and the Princess, as always, exquisite.'[1]

The following week, apparently no less nervous, Prince Eddy went down to Aldershot. He was to start his military career as a lieutenant in the Royal Artillery before being transferred to the famous cavalry regiment, the 10th Hussars. With him, as successor to first Dalton and then Stephen, went his newly appointed equerry, Captain the Honourable Alwyn Greville. Greville was the brother-in-law of Lady Brooke, the unconventional society beauty who, as 'Darling Daisy', was destined to replace Lillie Langtry as the Prince of Wales's acknowledged mistress.

Prince Eddy proved himself to be no more of a soldier than a scholar. The impression given by the official version of his military career – his steady promotion to major, his dedication to his duties, his 'soldierly bearing and spirit' – is hardly borne out by the private opinions of his contemporaries.[2] When Queen Victoria's cousin, the Duke of Cambridge, who was Commander-in-Chief of the British Army, once visited Aldershot during the Prince's time there, the gruff old warrior was astonished by the young man's backwardness. 'He cannot learn his drill, so that he is not *yet* in the ranks!' reported Lady Geraldine Somerset. 'The Duke wanted to try him in some most elementary movement, the Colonel begged him not to attempt it as the Prince had not an *idea* how to do it! The Duke of course not wishing to expose him, let it alone!'

Sitting beside the Prince one night at dinner at Sandringham, the Duke of Cambridge turned the conversation to military matters. The Duke had served in the Crimean War and as Prince Eddy's regiment, the 10th Hussars, had played a part in the campaign (the word 'Sebastopol' had been added to their colours) the topic seemed an obvious one. '*He knew nothing about it!!!!*' reported the astounded Duke. 'Knew *nothing* of the Battle of the Alma!!! It is past all conceiving!'[3] Even the Prince's official biographer had to admit that he 'was disinclined by nature, not so much to active exertion as to the act of entering upon it'.[4] The Duke of Cambridge put it more bluntly. 'He is an inveterate and incurable dawdler,' he thundered, 'never *ready*, never *there*!'[5]

Neither at Aldershot, nor at York, nor at the Curragh near Dublin, did Prince Eddy show much interest in soldiering. He disliked barrack life, he detested field days, he dismissed his General as 'a lunatic'. Such cavalry routines as the 'officers' ride' he found tedious in the extreme. 'One has to go jogging round and round the riding school in a very tight and uncomfortable garment called a stable jacket and very hot work it is I can assure you,' he once grumbled to a friend. His promotions were never earned or deserved; the authorities were obliged to promote him because of his position and because 'younger men were rising above his head'.[6]

A lackadaisical attitude characterized everything he did – or did not do. When the fiftieth anniversary of the Duke of Cambridge's joining the Army was being publicly celebrated in 1887, Prince Eddy forgot all about it. 'Prince Eddy *here*, at Marlborough House,' wrote the outraged Lady Geraldine at this ignoring of the Duke's great day, 'his own near relation, known him intimately from his birth, an officer under his command, neither comes to him, nor writes to him, nor takes the slightest notice!!!! His own uncle and Commander-in-Chief!!!! Too bad; it is no want of proper feeling, but sheer stupidity!! Alas! that fatal apathy and inertness, sleepy apathetic laziness and total want of initiative.'[7]

Once his first six months of training were over, Prince Eddy seems to have spent almost as much time away from his regiment as with it. Not only did he have various public duties to perform but he was to be seen at balls, dinners, family weddings, the theatre and weekend house parties. He often dined with a friend in some London club. He went to Cambridge to open the new buildings of the Union and, on another occasion, to receive an honorary Doctorate of Law. In spite of the Duke of Cambridge's complaint that he was 'hopelessly soft' and did not 'care even for any field sports', the Prince seems to have done his obligatory share of hunting and shooting.[8] He was hardly, though, what Vincent, in one of his frequent flights of fancy, calls 'a shot of real brilliance' and 'a hard Englishman' who 'possessed all the manly instincts and tastes of an English gentleman'.[9]

His son's continuing backwardness annoyed the Prince of Wales considerably. Prince Eddy's remaining in the Army, he sighed on one occasion, was 'simply a waste of time – and he has not that knowledge even of military subjects which he ought to possess'.[10]

In October 1886 Prince Eddy's old tutor, the Reverend Dalton, having been rewarded for his years of service by being installed as a Canon at Windsor, finally married. His bride was Catherine Evan-Thomas. The version given in official royal biographies, that Dalton married the sister of one of the officers aboard the *Bacchante*, is not quite accurate. The truth is more intriguing. On the *Bacchante*, the middle-aged Dalton, invariably described as a confirmed bachelor, had taken a fancy to a teenaged cadet; a mere three days after meeting the boy's sister, he proposed marriage. His bride was barely half his age. Best man at the wedding was Arthur Benson, also half Dalton's age and the 'object of adoration' of Dalton's days with Prince Eddy at Cambridge.

Just over eighteen months later, Catherine Dalton bore her forty-eight-year-old husband a son. The Canon decided on Edward, after Prince Eddy, as a first name for the baby and asked the Prince to be godfather.

Prince Eddy agreed but, to the Canon's regret, was unable to be present at the christening in St George's Chapel, Windsor, on 24 September 1887, as he was with his mother, Princess Alexandra, in Denmark. Characteristically, the Prince was late in sending his christening gift.

'You will I hope receive in a few days my gift for my Godson which was not ready before, or I would have sent it for the Christening on the 24th of last month,' he wrote to Canon Dalton. 'I hope you will think the cups suitable, as I got them in Copenhagen, and they took my fancy at once; and I think they ought to come in useful when my Godson grows older as I used to have the same kind of cups for drinking out of as a child ...'[11]

Although Dalton would have been delighted with the royal gift, his son – as he grew older – was not. In fact, he was acutely embarrassed at having a royal godfather. For the boy, who never used his first name of Edward, became celebrated as Hugh Dalton, that most dedicated of socialist Chancellors of the Exchequer, actively concerned with setting up the Welfare State after the Second World War. He grew up to loathe and distrust the royal family: an attitude they heartily reciprocated. Of all Labour politicians, the royal family disliked Hugh Dalton the most; they no doubt saw him, as did many Conservatives, as a 'class traitor'. Particularly displeasing to King George VI – Prince Eddy's nephew – was the insouciance with which Hugh Dalton sold off all his royal godfather's gifts, including those christening cups from Copenhagen.

An interesting sidelight on the situation is that Hugh Dalton appears to have shared, not only the socialism of his father's great friend Edward Carpenter, but also his ideals of brotherly love and friendship. 'Both before and after his marriage', writes Hugh Dalton's biographer, Ben Pimlott, 'his emotions were more stirred by men – increasingly by younger men – than by women.'[12]

For all Prince Eddy's manly and military inadequacies, his brother officers seem to have been fond of him. It was true that he had 'a certain shrinking from the robust horseplay which has been known to exist among subalterns', but he was popular for other reasons.[13] 'He was greatly beloved', it is claimed, 'for his kindly disposition, his unassuming modesty, his earnest simplicity of character. For display, for ostentation, for flattery ... he had no inclination.'[14] Those swaggering and mustachioed cavalrymen, expecting to be faced by an arrogant and conceited princeling, warmed to what can only be termed his more feminine characteristics. 'Kind', 'gentle' and 'dear' are the adjectives most frequently used by his contemporaries to describe Prince Eddy. His was the sort of dozy, well-intentioned personality that tends to bring out the protective instincts in others. And he was helped, of course, by the fact that he would one day be King.

The Reverend William Rogers, who had known the Prince since boyhood, once visited him at camp. His obsequious account makes — in the light of Prince Eddy's almost girlish diffidence and subsequent reputation for aberrant sexuality — amusing reading. The Prince had developed, the good cleric tells us, 'into a fine, manly character not easily seduced from the right path. I was very much struck by his manly bearing. In the exuberance of my spirits I said, "Well, Prince Edward, they have made a man of you." He was pleased with my remark, and asked me to send him my photograph ... Some of his brother officers had said that they would like to make a man of the world of him. Into that world he refused to be initiated, but he was a man of the world in the best sense — a Christian gentleman.'[15]

In a carefully considered report to the Duke of Cambridge, Lord Wolseley — who was one day to succeed the Duke as Commander-in-Chief — gave his honest opinion of the young man's abilities. 'I think', he wrote, 'HRH has far more in him than he is often given credit for, but I should describe his brain and thinking powers, as maturing slowly ... Some of our very best and ablest men have mentally matured with extreme slowness ... Personally, I think he is *very much* to be liked, has most excellent manners, thoughtful for others, and always anxious to do the right thing. He is, however, young for his age and requires to be brought out. I studied him closely when staying in a country house with him, and this is the result of my study.'[16]

Perhaps Wolseley was right. There were certainly indications, after the Prince had been in the Army for a couple of years, that there had been some improvement. Major Miles, one of the Prince's instructors at Aldershot, who had at first been 'quite *astounded* at his utter ignorance', subsequently professed himself 'equally astounded how much he has got on with him and thinks, under the circumstances, his papers are infinitely better than he dared to expect. He has his father's dislike for a book and never looks into one, but learns all orally, and retains what he thus learns.'[17] Even the Duke of Cambridge had eventually to admit that although it was true that Prince Eddy 'was not a devoted soldier … he has greatly improved in the last few months'.[18]

The Prince's letters to his Cambridge friends might have been unimaginative but they were articulate, and his handwriting was fluid and confident. He always signed himself 'Edward', never 'Albert Victor'. 'I am, as you see, signing myself in the name you knew me when I was a boy, which I prefer with old friends …' he once wrote.[19] He was also beginning to look more self-assured. His previously tentative-looking moustache was now fuller and curled up at the ends; his somewhat vague stare struck some observers as cool and impenetrable. He had inherited, from both parents, a passion for clothes. With his slender figure and exceptionally slim waist, he had the perfection of, and about as much animation as, a tailor's dummy. He was certainly a dandy. To minimize the length of his neck ('a neck like a swan', wrote one relation) he wore high starched collars. This led to the family nickname of 'Collars-and-Cuffs'. 'Don't call him Uncle Eddy,' the chaffing Prince of Wales would instruct visiting royal children, 'call him Uncle-Eddy-Collars-and-Cuffs'.[20] In an artfully posed photograph of himself in a kilt, with a fishing rod held stiffly in one hand, the Prince looks more like a fashion plate than someone about to get his boots muddy on some river bank.

But it was in uniform that he looked most impressive. The dress uniform of the 10th Hussars — as was to be expected from a regiment which had once numbered Beau Brummell in its ranks — was especially elegant. Rendered even more elegant by subtle changes on the part of the Prince's tailor — a longer tunic with rounded corners, a tighter waist, a higher collar – it gave him a decidedly dashing air. His top-boots were highly polished, his breeches skin-tight, his tunic glittered with gold braid, frogging and tassels, his busby sported an extra-long white plume.

This bandbox appearance, allied to his languid manner and hooded gaze, afforded Prince Eddy a mysterious, curiously seductive aura. As he smoked almost continuously, both Turkish cigarettes and cigars, he was usually seen through a haze of slowly drifting smoke. It comes as no surprise to learn that he was by now being drawn, ever more deeply, into the shimmering underworld of late Victorian London.

It is concerning this period of Prince Eddy's life that various bizarre legends have grown up. Most of them are connected to the famous Jack the Ripper murders in which five, and possibly eight, prostitutes were murdered and hideously mutilated in London's Whitechapel district in the autumn of 1888. Closely related to these murders is one of the strangest of the Prince Eddy legends: the story of his 'secret marriage'.

The story first came to light in 1973. In the course of making a series of television programmes on Jack the Ripper, the BBC researchers were put in touch with a man by the name of Joseph Sickert. Sickert, the natural son of the celebrated Victorian painter, Walter Sickert, claimed that he was Prince Eddy's grandson. The Ripper murders, said Joseph Sickert, had all been part of an elaborate attempt to cover up Prince Eddy's unsuitable marriage.

These startling revelations aroused the interest of the journalist Stephen Knight who, in collaboration with Sickert, produced a book entitled *Jack the Ripper: The Final Solution*. In it, Knight repeats, in a highly coloured version, Sickert's theory that Prince Eddy was his grandfather and that the Prince's clandestine marriage had led to the Ripper murders.

In 1978, two years after the publication of Knight's book, Joseph Sickert repudiated it. The Ripper connection had been a hoax, he said. The only truth in the book concerned his illustrious ancestry. Yet in 1991, after Knight's death, Joseph Sickert – in collaboration this time with Melvyn Fairclough – not only repeated, but also considerably expanded upon, the story. Because, he explained in the foreword to a new book

The Ripper and the Royals, he had realized that Knight was misrepresenting his material, the two of them had quarrelled and Sickert had decided not to give Knight the full story. He was now making good that omission. In *The Ripper and the Royals*, the whole extraordinary tale, as recounted to Joseph Sickert by his father Walter Sickert, was being presented for the first time.

And an extraordinary tale, as retold by Joseph Sickert through Melvyn Fairclough, it is.

They start their story by claiming that towards the end of 1883 Princess Alexandra asked the twenty-three-year-old artist, Walter Sickert, to introduce Prince Eddy 'to the artistic and literary society' of London. Walter Sickert's father and grandfather had apparently been 'employed in the Royal Palaces of Denmark'. At that time Walter Sickert had a studio in Cleveland Street, in the Bohemian quarter centring on Fitzroy Square and it was here, we are assured, that Prince Eddy frequently visited him. To pass undetected, the Prince would pretend to be the artist's brother, 'Albert Sickert'.

Before long, continues their account, Prince Eddy had met and fallen in love with one of Sickert's occasional models: a young woman by the name of Annie Elizabeth Crook, who was employed in a local tobacconist's and confectioner's shop. They had allegedly been introduced to each other by Prince Eddy's tutor, Jim Stephen; Stephen and Annie were second cousins. Jim Stephen, writes Fairclough, was in love with Prince Eddy and in order to protect the young Prince from the 'homosexual milieu' into which he had been drawn, Stephen introduced him to Annie Crook in an effort to 'divert' him. Stephen 'could handle the thought of Eddy with a woman, but became jealous if he was with other men and hoped that a relationship with Annie would serve to exclude them'.[21] The young couple became lovers and on 18 April 1885, Annie Crook gave birth to a daughter at the Marylebone workhouse. The girl was named Alice Margaret Crook.

It was after the birth of their daughter Alice, claims Joseph Sickert, that Prince Eddy and Annie Crook were married. As the bride was Roman Catholic, there were two ceremonies: an Anglican marriage at St Saviour's Parish Hall and a Catholic marriage at St Saviour's Chapel.

With the Act of Settlement of 1701 excluding anyone married to a Roman Catholic from inheriting the crown, and as the Royal Marriage Act of 1772 forbade any member of the royal family marrying without the monarch's consent, Prince Eddy's marriage had to be kept secret. Another reason for secrecy, runs Joseph Sickert's theory, is that had it been revealed, a combination of republicanism, class hatred and anti-Catholicism would have led to revolution and the fall of the monarchy.

But, inevitably, the news reached the ears of 'those in power'. Chief amongst these powerful men was the Prime Minister, Lord Salisbury. Fearing a national upheaval, he immediately ordered not only a cover-up but also a forcible separation of the young couple. One day, under cover of a purposely organized commotion in Cleveland Street, two closed carriages slipped into the area. One stopped outside Sickert's studio; the other outside No. 6, where Annie Crook lived in a basement room. Two men in 'brown suits' entered the studio to re-emerge with the struggling Prince Eddy between them. They bundled him into the carriage. In the meantime, a man and a woman were forcing Annie into the second coach. They were driven off in opposite directions, never to see each other again. The Prince was henceforth 'confined to Court and supervised'.

Annie, claims Fairclough, was more harshly treated. She was taken to Guy's Hospital where she was detained for several months and certified insane. This was ordered by Sir William Gull, Queen Victoria's Physician-in-Ordinary and physician also to the Prince of Wales's family. Gull, an expert on paraplegia and diseases of the nervous system, performed 'some kind of operation' on Annie which led not only to 'partial paralysis and later epilepsy' but to an impairment of her memory. Thus mentally and physically crippled, she could safely be set free.

For the rest of her life, Prince Eddy's 'wife' Annie Crook drifted in and out of infirmaries and workhouses. She died, aged fifty-eight, in 1920, in the Lunacy Observation Ward of St George's Union Workhouse.

The Ripper murders, claims Joseph Sickert, were instigated by 'a group of influential men' in order to protect Prince Eddy from being blackmailed by a handful of Annie's associates who knew about the clandestine marriage. But that was another story.[22]

So much for Prince Eddy's 'wife', Annie Crook. Joseph Sickert and Melvyn Fairclough now move on to outline the career of Prince Eddy's 'daughter', Alice, who bore her mother's surname of Crook. Alice is depicted as having lived an equally wretched and impoverished life. Twice, as a girl, she was almost killed in carriage 'accidents' organized by that coterie of 'influential men'. In 1905, at the age of twenty, Alice had a brief liaison with her mother's artist friend, Walter Sickert, and bore him a son. This son (who was, if Joseph Sickert is to be believed, Prince Eddy's 'grandson') was named Charles. One day, while Alice was in Holloway prison for some minor offence, she was told that her son Charles was to be taken from her; she had proved herself incapable of caring for him.

It is here that Joseph Sickert's story becomes more intriguing still. By now Prince Eddy was dead and his brother, Prince George, the future King George V, was Heir Apparent. The birth of Alice's son Charles had happened to coincide with that of a fifth son to Prince George and his wife Princess May, the future Queen Mary. Their son was christened John. Prince John – so runs Sickert's version – died in his first year and, instead of announcing this fact to the world, 'the royal family and their advisers' decided to snatch Prince Eddy's 'grandson' – Alice's illegitimate son Charles by Walter Sickert – and substitute him for the dead Prince John. The royal family had been worried 'that Charles might one day prove an embarrassment to the monarchy since, as Eddy's grandson, he was in line to the throne'. Having him 'within the confines of the palace walls, they could ... forestall any complications his existence might create'.

The substitute Prince John – ignored by his putative mother, Princess May, and doted on by his great-grandmother Queen Alexandra ('who knew that John's real mother was Alice') – was discovered to be epileptic. He died in 1919, aged thirteen.[23]

Prince Eddy's 'daughter' Alice, at the age of forty, had another brief affair with the sixty-four-year-old Walter Sickert, and bore him a second son. Alice died, aged sixty-five, in 1950. It is to her second son, Joseph Sickert, that we owe the above story of Prince Eddy's 'secret marriage'.

1. A sexual conundrum: Prince Albert Victor (Eddy),
Duke of Clarence and Avondale

2. Three of the telegraph boys involved in the homosexual brothel case

3. The Cleveland Street brothel, picturing clients, telegraph boys, a waiting cabby and an oblivious policeman

4. Charles Hammond, the brothel-keeper who was allowed to escape justice

5. Lord Arthur Somerset, whose visits to the brothel sparked off the
Cleveland Street Scandal

6. A male prostitute, in drag, soliciting in Piccadilly

7. The Prince and Princess of Wales holding Prince Eddy and Prince George, with the boys dressed, as was customary, as girls

8. Prince Eddy and Prince George, in miners' outfits, during the visit of
HMS *Bacchante* to Australia

9. The philandering, pleasure-seeking, undeniably
heterosexual Prince of Wales

10. 'Motherdear': the beautiful, elegant and
possessive Alexandra, Princess of Wales

11. The Wales family in the early 1880s. The Prince and Princess of Wales flanked by Prince George and Princess Victoria; Prince Eddy flanked by Princess Maud and Princess Louise

12. The malleable Prince Eddy, during his first year at Cambridge

13. Jim Stephen, the Prince's unstable, misogynous Cambridge mentor

14. Looking like a tailor's dummy, Prince Eddy poses elegantly on a river
bank, at the time of the Jack the Ripper murders

15. The Prince astride a buffalo, shot during his tour of India at the height of the Cleveland Street Scandal

16. A policeman taking statements from a telegraph boy

17. An artist's impression of a pimp handing Lord Euston a card advertising *'poses plastiques'* at the Cleveland Street brothel

18. Five of the boys involved in the brothel case

19. Resplendent in Hussar uniform and flanked by members of his staff, the newly created Duke of Clarence and Avondale

20. The lovelorn and ambitious Princess Hélène d'Orléans, who was determined to marry Prince Eddy

21. Princess May of Teck at the time of her arranged match with Prince Eddy

22. An artist's depiction of 'a nation's calamity'

23. Sir Alfred Gilbert's monument to 'a brave and blameless warrior'; the tomb of the languid and dissolute Prince Eddy, at Windsorv

Joseph Sickert's story is, to put it kindly, improbable. Its sensational-ism aside, at no stage does it take into consideration the character and circumstances of Prince Eddy himself. That Princess Alexandra would have wanted her son – at that stage newly arrived at Trinity College, Cambridge – to be introduced into London's artistic and Bohemian circles is highly unlikely. One of her chief concerns was to guard him against just such society; to keep him as unworldly and unsullied for as long as possible. Nor would she ever have chosen an unknown, twenty-three-year-old painter to effect such introduction. There was no shortage of well-established and respectable court paint-ers and sculptors to awaken whatever interest the Prince might have had in cultural matters. Two of Queen Victoria's children, Prince Leopold, Duke of Albany and Princess Louise, Duchess of Argyll, moved in what, by royal standards, were considered to be artistic circles. In any case, Prince Eddy never showed the slightest interest in art or literature.

Sickert claims that 'nearly three years elapsed between the first meet-ing of Prince Eddy and Annie Crook and their becoming lovers'.[24] As Annie's child must have been conceived in July 1884, this places their first meeting in the last months of 1881. This cannot be accurate. At that time Prince Eddy and Prince George were sailing in Far Eastern waters aboard the *Bacchante*. They did not reach home until August the follow-ing year. Contradicting himself, Joseph Sickert then puts Prince Eddy's introduction to Walter Sickert – and subsequently Annie – 'towards the end of 1883'.[25] But in October that year, after those months of intensive tutoring in the Bachelors' Cottage at Sandringham, the Prince went up to Cambridge.

Throughout 1884, the year in which Joseph Sickert claims that Prince Eddy and Annie Crook became lovers, the twenty-year-old Prince – slow-witted, unsophisticated, apathetic, immature – was up at Trinity College, under the eye, not only of Dalton, but of the possessive Jim Stephen. He was certainly not living *la vie bohème* in Fitzrovia. The one extended period during which he was not at university – the long summer vacation of 1884 – was spent at the University of Heidelberg, learning German. Annie's child must have been conceived in mid-July 1884; Prince Eddy was at Heidelberg from mid-June until the third week of August.

Sickert's theory – that a besotted Jim Stephen encouraged Prince Eddy's love affair with Annie Crook in order to keep him out of the arms of other men – is far too tortuous. Why, then, did Stephen allow him to consort with the likes of Lord Ronald Gower and Oscar Browning?

Nowhere, apparently, is there any written, official evidence of a relationship between Prince Eddy and Annie Crook. On the birth certificate of the girl born to Annie Crook in the Marylebone work-house on 18 April 1885, the space for the father's name is left blank. This is hardly significant: on many a Victorian birth certificate, the space for the father's name of an illegitimate child was left blank. Annie Crook, apparently illiterate, made a cross instead of signing her name. It is difficult to understand why Prince Eddy, who is alleged to have married Annie after the birth of her child, should not have ensured that the baby was born in more comfortable circumstances than in a workhouse.

Of a marriage certificate for Prince Eddy and Annie Crook there is no trace in the General Register Office. Sickert's collaborator, Melvyn Fairclough, has an explanation for this. 'Those in power', he says, 'can make sure the records say whatever they wish them to say – especially to save the throne.'[26]

Had the Prince's marriage to a Roman Catholic become known, argues Sickert, he would automatically have forfeited his right to the throne. Whether or not Annie Crook was a Catholic is a matter of debate but, in any case, by the terms of the Royal Marriages Act, a prince, who was still under twenty-five and who had married without the Sovereign's consent, would have been acting unlawfully. The marriage could simply have been declared illegal. Sickert's protest, that this would have created an uproar, is untenable. It could have been done – as he claims everything else was done – in secret. But if, as his collaborator Fairclough implies, 'those in power' had destroyed the marriage certificate, then there was really no reason for any further action; certainly not the sort of action likely to create a public scandal. There was simply no written proof of any such marriage. Nor is there any reason to imagine that news of the marriage would have led to violent revolution and the overthrow of the throne.

The melodramatic manhandling of the lovers leading to their forced separation makes no sense whatsoever. Why did the authorities have to wait until Prince Eddy was visiting Walter Sickert's studio to abduct him? Why did he have to be abducted at all? Surely the Prince of Wales could have called him to his study for a stern talking-to? How could the Prince from then on have been 'confined to Court and supervised'? Throughout the period when the abduction and confinement is alleged to have taken place, Prince Eddy was at Aldershot, pursuing, in desultory fashion, his military career.

And is it likely that Prince Eddy, who had apparently loved Annie enough to marry her, would have allowed her to live such a destitute life? Or that his mother, Princess Alexandra, renowned for her impulsive generosity, and who – claims Sickert – knew all about the marriage, would not have ensured, if only in secret, that her beloved Eddy's 'daughter' Alice was well provided for?

Sickert says that Princess Alexandra once visited her 'granddaughter' Alice in hospital and gave her a diamond brooch. This brooch was subsequently stolen during a burglary. He also tells us that, a month before her death in 1925, Queen Alexandra sent Alice a black-lacquered metal box containing 'a magnificent collection of jewels comprising a triple-row diamond-and-emerald necklace with matching earrings and bracelet; a single-row dark-red ruby-and-sapphire necklace with a central pear-drop, and matching earrings and bracelet; a single-row diamond necklace; a triple-row necklace and blue-and-red opals; a pair of diamond oval brooches, one framing a picture of the Duke of Clarence, the other a picture of Queen Alexandra and her father, Christian IX of Denmark; and, lastly, a pair of gold cuff-links which had belonged to Prince Eddy'. The lid of this treasure chest was decorated with two 'A's entwined, surmounted by a crown. 'The initials are those of Alice and Alexandra.'[27] Sickert does not say whether or not he still owns this priceless collection of jewels. This is surprising: the production of the jewels would prove, beyond the shadow of a doubt, the truth of his story.

His claim about the substitution of Alice's son Charles for the dead Prince John hardly warrants serious consideration.

So much then, for Joseph Sickert's story of Prince Eddy's 'secret marriage'. An amalgam of rumours, inferences, coincidences and contradictions, it is entirely lacking in any hard evidence. It could have been just another of those prince and peasant girl legends, so numerous in royal history, had it not been for the fact that Joseph Sickert cites the secret marriage as the motivation for the Jack the Ripper murders.

For Sickert's story takes one on into that 'autumn of terror'; that horrific series of crimes with which Prince Eddy's name has been repeatedly linked.

PART THREE

JACK THE RIPPER

7. ROYAL JACK

From September to November 1888, London's East End was terrorized by Jack the Ripper. Moving stealthily through the dark and fetid alleys of the Whitechapel district, he subjected at least five women to a horrifying death. His motivation was clearly sexual. All the women were prostitutes. Working at great speed, he would first strangle them (possibly from behind as they bent over in preparation for anal sex), slit their throats from left to right until their heads were all but severed, and then disembowel them in nightmarish fashion. With each murder the mutilations became more grisly. The victims, in the words of one shocked policeman, would be 'ripped up like a pig in the market', their entrails 'flung in a heap' about their necks.[1] Sometimes the uterus and its appendages and the upper portion of the vagina would be removed. In the final murder – of Mary Kelly – her cheeks and forehead were skinned. Even hardened police officers would blanch at the sight of these savage mutilations.

Quite obviously, the murders were the work of a sexual psychopath. Despite being highly sexed, indeed sexually obsessed, he was probably incapable of normal sexual relations. His actions were a particularly ghastly form of defloration.

The identity of Jack the Ripper has never been conclusively established. At the time, and ever since, there has been no shortage of suggested candidates. They range from the probable to the ludicrous. He was said to be a large ape who bounded over walls and hid his bloody knife in the branches of nearby trees; although trees were hardly a feature of Victorian Whitechapel. He was a man seeking revenge for having had his penis cut off. A sufferer from syphilis, he was using the stolen vaginas to 'suck off the virus from his ulcers'. One theorist suggested that he was one of those 'Hill tribesmen' who 'pay particular reverence to genital organs' or, worse still, a white man, affected by sunstroke, who had adopted the tribesmen's beastly customs.[2] Others claimed that he was a social reformer, anxious to draw attention to the wretched conditions in the East End. Many imagined that he was a physician avenging himself on prostitutes for having given him a venereal disease. He was a Jewish slaughterman, a Polish hairdresser, a Russian doctor, a German imperialist trying to get his hands on 'the Crown of England, the Colonies and India and the New World'.[3] He was not a man at all: he was Jill the Ripper.

'Theories!' Chief Inspector Abberline, in charge of the case, once sighed. 'We were lost almost in theories; there were so many of them.'[4] It is significant that out of this plethora of theories, Prince Eddy features in no less than five.

In Dr T.E.A. Stowell's celebrated article on the identity of the Ripper, published in the *Criminologist* in November 1970, the suspect is clearly Prince Eddy. It is worth quoting Stowell's description of the man whom he prefers not to name but to call 'S'.

'He was the heir to power and wealth. His family, for fifty years, had earned the love and admiration of large numbers of people by its devotion to public service to all classes, particularly the poor, but as well to industry and the workers. [By 1888 Queen Victoria had reigned for fifty years.] His grandmother, who outlived him, was very much the stern Victorian matriarch, widely and deeply respected. His father, to whose title he was heir, was a gay cosmopolitan and did much to improve the status of England internationally. His mother was an unusually beautiful woman with a gracious personal charm and was greatly beloved by all who knew her.

'After the education traditional for an English aristocrat, at the age of a little over 16 years, "S" went for a cruise round the world with a number of high-spirited boys of approximately his age group.

'He was, perhaps, too popular and gregarious for his own safety. It is recorded that he went to many gay parties ashore.'

That established, Stowell develops the main thrust of his theory. He claims that for someone of his age, personality and prospects, 'S' was not sufficiently protected by those responsible for his welfare. He was exposed to far too many temptations. It was during his stay in the West Indies, at one of the 'many shore parties' which he was so recklessly allowed to attend, that the young man contracted syphilis. This led, eventually, to madness.

Six weeks after leaving the West Indies, maintains Stowell, 'S' was obliged to cancel an important public engagement in what was then one of Britain's colonies. The excuse given was that he was suffering from 'a trifling ailment'. Such a cancellation, he argues, was highly unusual, permissible only if the subject were in severe pain or suffering from some obvious physical disfigurement, like toothache or a rash.

'This "trifling ailment" may well have been the appearance of the skin rash of secondary syphilis appearing six weeks after the primary infection acquired in the West Indies.'

Stowell doubted that this rash had been recognized for what it was or whether the patient had received any appropriate treatment. He believes that the syphilitic infection was simply allowed to develop unchecked.

The article then deals briefly with the young man's return to Britain and his subsequent military career. In the army he was 'successful, popular and happy'. The writer claims that 'S' was forced to resign his commission soon after the 'raiding' of Charles Hammond's homosexual brothel in Cleveland Street.

Stowell describes, at some length, a photograph of his suspect. This is quite clearly the well-known portrait of Prince Eddy, widely reproduced at the time.

'In this photograph he is seen by the riverside holding a fishing rod, wearing a tweed knickerbocker suit of perfect cut, not a fold misplaced and without a crease. On his head is a tweed cap set far too precisely, and he has a small moustache. He is wearing a 4 in. to 4½ in. stiff starched collar, and is showing two inches of shirt cuff at each wrist (I was told by my elders that he was given the nickname of "Collars and Cuffs"). This photograph of him is more suitable for a tailor's showcase than for the river bank, but it must be remembered that this was the period of extravagance of the "aesthetes", and also that the photographic plates of those days were slow, and subjects had to be "posed".'

Stowell then goes on to detail his suspect's reign of terror in the East End, his later life and his early death. This, allowing for minor errors on the part of an old man who did not pretend to be a historian, was quite obviously meant to be a pen-picture of Prince Eddy. It is, though, through his major errors that Stowell undermines his case for proving that the Prince was Jack the Ripper.

Stowell's contention is that the Ripper murdered his victims during fits of insanity brought on by syphilis. He claims that Prince Eddy, or 'S', contracted the disease during 'one of the many shore parties which he enjoyed in the West Indies on his world journey'. This is, to say the least, unlikely. Prince Eddy visited the West Indies only once, having just turned sixteen, in the course of his first cruise on the *Bacchante*. One cannot imagine the upright Mr Dalton allowing his precious charge – the backward and unworldly Prince Eddy – to attend what Dr Stowell calls the sort of 'gay parties ashore' at which he was likely to contract syphilis.

Six weeks after this visit, continues Stowell, the Prince was forced to cancel an important public engagement in 'one of our Colonies' because of what was probably 'the skin rash of secondary syphilis appearing six weeks after primary infection acquired in the West Indies'. In fact, six weeks after leaving the West Indies, Prince Eddy was not in 'one of our Colonies' but back home in England. That cancelled 'important public appointment' occurred, over a year later, in Australia. By the following day, the Prince was fully recovered.

In another part of his twelve-page article Stowell claims that the Prince's murderous activities were known to the royal family after the second, and possibly even the first, Ripper murder and that soon after the third and fourth murders, which occurred on the same night, he was placed under restraint 'in a private mental home in the Home Counties'.

From here he escaped to commit, on 9 November, the fifth and final murder.

But it has since been established – by, if nothing else, a reading of the Court Circular – that Prince Eddy had alibis for most of the nights when the murders were committed. Even one alibi – assuming the murders were all committed by the same man – would be enough. On the night of the double murder, for instance, he was in Scotland; on the night of the final murder, 9 November, when Stowell would have us believe that the Prince had escaped from that 'private mental home in the Home Counties', he was at Sandringham, celebrating his father's birthday. Immediately after these celebrations, far from being 'again apprehended', Prince Eddy set off on a visit to his grandfather, King Christian IX of Denmark.

After the Ripper murders, says Stowell, the Prince's health gradually deteriorated. During a five months' cruise 'he probably suffered a relapse and was brought home quietly for further intensive treatment'. From then on 'he was on the downward path from the manic stage of syphilis to the depression and dementia which in time must inevitably overtake him. We hear little more of him before his death a year or two later.'

In truth, during the three-year period between the Ripper murders and Prince Eddy's death early in 1892, he not only carried out a full, minutely documented and highly publicized tour of India but, once back home, fulfilled a stream of public and private engagements. Far from hearing 'little more' of the Prince during the last years of his life, those years were some of his busiest and most thoroughly reported. Stowell's claim – that his information about Prince Eddy's syphilis and eventual death from 'softening of the brain' in a private mental home near Sandringham – came from a study of the papers of the royal physician, Sir William Gull, cannot be true. Sir William Gull died in 1890, two years before Prince Eddy.

Gull had all along known that Prince Eddy was the Ripper, says Stowell. Indeed, the doctor had often been seen in Whitechapel on the night of a murder; he was probably there 'for the purpose of certifying the murderer to be insane'. But who had seen him? And why did he need to go to Whitechapel to certify that Prince Eddy was insane? There is, in fact, no evidence whatsoever to back up the contention that Gull was in Whitechapel at the time of the murders.[5]

Even without all these glaring implausibilities in Stowell's theory, the suggestion that Prince Eddy might have been Jack the Ripper is absurd. From the various descriptions of those who thought that they had seen the Ripper talking to his victims, there emerges a picture of a man in his mid-thirties, dark-haired, with a heavy moustache. He must have been, as a doctor carrying out two of the post-mortems put it, 'a man of physical strength and of great coolness and daring'.[6] He would also have had to have been astute, quick-witted and fast-moving. In 1888 Prince Eddy was twenty-four: a good-natured, impractical and, above all, listless young man. Can one really imagine this 'dawdly' Prince strangling a woman, slitting her throat until it was almost severed from her head, expertly eviscerating her body, carrying off her uterus and disappearing, in a flash, through the maze of Whitechapel? Hardly.

But the story died hard. It was revived in a book by the American writer, Frank Spiering, entitled *Prince Jack: the True Story of Jack the Ripper*. His book, claims Spiering, is the unmasking of a ninety-year-long conspiracy of silence on the part of 'Prime Ministers, members of Royalty and Scotland Yard officials in hiding the identity of the world's most infamous mass-murderer'.[7] His study (which is simply an elaboration of Stowell's theory) is a reconstruction of what he felt had happened but was based, he asserts, on a reading of official and unofficial sources.

What Frank Spiering's publishers describe as his 'impeccable research' included interviews with 'staff members at Buckingham Palace and people at Scotland Yard'.[8] But the chief and most important source was the copy of some notes, made by Sir William Gull, which the author discovered 'bound in an ancient portfolio, in the New York Academy of Medicine'. These notes, Spiering subsequently claimed, 'contained the confession of Victoria's grandson, HRH Prince Albert Victor Christian Edward, the Duke of Clarence and Avondale, whom the Royal Physician was treating for syphilis. They detail the Prince's account of the sordid murders he committed in Whitechapel and his motivation for these murders.'[9]

This sensational 'discovery' was converted by Frank Spiering into an even more sensational book. Purporting to be a serious, non-fiction account, it reads, according to one American reviewer, like 'concocted, Grade Z fiction'.[10] Here, in brief, is the plot of Spiering's book. Prince Eddy, wandering about Spitalfields one night, is so intoxicated by the butchering of horses in a horse slaughter-house that he grabs a knife and rushes out to murder and disembowel a prostitute. A subsequent visit to a Jewish abattoir results in a second murder. From the body he carries away a 'bloody portion' which he shows to his 'lover', Jim Stephen. To Stephen the Prince explains that the murders leave him feeling 'tremblingly afraid, yet wonderfully free'. He had been infected, years before, with syphilis by a prostitute; therefore he feels no remorse at getting rid of them. Overcoming his initial shock, Jim Stephen feels obliged to make his contribution to his friend's murderous exploits: he writes one of the famous Ripper letters, taunting the police.

After two more murders by Prince Eddy, Queen Victoria notices that her grandson is not looking well. Like any concerned grandmother, she packs him off to the doctor. This is the ubiquitous Sir William Gull who, realizing that his patient is suffering from syphilis, hypnotizes him. The horrified doctor discovers that the Prince, acting out his syphilitic obsessions, is responsible for the Whitechapel murders. Gull promptly communicates this astonishing news to Sir Charles Warren, Head of the Metropolitan Police.

But far from being equally astonished, Sir Charles Warren tells Gull that he has all along known about the Prince's activities; and so does the Prime Minister, Lord Salisbury. The result is that Gull is drawn into this top-level conspiracy of silence.

The best course, decide Gull and Warren, is for Prince Eddy to be kept under strict surveillance, in the House of Rest Sanatorium in Balham. Here, in spite of treatments of iodide of potassium, electrical therapy and drugs, the Prince remains uncontrollable. On 8 November 1888, in a violent fit of rage, he escapes from the sanatorium. He heads for Jim Stephen's house in De Vere Gardens, Kensington. Realizing that he would have sought sanctuary with his friend, Gull and Warren arrive in De Vere Gardens with a small party of hand-picked men to reapprehend him. But the Prince has slipped away. And, to his horror, Jim Stephen notices that one of the long knives is missing from the pantry.

That night the last victim, Mary Kelly, is murdered. The Prince's particularly nightmarish eviscerating work over, he puts on 'the woman's dress and shawl which he'd brought with him in the black handbag' and, moustaches notwithstanding, hurries to Sandringham in time to celebrate his father's birthday. He explains away his garb to the doubtless puzzled guests by pretending that he had attended a costume party the night before. Not surprisingly, the Prince of Wales promptly alerts Sir William Gull and, the birthday luncheon over, Prince Eddy is escorted back to London and into the care of the doctor.

For the rest of his short life he is so successfully controlled by drugs and hypnotism that he is able to lead an apparently normal existence. But on 13 February 1891 he has a relapse and commits yet another murder. Finally deciding that enough is enough, 'the powers who ruled England' realize that the business must be brought to an end. First the Prince's accomplice and lover, Jim Stephen, is committed to a lunatic asylum and then the Prince himself is gradually weakened. Instead of the customary doses of iodide of potassium, he is 'probably given daily injections of morphine'. He is finally confined to a rest home in Ascot where 'the doses were steadily increased until the sleep condition became permanent'.[11]

As no statement in Spiering's book is actually attributed to any palace or police official, one must assume that all this information comes from Sir William Gull's notes found in that 'ancient portfolio in the New York Academy of Medicine'. Donald Rumbelow, in his masterly compilation of Ripper material, *The Complete Jack the Ripper*, describes his own efforts to locate these important notes. A letter to the New York Academy of Medicine produced nothing.

'None of the entries in our catalogue for works by or about Sir William Gull contain the material referred to by Mr Spiering,' answered the Librarian. 'In a library the size and age of ours, it is possible that a set of notes bound with a larger work or other works could have gone unnoticed by our cataloguers, but it is highly unlikely. Mr Spiering was never able to remember or reconstruct the catalogue entry he submitted for retrieval from our stacks and in which he allegedly found the notes by Gull. Thorough searches by staff also proved fruitless.'

Equally fruitless was Rumbelow's direct appeal to Spiering. His letters, sent care of Spiering's publishers, have remained unanswered.

In 1978, just before the publication of his book, Frank Spiering publicly challenged Queen Elizabeth II to make available the material on Prince Eddy in the Royal Archives at Windsor. He offered to halt the impending publication of *Prince Jack* if she held a press conference and revealed what she knew about her 'great-uncle's acts of murder and his own extraordinary death'. With infinite politeness, a Buckingham Palace spokesman told Mr Spiering that his allegations were 'not sufficiently serious to warrant a special statement from the Queen' but that the Royal Archives would be opened to him as they were to other researchers.[12]

Spiering's answer — that he had no wish to see any files — led, in Donald Rumbelow's drily expressed opinion, 'to the inevitable conclusion that his challenge to the Queen had been made to publicize his book'.[13]

8. RIPPING
FOR THE PRINCE

If Prince Eddy was not Jack the Ripper, then the Ripper was acting, argue several theorists, on his behalf. This is certainly the contention of Michael Harrison in his book *Clarence* published in 1972. Harrison claims that Dr Stowell, in his article in the *Criminologist*, was not pointing the finger at Prince Eddy at all, but at his one-time Cambridge tutor, J.K. Stephen. This was why Stowell called his suspect 'S'. Finally realizing that his love for Prince Eddy was not reciprocated and that the relationship between them was cooling, Jim Stephen committed the murders as some sort of monstrous manifestation of his love.

Stephen had never fulfilled his early promise. Like many who shine too brightly in too many spheres at university, he shone in none once he left. Although he became a Fellow of his college and a barrister, he devoted much of his time to journalism. His prowess in debate, which had led his Cambridge friends to assume that he would enter Parliament, was frittered away in after-dinner conversation. In 1886 he suffered a severe blow on the head. Whether it was this, or inherited mental instability, which was the cause of his increasingly erratic behaviour, is uncertain. But from then on Jim Stephen veered recklessly from one interest to another.

He published a weekly journal, the *Reflector*, which folded after a few issues. He wrote a pamphlet in defence of the compulsory study of Greek at university. He brought out two slim volumes of poetry, in which both his snobbery and his hatred of women was only too apparent.

In desperation his father, Mr Justice Stephen, had him appointed to a Clerkship of Assizes on the South Wales Circuit. This, too, he abandoned after a short spell, having anyway left most of the work to his deputy. Stephen then decided that he would become a painter. To his cousin, the young Virginia Stephen, afterwards Woolf, whom he sometimes used as a model, he once announced 'as though it were an amusing incident, that the doctors had told him that he would either die or go completely mad'.[1]

Michael Harrison's reasons for identifying Jim Stephen as Jack the Ripper are extraordinarily convoluted. To follow them here would be tedious. In the absence of any hard facts, Harrison analyses every line of Stephen's poetry, uncovers every double meaning, parades every literary allusion, hammers home every coincidence, gives significance to every number and date. He discovers a similarity of both style and handwriting between Stephen's poetry and Jack the Ripper's taunting letters to the police. Ignoring such evidence as does not suit his case, he overemphasizes such scraps as do.

In essence his theory is this. Jim Stephen was in love with Prince Eddy in a 'dominant, demanding' fashion. The gradual slackening of their relationship, once the Prince had left Cambridge and joined the Army, allied to the frequent sight of him in the company of other homosexuals in pubs and clubs, roused Stephen's jealousy to 'dangerous heights'.[2] Already mentally unstable, Stephen's balance was finally tipped by the thought of the Prince's association with a woman – it might have been an actual association with a 'harlot' or simply the Prince's loving relationship with his possessive mother, the Princess of Wales. (The Ripper's removal of the uterus, claims Harrison, is a symbolic attack on women, not as whores, but as *mothers*.) Jim Stephen then committed his series of horrifying murders which Harrison deftly extends to ten to fit in with Stephen's poem about 'ten harlots of Jerusalem'. The murders were committed as an act of revenge by a discarded lover during a period of insanity: Stephen was offering up some sort of dramatic blood sacrifice.

According to Harrison, the Ripper's identity, well known to the authorities, was suppressed, not only because Stephen was the son of 'one of Britain's most famous judges' but because of his suspect friendship with the Heir Presumptive to the British throne. 'One could imagine', argues Harrison, 'what might have happened to the Crown and the Judiciary had a Stephen been shown to be the Ripper.'[3]

This is all too baroque by half. Indeed, from the very outset one of Harrison's chief clues is rendered worthless. He claims that Stowell had chosen the initial 'S' as a code letter for Prince Eddy for a very good reason: 'S' was the first letter of Stephen's name. By doing this, Stowell was dropping a hint that the Ripper was actually Stephen and not Prince Eddy. But had Harrison bothered to ask the editor of the *Criminologist* about it, he would have been told that Stowell had originally wanted to use the more conventional 'X'. Only on being told by the editor that 'X' was too trite did Stowell agree to change the initial to the first letter of his own name – 'S'.

The one verifiable fact to emerge from the welter of Michael Harrison's arguments is the refusal of Jim Stephen to take any nourishment after hearing of Prince Eddy's death; and of his own death, in a lunatic asylum, twenty days later. The relationship between the two men is certainly intriguing. Perhaps, as Stephen became progressively less successful and more unbalanced, he began to look back on their time together as a sort of idyll.

Even more tortuous are the paths by which Joseph Sickert sets out to solve the Ripper mystery. His theory, as told by Melvyn Fairclough in *The Ripper and the Royals*, is that the murders were committed, not by one man but by a group of high-ranking Freemasons determined to keep secret the marriage of Prince Eddy to Annie Crook.

While working in that confectioner's and tobacconist's shop in Cleveland Street, runs Sickert's version, Annie Crook had been joined by a girl named Mary Kelly. When Annie gave birth to her daughter by Prince Eddy, Annie's friend Walter Sickert arranged for Mary Kelly to move in with her as companion and nurse. The arrangement did not last long. Mary Kelly soon took to prostitution and gin-tippling in the East End. In 1888 she, together with three other prostitutes, decided to take advantage of Mary Kelly's one valuable asset: her knowledge of

Prince Eddy's secret marriage. The four of them set out to blackmail Walter Sickert. Unless they were paid for their silence, they threatened, they would make public everything they knew about Prince Eddy, Annie Crook and their daughter.

Walter Sickert immediately alerted Prince Eddy. He consulted his younger brother, Prince George, who happened to be home on leave from the Navy. Prince George told their father, the Prince of Wales who, in turn, told not only 'some of his friends' but also the Prime Minister, Lord Salisbury. Between the lot of them, they decided that the blackmailers must be silenced. If the marriage were to be revealed the throne 'might be swept away forever' and with it, 'the Freemasonic Royal Alpha Lodge No. 16'. The 'real power behind the throne in the 1880s', explains Joseph Sickert, 'was Freemasonry'.[4] The Prince of Wales was Grand Master of England, Prince Eddy had been initiated into the movement in 1885 and 'many peers of the realm, especially those close to the throne' were Freemasons.[5]

The most effective way of silencing these blackmailing prostitutes was to murder them. So a great Masonic conspiracy, including Sir Charles Warren, head of the Metropolitan Police, and Sir Robert Anderson, head of the Metropolitan CID, set about accomplishing this task. The actual killing was done by Sir William Gull. On each occasion he would be driven to the East End by a coachman named John Netley. The victim would be lured into the curtained coach where they would be fed by Gull with grapes 'liberally treated with laudanum'. Once they were unconscious, Gull could begin his task of throat-slitting and disembowelling. The coach was lined with 'American cloth' which prevented the blood from soaking into the floor and could afterwards be washed down by the obliging Netley. The bodies would then be deposited by Netley 'in a manner prescribed by his Masonic masters'.[6] Indeed the places, dates, method of murder and arrangement of the intestines were all rich in Masonic symbolism.

If Sir William Gull was the actual murderer, the instigator of the murders was Lord Randolph Churchill, brother of the 8th Duke of Marlborough and father of the future Sir Winston Churchill. He was, says Sickert, 'the highest Freemason in England: Magister Magistrorum or Master of Masters'.[7] Determined to prevent the wholesale sweeping away of 'the monarchy, the aristocracy, the landed gentry and the government' which would doubtless follow the revelation of Prince Eddy's marriage, Lord Randolph was tireless in the organizing of his fellow Masons in these murderous expeditions.[8] For Gull and Netley were not the only ones directly involved. On the occasion of the last murder – of Mary Kelly – Lord Randolph was himself present in the room in which she was so hideously mutilated. 'Like a shooting party making a foray into the country …' explains Sickert, 'other gang members went along to oversee the job in hand, or to act as look-outs, or simply for the ride.'[9] Sometimes as many as twelve would set out.

One leading gang member was, apparently, the inevitable Jim Stephen. 'It was due to his love for Eddy and his loyalty to his Royal Alpha brothers that he became involved in the conspiracy in the first place', but when the 'feverish' Lord Randolph decreed that Annie Crook and her daughter Alice must also be killed, Stephen rebelled.[10] His love for Eddy overcame his Masonic loyalty. He reported the plan to Inspector Frederick Abberline, who was in overall charge of the investigation. He also, apparently, told Abberline the full story of the Masonic conspiracy. But as Abberline's superiors, Sir Charles Warren and Sir Robert Anderson, were part of the conspiracy, there was nothing that Abberline could do about the murders. In fact, he was subsequently 'advised' not to pursue his investigations.[11]

Stephen also told Prince Eddy about the proposed murder of his wife and child. The Prince's reaction to this was to suggest that his grandmother, Queen Victoria, be murdered instead. Having been brought up by his mother, the Danish Princess Alexandra, to hate everything German, and regarding Queen Victoria as the personification of all things German, Prince Eddy's 'tortured mind formulated the madcap scheme of having his grandmother murdered'. But at this, apparently, even Lord Randolph Churchill balked. 'Who?' he exclaimed. 'The great whore herself?'[12]

And so Joseph Sickert's fancifully fashioned edifice soars skywards. Speculation is piled upon speculation, conjecture heaped upon conjecture.

The reasoning becomes progressively more involved; the motives less comprehensible. Towards the end of the book he tells us that the last woman murdered was not – as is generally believed – Mary Kelly at all: by then, or soon after, she was safely in Canada, having had her passage paid in exchange for Prince Eddy's marriage certificate. (Had this been done at the start, one cannot help thinking, a great deal of trouble, and blood, would have been saved.)

To back up his claims, Joseph Sickert quotes the diaries of Inspector Abberline. Three such diaries had apparently been bequeathed to Walter Sickert but are now in Joseph Sickert's possession. He was prepared, Joseph Sickert announces on one page, to present these important diaries to the Metropolitan and the City of London police. But on the next page he claims that the Special Branch had 'forcibly' entered his home in search of Abberline's diaries. Luckily, they were not in his possession at the time and he fobbed off the intruders with a few unimportant papers. On another occasion a number of Crown Prosecution Service officials, who had somehow managed to read the still unpublished manuscript of *The Ripper and the Royals*, came to warn him that the book had 'political implications and could embarrass the Royal Family'. Two days after this, three men purporting to be from the Special Branch came to check if the manuscript was 'treasonable'.[13]

The whole story is incredible. Indeed, it is difficult to believe that Joseph Sickert is being serious. Even if the story of Prince Eddy's secret marriage were true, can one really believe that dozens of Freemasons, including the Prince of Wales, the heads of the Metropolitan Police and of the Metropolitan CID would countenance a series of horrific murders? Or that the truth would never, until now, have leaked out? Or that five derelict and drunken prostitutes would have been believed? That only by murdering them could they have been silenced? Or that they, in turn, would not have told their friends about it? How could the seventy-year-old Sir William Gull, who had suffered a stroke the year before, have carried out the murders? For although he had recovered from his stroke, its effects had obliged him to give up his medical practice. He died just over a year after the Ripper murders. And why was Walter Sickert, who knew more about the alleged marriage than anyone, not murdered?

Osbert Sitwell, in his book *Noble Essences*, says that Walter Sickert claimed to know the identity of Jack the Ripper. According to the painter, he had been given his name by the landlady in whose house Sickert had once had lodgings. She told him that the previous occupant of his room had been Jack the Ripper. She and her husband had often heard their lodger, a quiet veterinary student, return home from having been out all night; from traces in the fireplace, they would know that their lodger had burnt the suit he had been wearing the previous evening.

Walter Sickert had scribbled the name of the Ripper in the margin of the book he happened to be reading; a book which he subsequently gave away. If Osbert Sitwell wanted to know the name, said Sickert, he should try and track down the book. But by the time Osbert Sitwell tried to trace it, it had been destroyed in the bombing during the Second World War.

If Walter Sickert was telling Osbert Sitwell the truth, it proves that the name he scribbled down could not have been a particularly well-known one, and that he was given it by a landlady only 'some years after the murders'.[14]

All these theories – Stowell's and Spiering's of Prince Eddy as the Ripper, Harrison's of Jim Stephen killing for love of the Prince, and Joseph Sickert's of a Masonic conspiracy to keep a royal marriage secret – can safely be discounted. Not so easily dismissed is the theory of Martin Howells and Keith Skinner. In their book *The Ripper Legacy*, published in 1987, they establish a link between Prince Eddy and a man named Montague John Druitt.

It has long been suspected that there was an official conspiracy of silence about the true identity of Jack the Ripper; that his name was known to what has since come to be called the Establishment and to the upper echelons of the police force. It seems to have been realized, by the end of 1888 – seven weeks after the last and most ghastly murder – that there was no further need to hunt for the Ripper. The exceptional number of police patrolling the streets of Whitechapel and Spitalfields was gradually reduced. By 1892, with the Ripper still not caught, detained and brought to trial, the file on the case was closed. No official explanation was given for this closure. It was afterwards claimed, by an Assistant Commissioner of the Metropolitan Police, that the Ripper had 'escaped justice'; and by Chief Commissioner James Munro that 'he *should* have been caught'.[15] The apparent belief, at the highest police levels, was that the Ripper had committed suicide.

On 31 December 1888 a body was fished out of the River Thames. It was estimated to have been in the water for about a month. It was identified as that of a thirty-one-year-old man named Montague John Druitt. He was subsequently described as a barrister. He was, in fact, a failed barrister and an obscure schoolteacher who had recently been sacked from his post. At the inquest the dead man's brother, William Druitt, gave some misleading information and produced what appeared to be a suicide note, found in his brother's lodgings.

No official indication was given, at the time, that Druitt might have been Jack the Ripper. Not until many years later, in the private notes of yet another Assistant Commissioner, Sir Melville MacNaghten, was Druitt found to be listed as the prime suspect. This information had been given to MacNaghten 'privately'. At the time of Druitt's death, no evidence appears to have been brought against him; there is apparently no mention of him in any of the police files; nor was a police report on his death sent to the Home Office. The lower levels of the police – the men who had so tirelessly been hunting the Ripper – knew nothing about him.

Quite obviously Druitt – this unsuccessful barrister and insignificant schoolteacher – was being protected. But why should his identity have been kept secret? What reason could there possibly be for an Establishment cover-up?

Montague Druitt had been born in 1857 into a respectable upper middle-class family in Wimborne, Dorset. One scholarship took him to Winchester College; another to New College, Oxford. Like Prince Eddy's mentor, Jim Stephen, Druitt was an accomplished scholar and a successful sportsman. But, again like Stephen, he failed to live up to his early promise. In 1885, after completing his training, he was called to the bar but in the three years that he spent at the Inns of Court as a barrister, he received not a single brief. With no private income, he was forced to take a teaching job. He taught in a private school in Blackheath until he was dismissed in the autumn of 1888. Both in the privileged and highly competitive world of the bar and in the less demanding post of a schoolteacher, Druitt had proved himself a failure.

But Montague Druitt moved in another world as well. He was an attractive young man and, before his life began to fall apart late in 1888, very popular. He was a dedicated cricketer, a keen debater and a good mixer. At the Inns of Court, during his early, more optimistic days, he found himself in the company of many like-minded young men; many, in fact, who belonged to that coterie of Apostles who had once surrounded Prince Eddy at Cambridge. Some of the Prince's closest companions, including Jim Stephen and his brother Harry, and Harry's close friend Harry Wilson, had chambers at the Inns of Court during this period. Druitt was also known to have played cricket with many of the Prince's Cambridge set.

The writers of *The Ripper Legacy*, and others, believe Druitt to have been homosexual. 'As a resident,' claim Howells and Skinner, Druitt 'would have dined at the Inns of Court more regularly than most, and he would have been drawn into the same cosseted homosexual circle as other men of similar disposition.' He would almost certainly have been able to attach himself to that 'privileged and clandestine league' who had been together at Trinity.[16] Druitt was exactly the apparently heterosexual but secretly homosexual type characteristic of the Apostles.

Obliged to keep their private lives secret, this group of young barristers did what homosexuals have always done: arranged to meet each other, and their less presentable companions, in some place safe from prying eyes. In this case the haven was provided by the leading member of the group – Harry Wilson. In a tribute to Wilson, his old friend Harry Stephen gives a picture of this haven. Reading between the lines – or indeed, the lines themselves – Harry Wilson's homosexual milieu is only too apparent.

At Cambridge, writes Stephen, Wilson 'joined the mysterious company of the Apostles of whom nothing can be said because their very existence is a secret, and he also made a host of friends who were not leading men, and who had no particular intellectual gifts, but did possess certain common but very definite qualities which were necessary to gain his friendship ... During this later period [1885–8] he was able to carry out an idea that he had long had in his mind by establishing a "chummery" in a picturesque little house called "The Osiers", in Chiswick Mall, where a succession of young men, chiefly from Cambridge, found an ideal substitute for the lonely and uncomfortable lodgings which would otherwise have been their lot, and where other friends could always find youthful and cheerful company.'[17] This is the same Harry Wilson who had been Prince Eddy's closest friend at Cambridge, whom he still often met and who was destined, it was widely believed, to become the Prince's private secretary.

An understanding of Wilson's circle at 'The Osiers' makes the discreet letter from Prince Eddy, written in 1888 and innocently quoted by James Vincent in his official biography, especially significant.

My Dear Harry,

I put off writing to you before in the hope of still being able to give a favourable answer. But I now find, very much to my regret, that I shall not be able to get away for next Saturday, which is very tiresome, for I should have much enjoyed paying you a visit at Chiswick and seeing some of my old friends again ...[18]

That Montague Druitt was not only a member of this particular barristers' inner circle but that he actually knew Prince Eddy seems to be indicated by the fact that when the Prince paid a visit to Lord and Lady Wimborne in Dorset that year, Montague Druitt – who lived in London, and not his elder brother William who lived in nearby Bournemouth – was invited to a ball in his honour. One can only assume that the Wimbornes knew of the Prince's friendship with Montague Druitt.

This is not the place to follow the reasoning by which Druitt has become one of the chief suspects in the hunt for the Ripper's identity. By the autumn of 1888, with the failure of his career as a barrister and his sudden dismissal from his teaching post, he had become a brooding and embittered man. There was insanity in the family: his mother, to whom he was devoted, was by now in a lunatic asylum. The one detailed description, by a young policeman, of the man who was undoubtedly the Ripper, is an uncannily accurate portrait of Druitt. As we have seen, he was the principal suspect of Sir Melville MacNaghten: the truth of the Ripper's identity, the Assistant Commissioner afterwards declared, lay 'at the bottom of the Thames'.[19] What is certain is that once Druitt's body, weighted down with four large stones, was fished out of the Thames on the last day of 1888, the hunt for the Ripper ceased. When Albert Bachert, a member of the Whitechapel Vigilance Committee, complained about the fact that the police seemed to be making no more effort to apprehend the Ripper, he was told, in strictest confidence, that 'The man in question is dead. He was fished out of the Thames two months ago.'[20]

But why should Bachert have been sworn to secrecy? Surely the police would have been only too eager to broadcast the fact that the notorious Ripper had been caught. Druitt, on the face of it, was an obscure and unimportant person. What possible reason could there have been for this conspiracy of silence about him?

The theory is that any investigation into Druitt's background would have led the police and, more importantly, the newspapers and the general public, straight into that circle of ambitious, socially prominent and, above all, homosexual members of the Establishment. Among their number were a private secretary to the Home Secretary, a future Lord Mayor of London, the sons of one of the country's leading judges, and Harry Wilson himself, who had been marked out as a future private secretary to Prince Eddy. At the head of this band of 'faithful servants of the Crown and State' stood the future wearer of the Crown and the embodiment of the State – Prince Albert Victor, Heir Presumptive to the throne.[21]

In one of the dead Montague Druitt's pockets was found the return half of a ticket from Charing Cross to Hammersmith – the nearest station to Chiswick Mall. The body itself, heavily weighted, was fished out of the Thames just yards from Harry Wilson's 'chummery', The Osiers. Had Druitt visited his friends and had they advised him that suicide was the only honourable course? Or had they, as Howells and Skinner imply in their study of the case, taken it upon themselves to rid the Establishment of this risk to its position of power and privilege? Had Druitt been murdered to save the skin of the future King-Emperor?

The whole exercise bore a striking resemblance to the cover-up of that other great *cause célèbre* of the period: the Cleveland Street scandal.

9. KINGS AND QUEENS

In January 1889, Prince Eddy turned twenty-five. By now, apparently, this mysterious young man was leading what has been described, by the official biographers of several other members of his family, as an extremely 'dissipated and unstable life'. He indulged in 'every form of vice and dissipation'; his 'dissipations were beginning to undermine his health'.[1] Yet the precise nature of these dissipations is never made clear. His younger brother, Prince George, kept a girl in St John's Wood: 'a ripper' whom he is said to have sometimes shared with Prince Eddy.[2] One cannot know how often or how eagerly Prince Eddy took advantage of her services but an occasional visit to a kept girl can hardly be regarded as debauchery.

Apart from this, Prince Eddy's name has not been linked with that of any woman during this period of his life. Joseph Sickert's story of his 'secret marriage' is hard to believe, and until the worried royal family began dragooning Prince Eddy into marriage, he seems to have shown very little interest in the opposite sex. His father, by the same age, was an ardent womanizer; even the younger Prince George, generally regarded as sexually abstemious, not only kept one woman in St John's Wood and another in Southsea but was also embarked on a more chaste love affair with a Miss Julie Stonor. He was even rumoured to have married a woman on Malta.

On the other hand, the allegations of Prince Eddy's homosexuality must be treated cautiously. Michael Harrison's contention, in his book *Clarence*, that Jim Stephen was in love with Prince Eddy, has led subsequent writers to refer to the two men as 'lovers'. There is no proof of this. Nor is there any proof for Harrison's claim that the Prince was 'a regular and popular guest' at a string of homosexual clubs and pubs, and that he was known, at the notorious transvestite Hundred Guineas Club, as 'Victoria'.[3] The allegations may be true but Harrison gives no source for them.

Yet the contention that Prince Eddy would never have dared to visit homosexual meeting-places, or even brothels, for fear of being recognized, is not valid. In those days, before the widespread reproduction of photographs in newspapers and magazines, readers had to rely on line drawings for likenesses. These bore little resemblance to the subject. Even the future King Edward VIII, later Duke of Windsor, claimed that, until the First World War, it was quite possible for him to walk largely unrecognized through the streets of London. For Prince Eddy, in the 1880s, it would have been even easier. With his waxed moustache and his well-cut clothes, he would have been indistinguishable from any other young man-about-town.

The weight of – admittedly circumstantial – evidence seems to indicate that the Prince's unspecified 'dissipations' were predominantly homosexual. So many factors seem to bear this out: the personalities of, and relationship between, his parents; his fear of his busy and aggressively heterosexual father and his adoration of his elegant and possessive mother; his 'want of manliness', his 'shrinking from horseplay', his 'sweet, gentle, quiet and charming' nature;[4] the submissive, easily influenced qualities which would make any highly sexed young man such as he amenable to the advances of a bolder, more predatory male. Prince Eddy seems to have been typical of a sort of lazy, feather-brained voluptuary who can become obsessed by sex. For someone like that, sexual activity can quickly lead to overindulgence.

By all accounts, Prince Eddy seems to have been most at ease in the company of men younger than himself. Indeed, in common with many backward and inadequate men, he enjoyed being with boys. James Vincent, in his official biography that tells one so little about Prince Eddy's tastes or personality, suddenly brings him to life in a paragraph about the Prince's interest in boys. 'If the people to be addressed were boys – the lads of a Boys' Home for example – the Prince addressed them in words exactly appropriate to their needs, and in a tone which, without being for a moment lacking in dignity, was friendly and kindly and went straight to their hearts. He had, indeed, always the tenderest corner in his heart for boys and for little children and his simple kindness towards them never failed to rivet their affections to him …'[5] On the Prince's coffin, continues Vincent, was placed a wreath from two boys whom he had befriended: the inscription read simply, 'From Norrie and Charlie'.

Another observer claims, with no apparent awareness of a *double entendre*, that Prince Eddy 'interested himself in those efforts which modern philanthropy, taught by experience, is making to get hold of the young lads at the dangerous age between school and manhood'.[6] Boys' activities were something in which the Prince seems to have shown a real, and a rare, interest. He opened numberless clubs and homes for boys; not only in London but in cities such as Manchester and York. Given his reputation for yielding to temptations of every sort, it must have been with a degree of cynicism that his entourage listened to the words which the Prince's speech-writers put into his mouth on these occasions. 'Never do what you know is wrong,' he told a gathering of boys in Bethnal Green. 'Often you will feel inclined, either through your own wishes or through the promptings of companions, to do something you would like but which your conscience tells you ought not to be done. Then is the time not to give way: be brave, stand firm, refuse under any circumstances to do what you are not sure is right.'[7]

In his book *The World's Tragedy* published in Paris in 1910, Aleister Crowley – admittedly an unreliable source – claimed to possess some compromising letters written by Prince Eddy to a boy named Morgan. 'And a pretty penny [the letters] have cost me!' he complained.[8] Apparently the boy's mother ran a shop in Cleveland Street. Perhaps – if the claim is true – the Prince had met young Morgan while visiting the male brothel in Cleveland Street.

None of this is to assert that Prince Eddy was exclusively homosexual. But there is a strong possibility that his sexual orientation was not entirely straightforward. Elements of maleness and femaleness, in varying proportions, are present in all human beings. There is, to a greater or lesser extent, a certain amount of homosexuality in all men. The celebrated psychologist, Alfred Kinsey, in *Sexual Behaviour in the Human Male*, divided men into seven groups – from the exclusively heterosexual Group 0 to the exclusively homosexual Group 6. Prince Eddy probably fitted somewhere into the upper half of this scale.

Bisexuality, in different degrees, is far more common than is generally realized. Kinsey claimed that two out of every five men have had homosexual experience; this means that over one-third of the male population is bisexual. Being heterosexual does not preclude a man from having sex – if the circumstances are favourable – with another man; any more than being homosexual prevents a man from getting married and fathering children. This was particularly true of late Victorian England when social conventions were more rigid. Hardly one of the prominent homosexuals of the period was not also a husband and a father.

The fact that Prince Eddy was later to profess himself in love with a couple of women and that he would eventually become engaged to be married, does not prove that he was not homosexual. Still less does it prove that he would never have visited a homosexual pub or brothel. Love and sex were then two very different things: love was often cerebral, romantic, poetic, expressed in fan language, piano duets, scented *billets-doux*. Sex was something altogether more robust. In fact, love was often regarded as the enemy of lust. The average Victorian aristocratic husband slept with his wife for reasons of procreation but enjoyed sex with other men's wives, mistresses, servant girls, prostitutes or, if so inclined, rent boys. For a highly sexed young man, whether homosexual or not, the sort of quick, anonymous, uncomplicated sex that can be enjoyed in parks or public lavatories, can be very convenient. It can also prove very addictive.

For Prince Eddy to have earned his reputation for debauchery, in an age when upper-class male licentiousness was regarded as the norm (and when not even his sexually insatiable father was regarded as dissipated) can only mean that his sexual activity was in some way unusual. There would have been nothing reprehensible about a young unmarried prince sowing a few wild oats. Prince Eddy must have been committing dark and different sins. When Princess Alexandra, who had always imagined him to be such a good boy, began to describe him as 'a naughty, bad boy',[9] it is unlikely that she was ever told exactly what form his naughtiness and badness was taking. For everything seems to indicate that the love – or lust – in which Prince Eddy was indulging was the love which, in high Victorian Britain, dared not speak its name.

Homosexuality was nothing new in the British royal family. Indeed, as far back as the Norman Conquest, two of William the Conqueror's sons, William Rufus and Robert, Duke of Normandy, were being accused of homosexual practices. While Duke Robert was apparently bisexual – having developed a taste for his own sex during the Crusades – his elder brother William, afterwards King William II or the Red King, was undoubtedly homosexual. Contemporary witnesses professed themselves shocked at the 'foulest practices of Sodom' which characterized William II's court.[10] 'Vices before unknown, the vices of the East, the special sin, as Englishmen then deemed it of the Norman, were rife among them,' wrote a later historian. 'And deepest of all in guilt was the Red King himself.' No one was surprised when the tower under which William II was buried crumbled and fell. With 'so foul a corpse' beneath it, what else could one expect?[11]

The next undeniably homosexual monarch was King Edward II, who reigned in the early fourteenth century. To the increasing consternation of his Queen and her entourage, Edward II made no secret of his sexual preferences; chief among his many favourites was the humbly born Piers Gaveston. Eventually, in 1327, at the instigation of the Queen and her lover, the King was murdered while being held prisoner in Berkeley Castle. His murderers had obviously given careful consideration to the method by which he should be done to death: Edward II was killed by having a burning stake thrust up his anus.

The most celebrated homosexual monarch was King James I, who succeeded Queen Elizabeth I in 1603. 'Elizabeth was King, now James is Queen' was a quip that was soon going the rounds. 'The King is wonderous passionate,' claimed one member of the court, 'a lover of his favourites beyond the love of men to women. He is the chastest prince for women that ever was, for he would often swear that he never kissed any other woman than his own queen. I never yet saw any fond husband make so much or so great dalliance over his beautiful spouse as I have seen King James over his favourites …'[12]

Ambitious courtiers, anxious to win the King's favour and failing to do so by offering their own sons or grandsons, would hire troops of handsome young urchins whom they would proceed to have washed, powdered, perfumed and dressed in fine clothes before parading them in front of the monarch. The 'mustering of minions' they called it. But James I had no difficulty in mustering his own minions. He had innumerable favourites, the greatest of whom was the young George Villiers, whom he created Duke of Buckingham. Although both men were husbands and fathers, they behaved, even in public, like lovers. 'In wanton looks and wanton gestures they exceeded any part of womankind,' wrote one astonished observer. Their love letters were extremely outspoken. Sometimes the King would address Buckingham as 'my sweet child and wife' and sign himself 'Thy dear dad and husband'; at other times, switching roles, he referred to himself as Buckingham's wife. 'I desire to live in the world for your sake, and I would rather live banished in any part of the world with you', James I once declared, 'than live a sorrow widow-life without you.'[13]

The sexual preferences of King William III, who reigned jointly with Queen Mary II from the time of the 'Glorious Revolution' of 1688, were much less obvious. William III had none of James I's lust for life: he was a cheerless man, unattractive, abstemious, impassive. 'He had no vice but of one sort in which he was very cautious and secret,' claimed one of his contemporaries, Bishop Gilbert Burnet.[14] The only occasions on which William III looked anything other than morose was when he was out hunting with a party of attractive young men. Usually so censorious, he would forgive these roistering blades any indiscretions.

In 1697 William III's partiality for male companionship caused an open scandal. For some years his close relationship with Hans Willem

Bentinck who, as a young man, had accompanied William III to Britain from his native Holland, and whom the King had created Earl of Portland, had been showing signs of wear. For one thing, Bentinck was getting a bit old and staid for the King's taste; for another, his place in William III's affections had been taken by a much younger man, the handsome and swashbuckling Arnold Joost van Keppel. The entertaining Keppel had risen, with spectacular rapidity, from page to secretary, to Gentleman of the Bedchamber, to inseparable companion. By now he had been created Earl of Albemarle. Keppel, noted one observer, was 'King William's closest companion in all his diversions and pleasures, entrusted at last with affairs of the greatest consequence, had a great influence on the King; is beautiful in his person, open and free in his conversation, very expensive in his manner of living'.[15]

Not unnaturally, Bentinck was violently jealous of Keppel's position. In fact, on one occasion, the King was obliged to separate the two courtiers as they started hitting out at each other. Unable to bear the situation any longer, Bentinck resigned his offices and left the court. William III begged him to return. In a series of anguished letters, Bentinck gave the King the reasons for his decision. He also told him about the 'malicious gossip' concerning William III's relationship with Keppel that was going the rounds of the army. The King was appalled. But he was not so appalled as to break with Keppel. Bentinck had to admit defeat.

In no time, the story of this emotional triangle was being gleefully bandied about; with each telling it became more *risqué*. Few doubted that the homosexual allusions in Vanbrugh's new comedy, *The Relapse, or Virtue in Danger*, were aimed at the court. Whether William III's passionate friendships with Bentinck and Keppel actually manifested themselves in sexual terms is uncertain but there were few of his contemporaries who did not believe that the King belonged to what the Duchess of Orleans called 'the brotherhood of the *château de derrière*'.[16]

But there is no need to look so far back for evidences of homosexuality at the British court. Throughout these later years of her reign, Queen Victoria was surrounded by homosexual or bisexual personalities. The list included the notorious Lord Ronald Gower, Lord in Waiting; Roden Noel, Groom of the Privy Chamber; Lord Henry Somerset, Comptroller of the Royal Household; Sir Horace Farquhar, financial adviser to the royal family and, under Edward VII, Master of the Household; Reginald Brett, afterwards Viscount Esher who, as Secretary to the Office of Works, organized Queen Victoria's Diamond Jubilee and who subsequently became one of the powers of Edward VII's court; Alick Yorke, the flamboyant member of the Household who produced the amateur theatricals and who kept the Queen in 'fits of laughter' with his 'killingly funny stories'. But not always. It was apparently to Alick Yorke that the Queen, on forcing him to repeat an improper story, made the withering remark, 'We are not amused.'[17]

One of Queen Victoria's own sons-in-law, the Marquess of Lorne, afterwards Duke of Argyll, husband of her 'artistic' daughter Princess Louise and at one time Governor General of Canada, was apparently homosexual. He was a frequent guest at the 'masculine entertainments' given by his uncle, Lord Ronald Gower, and he was implicated in a homosexual scandal concerning the theft of the Irish crown jewels from Dublin Castle. The Royal Commission, appointed to examine the theft, was hastily adjourned, never to meet again, on hearing of the Duke of Argyll's possible involvement. It has been claimed that Princess Louise, Duchess of Argyll, was obliged to brick up the door that led directly from their apartments in Kensington Palace into Hyde Park, in an effort to stop her husband's nightly prowlings in search of soliciting guardsmen.

In even closer contact with Prince Eddy would have been a certain equerry to his father, the Prince of Wales. Young George Merrill, the working-class boy who was to become the lover of Edward Carpenter, has a story to tell about his meeting with this unnamed equerry.

'One day I was at the station there,' he later told Carpenter, 'and the Prince of Wales ... was in the station just going off to Tranby Croft on a visit with some of his suite. Of course, they were all very smart with frock-coats and tall hats and flowers in their button-holes; but one of them was a very good-looking fellow – real nice and kind-looking – and only about 26 or 7. And he got into the last carriage just where I was standing on the platform outside, and as soon as he got in he put his head out of the window and made a movement to me to speak to him; and directly I went up he said quite sharp – "businesslike" – "Where will you be this evening at nine o'clock?" And I said "Here", and he said "All right. Mind you come." And the train went off. And in the evening he came all right – only in a tweed suit and cap. Oh! he was nice – such a real gentleman and such a sweet voice. And we walked along by the river, and sat on a seat under the trees, and he had brought some lovely grapes for us to eat.

'And after that we met several evenings in the same way.'[18]

The equerry was anxious for Merrill to come to London to stay with him but Merrill lost his address. In any case, he would have been too shy and too conscious of his humble birth to take advantage of the invitation. Would this bold equerry, in turn, one wonders, have been too conscious of the gulf between Prince Eddy and himself to risk dropping a hint about his own sexual tastes?

Another of the Prince of Wales's equerries was, of course, Lord Arthur Somerset. As Extra Equerry and Superintendent of the Stables, he would have been often in contact with Prince Eddy. But although Somerset was to deny that he had ever encouraged Prince Eddy's alleged forays into London's homosexual underworld, the revelation of his own forays were to be responsible for the spread of the allegations.

By the beginning of 1889, the Prince of Wales was in despair about his eldest son. Prince Eddy seemed to care for nothing other than clothes and those unspecified dissipations. It was true that, at the same age, the Prince of Wales had been equally dedicated to dress and debauchery but at least he had always carried out his public duties with great flair. Prince Eddy, on similar occasions, was hopeless. When he went to Dublin to be made a Knight of the Order of St Patrick, the ceremony at Dublin Castle was acutely embarrassing. The Viceroy, Lord Londonderry, who was initiating the Prince into the Order, was astonished at the young man's ignorance about procedure. The Viceroy's loudly hissed commands – 'Get up!', 'Kneel down!', 'Get up!' – could be distinctly heard throughout the hall.[19]

Equally embarrassing were the Prince's conversational *faux pas*. Once, at dinner, he asked Lord Spencer, Leader of the Liberal Party in the House of Lords, if he was a Tory. One can appreciate why the Prince of Wales was so often driven to growl, 'Eddy, you are a damned fool!'[20]

One of the troubles was that Prince Eddy simply did not have enough self-confidence to break through the deference with which, as a member of the royal family, he was invariably treated. Except in the company of his mother and sisters, he was tongue-tied. Conversation with him tended to be stilted and unnatural; only very rarely did he feel relaxed enough to exercise a certain quiet charm.

His worth – and that of the rest of the royal family – was brought into question during the parliamentary session of 1889. Prince Eddy's oldest, and plainest, sister, Princess Louise, was about to escape her mother's smothering possessiveness by marrying one of her father's sporting companions, Viscount Duff, who was soon to be created Duke of Fife. Almost twice as old as his bride-to-be, parsimonious and ill-mannered, Macduff was gratifyingly rich. This did not prevent Queen Victoria from using the impending marriage to ask the House of Commons for extra provision to be made for Prince Eddy and Princess Louise. The matter was hotly debated, with the maverick Henry Labouchere (whom Joseph Chamberlain dubbed 'the Nihilist of English politics'[21]) questioning the cost of the monarchy and Gladstone making a spirited speech in its defence. The matter was settled in the time-honoured way by the appointment of a Royal Commission to look into future royal financing, and by the eventual passing of the Prince of Wales's Children's Bill, whereby an annual sum of £36,000 was assigned to the Prince of Wales in trust for his children.

Prince Eddy's approach to his military career remained as half-hearted as ever. Soldiering never seemed to prevent him from spending August and September in Scotland, from accompanying his adored mother on her prolonged visits to her native Denmark or from slipping out from Marlborough House to yield to the temptations of London's night life.

The Prince of Wales, who considered his son's military career to be 'simply a waste of time', had at one stage appealed to the

Duke of Cambridge for advice. As tactfully as possible, the gruff old Commander-in-Chief, who had also heard something of Prince Eddy's sexual adventuring, put forward his proposals. 'You were kind enough to ask my opinion the other day as regards the best course to be adopted, from a general point of view, for Eddy's future plans,' he wrote, 'and I therefore now, after full consideration, think it well to point out to you that I would consider it would be for his advantage to leave the 10th Hussars ... The Head Quarters of the Regiment will soon move to Hounslow for London duties, and I do not think that this will be a desirable station at present for so young and inexperienced a man, who would be surrounded by temptations *of every description*, which it requires great firmness of character to resist ... I would suggest his being sent for a time abroad, to a Garrison Town like Gibraltar, where his whole time and attention would reasonably be expected to be devoted to military duties ... Sir Arthur Hardinge, the present Governor, happens to be well known to the Queen, as also to yourself and Alix, and he could receive such personal instructions from you, regarding your intentions and wishes, as you might think desirable, and you would have perfect confidence in his carrying them out most conscientiously ... Great interests are involved in Eddy's future career, and certain sacrifices must be made to attain the objects in view to teach him and accustom him to habits of discipline and the knowledge of the business which he can better attain in the manner proposed than in any other way that presents itself to my mind.'[22]

The Duke of Cambridge's advice was not followed. Prince Eddy remained with the 10th Hussars in their London and other home postings. Although the Prince of Wales would have been ready enough to send his son abroad, Princess Alexandra was not. She firmly believed that the closer Prince Eddy was kept to Marlborough House, the more chance there would be of her influencing his behaviour. But she was fighting a losing battle. Eventually, rumours of the Prince's debaucheries reached even the normally inaccessible ears of his grandmother, Queen Victoria. 'I ask you again,' wailed Sir Francis Knollys, the Prince of Wales's private secretary, to Sir Henry Ponsonby, the Queen's private secretary, '*who* is it tells the Queen these things?'[23]

In the end, even Princess Alexandra was forced to agree that her son should be removed from the temptations of London, if only for a while. It was decided that he should be sent to India for six months. The Prince and Princess of Wales were due to join what Queen Victoria disparagingly referred to as 'the Royal Mob' at a family wedding in Athens towards the end of October 1889. Prince Eddy would accompany them and, at the end of that month, set sail from Port Said for India.

Nothing could have been more fortuitous. By the time Lord Arthur Somerset was discovered to have been a visitor to the Cleveland Street brothel, plans for Prince Eddy's journey were well under way. And by the time the Prince's own name was being mentioned in connection with the affair, he was safely in India.

PART FOUR

THE SCANDAL

10. 'MY LORD GOMORRAH'

Badminton House, the palatial home of the 8th Duke of Beaufort in the quiet Gloucestershire countryside, where the Somerset family had lived for almost three centuries, seemed an unlikely springboard for the sexually unorthodox career of Lord Arthur Somerset. But appearances, in this case, were deceptive. The current generation of Somersets were well known for their sexual aberrations. The 8th Duke was a notorious womanizer with a marked taste for what was delicately described as 'unripe fruit': prepubescent girls supplied to him by the likes of those celebrated late Victorian procuresses, Madame Marie and Mrs Jeffries.

Obligingly, the Duchess of Beaufort turned a blind eye to the Duke's amorous activities in his bachelor rooms in London. But on at least one occasion his interests intruded on her more decorous way of life at Badminton. The Duke was away at the time and just as the Duchess was about to lead a party of guests into lunch, the butler announced that a large picture had arrived from London. Where, he wanted to know, should he hang it? Together with her guests, the Duchess went into the hall to inspect the painting. It was a portrait of a pretty girl whom everyone present knew to be the Duke's latest mistress. With characteristic aplomb, the Duchess announced the picture to be 'charming'. His Grace, she imagined, would prefer to have it in his own rooms. The butler had better arrange to have it hung there. It would come as such a pleasant surprise to the Duke on his return.

The sexual tastes of the Beauforts' eldest son, the Marquess of Worcester, seem to have caused no scandal, but those of the second son, Lord Henry Somerset, always known as 'Penna', were highly unconventional. After five years of marriage Lord Henry's wife, Isabella, left him because of what she described as a crime mentioned only in the Bible: his infatuation for a seventeen-year-old boy named Henry Smith. With her, she took their only daughter. 'We have nothing whatsoever to say in defence of Penna,' wrote the Duchess to her daughter-in-law, 'and, unless he is mad, cannot understand his behaviour.' The Duke, while admitting to his son that 'a man may get tired of his wife', condemned his conduct in what he considered to be the strongest possible terms: it was not that 'of a gentleman'.[1] After a much publicized divorce case, the wife was given custody of their daughter. But such were the social conventions of the period that, instead of winning sympathy, Lady Isabella was ostracized by society for violating the code whereby a woman never made a public display of her marital difficulties. She devoted the rest of her life to good works, particularly to the celebrated nineteenth-century crusade of Temperance.

Temperance, of any sort, played very little part in Lord Henry Somerset's subsequent life. He retired first to Monaco and then to that haven for expatriate homosexuals, Florence. In the very year of the Cleveland Street scandal he published a book of poems, inspired by his love for Henry Smith. As Smith had, by then, left him, these lovelorn poems were entitled *Songs of Adieu*. Reviewing them in the *Pall Mall Gazette*, Oscar Wilde ended his piece with the words 'He has nothing to say, and he says it.'[2] Lord Henry made a more lasting reputation as a composer of sentimental ballads, the most famous of which had the not inappropriate title of 'All through the Night'.

So one can appreciate why the third son, Lord Arthur Somerset, should be so anxious for the news of his visits to the Cleveland Street homosexual brothel to be kept from his mother. For a while, it seemed as though it might be: for there was – so it appeared to many of the policemen concerned with the case – a curious reluctance on the part of those in authority to take any action against Somerset. The excuse was that he had not been sufficiently identified.

This was nonsense. For one thing, the thirty-seven-year-old Lord Arthur Somerset was unmistakable. He was a big man, well over six feet tall, his bald head compensated for by his luxuriant gingery moustache and whiskers. He had a pronounced Roman nose and his bearing was upright, confident, military. He looked every inch of what he was – a much-decorated major in the Royal Horse Guards (The Blues) who had seen service in various campaigns in Egypt during the 1880s.

As soon as Newlove, that tireless procurer of his fellow telegraph employees, had told Inspector Abberline who was in charge of the case, that Lord Arthur Somerset had frequently visited the Cleveland Street brothel, a watch was put on the house. Although the police knew that the proprietor, Charles Hammond, had by now fled to France, it was only too obvious that his clients did not. In the course of the next few days dozens of men, reported a watching policeman, called at the *maison de passe*. They ranged from men 'of superior bearing and apparently good position' to soldiers and young boys. Twice a man resembling Lord Arthur Somerset arrived; on each occasion he was met by a corporal of the 2nd Battalion Life Guards. They had clearly arranged to meet there. Their knocking not being answered, the two men walked off together in the direction of Oxford Street.

A week or so later, the same policeman took two of the suspended telegraph boys, Swinscow and Thickbroom, to a spot opposite a club in Piccadilly. When Somerset emerged from the club, he was immediately identified by the boys. All three followed him to Hyde Park Barracks, where his regiment was headquartered. After he had gone in, Somerset was again identified, this time by a sergeant. The accompanying policeman, who had at first been suspicious of the telegraph boys, was eventually won over by their unworldliness. They were just simple lads, quite different from the usual homosexual prostitutes. Accustomed to 'playing with each other', they were quite unaware of the seriousness of their 'crimes'. 'It is not likely', added the policeman, 'that they would have identified Lord Arthur Somerset unless they honestly believed that he was the man who had tempted them.'

A still more positive identification came on 19 August when a warrant was issued for the arrest of Hammond's accomplice – the self-styled Reverend G.D. Veck. When the police arrived at Veck's new lodgings at seven in the morning they found that he was away. In his bed, however, was a seventeen-year-old boy who described himself as Veck's 'private secretary'. The Reverend Veck had just left for Portsmouth, explained the boy; he would be back later that day. Veck was arrested at Waterloo station on his return.

In Veck's pockets the police discovered letters from someone called Algernon Allies; in them Allies mentioned a 'Mr Brown' who had apparently been giving him money. Allies, who had once lodged with Hammond at 19 Cleveland Street, was now living with his parents in Sudbury, Suffolk. Inspector Abberline immediately sent the dependable PC Hanks – the policeman responsible for unearthing the Cleveland Street brothel in the first place – to interview Allies at his parents' home in Sudbury.

Here Hanks found a good-looking, curly-haired, nineteen-year-old youth. On being questioned about the mysterious 'Mr Brown' who had been giving him money, Allies admitted that, as the result of an anonymous tip-off the previous day, he had destroyed all 'Mr Brown's' letters. On being pressed, he confessed that 'Mr Brown' was really Lord Arthur Somerset. Somerset had been supplying Allies with money 'for services rendered'. This was confirmed when Hanks visited the local post office and tracked down three postal orders sent by Somerset and cashed by Allies.

Allies then told Hanks the whole story. He had met Lord Arthur Somerset the year before, when he had been employed as a 'house boy' – a waiter – at the Marlborough Club: the club established by the Prince of Wales and patronized by many of the Prince's circle. Allies had very soon caught Somerset's eye and a sexual relationship had developed. When the boy was found to have stolen money from the club's premises, he appealed to Lord Arthur for help. Although Somerset could not save his job, he was able to prevent him from going to prison. As Allies had lost his accommodation in the club as well as his job, Somerset arranged for him to go and live in Hammond's house in Cleveland Street. To his trusting mother, Allies explained that he was employed by Hammond as a waiter; Mr Hammond, she unblinkingly assured Inspector Abberline, used to entertain a great many guests. In spite of being able to earn his keep as one of Hammond's male prostitutes, Allies continued to pester Somerset for money. Even after he left Cleveland Street, just ahead of Hammond and Veck, Allies was sent money by Somerset.

But not even in the face of this irrefutable evidence was a move made against Lord Arthur Somerset. In spite of the fact that he had been interviewed twice at the Hyde Park Barracks by the police (Somerset denied all knowledge of the Cleveland Street brothel), no proceedings were taken against him. Responsibility was simply shuffled from one government department to another. Even when the Home Secretary eventually decided that the case should be dealt with by the Director of Public Prosecutions which, bewilderingly, really meant the Treasury, the matter was treated with the utmost discretion. In fact, it was considered so delicate that in the document drawn up by the Treasury Solicitor's office, pieces of paper were pasted over Lord Arthur Somerset's name. Apparently the idea of an aristocrat, a royal equerry and a major in The Blues being arraigned was too appalling to contemplate.

Not one of the authorities involved – Scotland Yard, the Director of Public Prosecutions, the Home Secretary, the Attorney General, even the Prime Minister, Lord Salisbury himself – was ready to grasp the nettle. Any proposal to go ahead was immediately countermanded or, if not actually countermanded, delayed. The excuse that Somerset had not been 'properly identified' was now replaced by one to the effect that there was not 'enough evidence'. Towards the end of August, Somerset, who seems to have been kept well informed on these matters, quietly obtained four months' leave of absence from his still unsuspecting regiment and slipped off to the Continent. The Treasury Solicitor, Sir Augustus Stephenson, who was now in charge of the case, was not sorry to hear the news of Somerset's disappearance.

'It is quite possible (in my judgement it is probable), that he will not return,' he wrote. 'It may be the best thing that could happen.'[3]

On 18 September 1889, two and a half months after PC Hanks had first uncovered the activities at 19 Cleveland Street, two of the accused were brought to trial. They were Veck and Newlove, who had been indicted on thirteen counts of procuring six boys 'to commit divers acts of gross indecency with another person'.[4] The brothel-keeper, Charles Hammond, who had been indicted with them, was nowhere to be seen. Having fled, first to France and then to Belgium, he was arranging to put himself even further beyond the reach of the British police. On 5 October, with money supplied by Lord Arthur Somerset's solicitor, he set sail for the United States.

But Hammond, who imagined himself to be in constant danger of arrest, need not have worried. No less a person than the Prime Minister, Lord Salisbury, had come to his aid. Lord Salisbury was generally regarded as the very embodiment of the Establishment: patrician and urbane, he was always ready to look the other way when it came to preserving the *status quo*. In this instance, the Prime Minister had let the Home Secretary know that he did not 'consider this to be a case in which any official application could justifiably be made' to extradite the escaped Hammond.[5] In other words, it would be better if Hammond were not brought to trial. The Home Secretary had taken the hint and had passed it on: the Cleveland Street enquiry need not be pursued too vigorously.

In his hurry to get away from 19 Cleveland Street in early July, Charles Hammond had apparently left behind one very valuable possession. This was the book in which a prostitute named Emily Baker, who had lodged with Hammond in Cleveland Street for several years, had kept a careful record of 'all the gents who used the house', together with the dates of their appointments. The book had been appropriated by the police, after which it mysteriously and conveniently 'disappeared with certain other papers which passed between police headquarters and the Treasury'.[6]

Then, on the very morning that Veck and Newlove were to be tried, a deal was struck between the defence and the prosecution. If the accused pleaded guilty of indecency, the more serious charges of conspiracy and procuring would not be pressed. In this way the case could be speedily dealt with and, more important, no names be mentioned. To this bargain, the Attorney General wired his immediate sanction. Except for the clearing, by the outraged judge, of a lone woman from the court, the case went like clockwork. Newlove's solicitor pleaded for leniency on the grounds that the telegraph boys whom he had recruited 'had all indulged in indecent practices' before he had approached them, even if only with each other and not grown men.[7]

'The whole thing was hustled through in half an hour,' reported one observer. Veck was given nine months' hard labour and Newlove four. These sentences were considered to be 'ridiculously light'.[8] (A minister of religion, found guilty of a similar offence a few months before, had been condemned to life imprisonment.) The Assistant Director of Public Prosecutions, Hamilton Cuffe, described the trial as a 'travesty of justice', but its brevity did allow him, he was glad to say, to catch his 6.15 train from Waterloo.[9]

And still nothing was being done about Lord Arthur Somerset. Documents concerning the case were simply passed from one department to another. The whole business developed into a saga of inexplicable delays, wrong addresses, shifted responsibilities and, as this was September and most of the lordships concerned were on holiday, of telegrams having to be delivered over rough country tracks, by hand. A letter from the Home Secretary to the Prime Minister, to the effect that the Attorney General agreed with the Director of Public Prosecutions that 'the case against Lord Arthur Somerset is complete' and that 'there is no doubt whatever as to his identity', was shuffled off by the Prime Minister to the Lord Chancellor.[10] The Lord Chancellor, unfortunately, was in Scotland shooting grouse. He was in no mood to put his mind to the embarrassing business.

Not even the return of Lord Arthur Somerset to England could stir the authorities into action. To the increasing exasperation of the police, nothing seemed able to ruffle the aristocratic insouciance of their superiors.

In the meantime, Somerset was doing his best to get rid of the evidence against him. As Hammond was about to be safely shipped off to the United States, the most damaging evidence now took the shape of Algernon Allies, the one-time waiter at the Marlborough Club to whom Somerset had been sending postal orders. The boy had been under police protection for over a month and was at present lodging in the Rose Coffee House in Houndsditch. Somerset's instructions to his solicitor, Arthur Newton, were that he 'must look sharp and get Algernon Allies away'.[11]

This was why, on the afternoon of 25 September, young Allies had a caller. By now an authority on the way gentlemen dressed, or indeed undressed, Allies was later able to describe his caller's clothes in considerable detail. This well-dressed gentleman, who was tall and fair and about twenty-five, had a proposition to put to Allies. If the boy agreed to go to America, he would be supplied with whatever clothing he needed plus the sum of £15 on his arrival in the United States. To this Allies agreed. There and then he listed his requirements: he would need 'underlinen, two suits, a pair of boots and a hat'. The gentleman duly noted these down. He had come, he explained in answer to Allies's query, from the solicitor, Mr Newton. 'The reason we wanted to get you away is that you should not give your evidence against you know who.'[12]

The two agreed to meet again that evening outside the A1 public house in Tottenham Court Road; by then the gentleman would have made arrangements for Allies to set sail from Liverpool the very next day. Allies, a past-master at getting money out of gentlemen callers, touched this particular caller for enough to buy himself a shirt, a collar and a tie. No sooner had his visitor left than Allies went straight to Inspector Abberline to tell him the whole story. A trap was set.

At nine that evening, watched at a discreet distance by Inspector Abberline and the indispensable PC Hanks, Allies kept his appointment in the Tottenham Court Road. The young man then hailed a cab and he and Allies set off, closely followed in another cab by Abberline and Hanks. The first cab stopped outside the Marlborough Head public house where the two policemen moved in on the young man. He admitted that his name was Taylorson and that he was the managing clerk to the solicitor Arthur Newton. But he would answer no other questions. Allies was taken back under police protection, while Taylorson hurried off to warn Newton of the failure of the scheme. He also told the solicitor that a warrant was about to be issued for Somerset's arrest. Newton lost no time in warning Somerset to get out of the country. Lord Arthur returned to France the very next day.

But no warrant was issued. The documentation on this recent turn of events was duly sent off to the Lord Chancellor in Scotland where it was added to the pile of documents already gathering dust on his lordship's desk. While the pile remained there, unattended, every other department head felt absolved of the responsibility for doing anything.

Reassured by this lack of activity, Somerset returned to England on 30 September 1889. A few days after he had slipped back, his grandmother, the Dowager Duchess of Beaufort, died and he went to Badminton for her funeral. Also attending was a police officer, poised to arrest him. But still no warrant was forthcoming. Returning to London, Somerset visited the Turf and Marlborough clubs where he was given a gratifyingly warm welcome by his fellow members. Not one of them, apparently, was prepared to believe the 'disgusting rumours' about him. 'My Lord Gomorrah', as one newspaper later dubbed him, seemed to be getting away with it.[13]

But Lord Arthur Somerset's relief was short-lived. As he had all along feared, the affair was about to take on another, royal, dimension.

When the Prince of Wales first heard of Lord Arthur Somerset's involvement in the Cleveland Street brothel case he refused to believe it. For the forty-seven-year-old Prince of Wales, much of whose time was given over to the pursuit of beautiful women, the idea of any man preferring sex with boys was incomprehensible. Nor could he credit that 'Podge' Somerset – his hearty, soldierly, sports-loving equerry, the Superintendent of his Stables – could possibly be such a man. 'I don't believe it,' he exclaimed, 'I won't believe it any more than I would if they had accused the Archbishop of Canterbury.' The Prince had not chosen an altogether appropriate example. The current Archbishop of Canterbury was Edward White Benson who, when at Cambridge, had been taken under the wing of a middle-aged bachelor, Francis Martin, bursar of Trinity College, who had paid all his expenses. One of the Archbishop's sons always claimed that Martin had had a romantic affection for young Benson. The Archbishop's wife, who was almost certainly a lesbian, left him to go and live with another woman. His sons, A.C. Benson, E.F. Benson and R.E. Benson, all seem to have been homosexual.

The Prince of Wales immediately instructed his Comptroller, Sir Dighton Probyn, a man with a splendid military record and with an even more splendid reputation for discretion, to look into the matter. 'Go and see Munro [the Police Commissioner], go to the Treasury, see Lord Salisbury if necessary,' he commanded.[14] Somerset's name must, at all costs, be cleared.

In his efforts to carry out his royal master's wishes, Sir Dighton Probyn was joined by Sir Francis Knollys, the Prince of Wales's private secretary and a man of equal tact and discretion. The loyalty of these two men, and indeed of all those who stood close to the throne, was absolute. Their chief concern was the protection and preservation of the monarchy. Beside this overriding obligation, all other considerations – even of justice – were secondary. To the ticklish question of Lord Arthur Somerset's complicity, and to its even more ticklish sequel, these two seasoned courtiers now applied all their diplomatic skills.

The two men met Lord Arthur at the Marlborough Club on 16 October. The meeting was extremely amicable. Clearly the two royal envoys had no idea that there was any truth in the rumours. Somerset denied everything. At subsequent meetings – all on the same day – with Somerset's solicitor, the Police Commissioner and the Assistant Director of Public Prosecutions, the two courtiers stressed the fact that the Prince of Wales was 'in a great state', that he 'did not believe a word of it and wished that he could come himself to clear Lord Arthur Somerset', and that 'he must have something settled'.

At each of these meetings they were given bland assurances by the officials but at no stage were the rumours actually denied. 'Of course I ought to tell you that I know nothing, but I know all about it but am telling you nothing,' was how the Assistant Director of Public Prosecutions put it to them.[15] This was backed up by a letter to Sir Francis Knollys in which the royal secretary was told that the Attorney General was unable to reveal the contents of any papers concerning the case.

Stalled by these lesser lights, Knollys approached a brighter one: the Prime Minister, Lord Salisbury. He arranged a meeting between Salisbury and Sir Dighton Probyn. The two men met at King's Cross station on the evening of 18 October, just before the Prime Minister was due to catch the 7.30 p.m. train to his country home, Hatfield. It was here, for the first time, that Probyn heard that there were grounds for the accusations against Somerset. He was appalled. 'The conversation principally consisted of expressions on the part of Sir Dighton Probyn of absolute disbelief in the charges,' reported Lord Salisbury afterwards. 'Until I saw you last night,' admitted Probyn to the Prime Minister next morning, 'I always thought it was a case of *mistaken identity*.'[16]

The Prime Minister was afterwards accused, on the floor of the House of Commons, of having told Probyn that a warrant for Somerset's arrest was about to be issued and that Probyn had immediately passed the news on to Somerset, with the result that Somerset fled back to France the next day. This Lord Salisbury vehemently denied.

But there is reason to believe that at least part of the accusation is valid. Although Salisbury did not say that a warrant was due to be issued immediately, he apparently led Probyn to believe that one might be issued at some future date. There seems to have been no other reason for Somerset's sudden decision to flee. He had been due to dine in the officers' mess at the Hyde Park Barracks on the night of 18 October and when he did not appear, some of his fellow officers, who had heard the rumours of his complicity in the brothel case, imagined that he had taken the 'honourable' way out by shooting himself. But on going to his quarters, they found his room empty and his belongings gone. Somerset had bolted.

Had Probyn warned him? Lord Salisbury's assertion that Probyn had not seen Somerset after the meeting between the Prime Minister and the Comptroller at King's Cross – or ever again – cannot be true. In his letter to Salisbury the following day Probyn wrote, 'I fear what you told me last night was all too true,' which can only mean that Salisbury's information had been confirmed: Probyn had seen Somerset and Somerset had admitted the truth.[17] As Marlborough House was only a stone's throw from the Marlborough Club, where Somerset was staying, a meeting could have been easily arranged. This is backed up by a letter to Probyn from the Prince of Wales. 'Your interview with Somerset must have been a very painful one,' he wrote. The Prince must have been referring to a second interview as the first one, two days before, at which Somerset had denied everything, had been very amicable.

'I had a very kind but sad letter from the poor Duke [of Beaufort],' continued the Prince of Wales to Probyn, 'and I cannot say *how* deeply I feel for him and the Duchess. His having to break the news to her will be terrible. Since this dreadful affair names of other people who we know will have been mentioned … It is really *too* shocking! One a married man [the Earl of Euston] whose hospitality I have frequently accepted! If these people are in the same boat as poor Podge – are they to be allowed to go about as before – whilst he has fled the country?'[18]

Not until 4 November, three weeks after the flight of Lord Arthur Somerset, did the Duke of Beaufort break the news to his wife. This means that the Prince of Wales's letter must have been referring to the final meeting between Probyn and Somerset, which must, in turn, have taken place after Probyn's meeting with Salisbury. So it is more than likely that Somerset was tipped off by Probyn. In fact, Somerset later wrote to Probyn to 'thank him for all that he has done'.[19]

One would have imagined that, with the flight of Lord Arthur Somerset, Sir Dighton Probyn would have let the matter drop. By now the Prince of Wales, accompanied by his family, including Prince Eddy, had set sail for that family wedding in Athens. But for reasons probably unsuspected by his royal master, Probyn persisted. Once again he approached the

Prime Minister. 'I write now to ask you, to implore of you if it can be managed to have the prosecution [of Lord Arthur Somerset] stopped. It can do no good to prosecute him. He has gone and will never show his face in England again. He *dare* never come back to this country.

'I think it is the most hateful, loathsome story I ever heard, and the most astounding. It is too fearful, but further publicity will only make matters worse ...'[20]

The Prime Minister answered this plea with a letter to the Prince of Wales in which he appears to have given the impression that he had responded favourably to Probyn's appeal. The Prince wrote to say that he was 'glad to gather ... that no warrant is likely to be issued against the "unfortunate Lunatic" '. And then, because he was a kind-hearted man, the Prince added that 'I shall be greatly obliged by your kindly letting me know whether the man might return to England now, or at any future date, without fear of being apprehended on this awful charge. I have no idea where he has gone, or if he would ever dare show his face in England again even if he were free to do so, but I would like, if I may, to let his Family know if their Relative will at any time be at liberty to visit his native country.'[21]

The Prime Minister now found himself torn between his half-promise to the Prince of Wales that Somerset would not be prosecuted and the growing exasperation of Scotland Yard at the continued delay. 'I have to press for a very early reply to this letter,' demanded James Monro, the Metropolitan Police Commissioner, on 21 October. 'Proceedings in the case have been pending since the month of July, and I cannot but consider that it is unfair to the Metropolitan Police that the action should be, on account of this delay, exposed to the criticisms and misinterpretation to which I have called your attention ...'[22]

But not until Somerset had been given time to resign his army commission honourably and his resignation had been gazetted on 4 November was Salisbury finally goaded into taking action. On 12 November 1889 a warrant was issued against Lord Arthur Somerset. In the warrant Somerset was specifically charged with 1) committing acts of gross indecency with other male persons, to wit, Allies, Swinscow and Thickbroom; 2) procuring Allies to commit similar acts with other male persons; and 3) conspiring with Hammond to procure the commission of such acts contrary to the Criminal Law Amendment Act, 1885.

According to a piece of confidential information passed on by one of Somerset's fellow officers, his acts were not as 'gross' as everyone imagined. Somerset did not commit sodomy but merely indulged in what was charmingly described as 'gentle dalliance with the boys'.[23]

With the issuing of the warrant, Sir Dighton Probyn's plans were foiled. But why had this loyal courtier been so anxious to have the matter swept under the carpet? Was his sole concern, as he so piously claimed, to spare the feelings of Lord Arthur Somerset's parents? The Duke of Beaufort was no saint and, as Lord Arthur's brother, Lord Henry Somerset, had proved, homosexuality was nothing new in the family. Was there a stronger reason for Probyn's determination to keep the matter quiet?

Sir Dighton Probyn's chief aim was to prevent Lord Arthur Somerset from giving evidence in open court. This was in order to scotch a sensational rumour that was going the rounds; a rumour that Prince Eddy was involved in the affair. The confidential allegation of the Prince's complicity, previously known to only a handful of departmental heads, was by now being discussed in every club in London.

11. 'THE WHOLE TERRIBLE AFFAIR'

The rumours of Prince Eddy's alleged visits to the Cleveland Street brothel remained, for the moment, no more than that. English libel laws prevented the allegations from appearing in print. But the American and Continental newspapers, unshackled by any such laws, showed no restraint. They were able to give their readers full, if sometimes fanciful, accounts of what were described as 'the West End Scandals'. In Paris *La Lanterne* claimed that at least *une douzaine de Lords* were implicated. *Figaro* spoke of Lord Arthur Somerset's *tendresse étrange pour les jeunes télégraphistes*. *Le Matin* referred to London as *La Sodome Moderne*. But it was in the United States that the most serious charge was levelled. Under a portrait of Prince Albert Victor, one New York journal gave full coverage to the rumours about his involvement in the scandal. Why, it asked, had the Prince been despatched to India just before the Cleveland Street affair became public?

The *New York Times* claimed that 'current rumor says that Prince Albert Victor will not return from India until the matter is completely over and forgotten, but there are certain stubborn moralists at work on the case who profess determination that it shall not be judicially burked, and the prospects are that the whole terrible affair will be dragged out into the light. The character of the threatened disclosures and the magnitude of personal interests involved may be gathered from the fact that a Privy Council meeting has been held to discuss the subject.'[1]

Whatever the truth of the other accusations, there was none in the accusation that Prince Eddy had been bundled off to India to avoid implication in the scandal. The tour – as was the way with all royal tours – had been arranged long before there was even a suggestion of scandal. On 25 September 1889, before the Prince of Wales and his entourage knew anything about Lord Arthur Somerset's involvement, Somerset was summoned to Marlborough House to discuss with the Prince of Wales the saddlery and other equipment for Prince Eddy's forthcoming tour. If, at that stage, the Prince of Wales had known nothing about Somerset's guilt, then he had certainly known nothing about the Prince Eddy rumours.

On the other hand, it was very fortunate that Prince Eddy should be out of the way during the seven crucial months from late October 1889 to late May 1890. It allowed him to remain, in the eyes of the general public at least, one stage removed from the swirl of gossip and speculation.

Prince Eddy arrived in Bombay, on board the *Oceana*, on 9 November. He was accompanied by, among others, his equerry Captain George Holford of the 1st Life Guards and Sir Edward Bradford VC, later Chief Commissioner of the Metropolitan Police. From then on, he was subjected to all the strains, exhaustions and formalities of a full-blown royal tour. Like an automaton, he was shunted from government house to maharajah's palace, paraded along troop-lined streets, presented with addresses of welcome, fêted at full-dress dinners, shepherded through historic sites, curtsied and bowed to at garden parties, entertained by dazzling displays of fireworks.

'The splendour of the reception accorded by the Nizam was beyond description,' writes Captain Holford in his meticulously detailed but sadly uninspiring journal. 'HRH received separate visits from about five-and-twenty of the principal chiefs and natives, each coming with his attendants and staying about five minutes. This took up nearly the whole morning ...'[2]

Much of Prince Eddy's time was spent on those sporting activities which were such a feature of life during the British Raj. Tirelessly Holford catalogues the polo, pig-sticking, tent-pegging, elephant hunting, elephant riding, tiger stalking and the shooting of snipe and partridge. 'Some idea of the royal scale of the Maharajah's hospitality may be gathered from the fact that, about the shooting camp, and as beaters, no less than five thousand men were employed.'

There was one embarrassing, and potentially fatal, incident. The Prince's uncle, Prince Arthur, Duke of Connaught, was also in India at the time (as Commander-in-Chief of the Bombay Army) and one day Prince Eddy and the Duchess of Connaught clambered into the howdah on an elephant's back in order to visit a temple. On the way, the elephant suddenly let loose a cascade of excrement. The nervous mahout panicked and the elephant started to move back, slithering on its excrement as it did so. The howdah pitched perilously, and if the mahout had not managed to gain control of the lurching beast, it might well have bolted. The results could have been catastrophic. A ladder was rushed to the scene and the badly shaken Prince and Duchess climbed down to safety.

The Connaughts were astonished at the trunkloads of clothes which Prince Eddy had brought with him. He had an impeccably tailored outfit for every possible occasion. Whatever his other shortcomings, this future Emperor of India certainly looked the part. He spent so long dressing that he once kept the punctilious Duke of Connaught waiting for twenty minutes before they could set out on their morning ride. But just now and then one glimpses a real person within the splendidly uniformed and accoutred figure of HRH Prince Albert Victor. When he had occasion to exercise it, his languorous charm could be very winning. Far from being an autocratic and petulant princeling, he struck those whom he met as very considerate and well-mannered. The Connaughts found him quite unspoilt but very young for his age. He was slow at taking things in and seemed happiest in the company of men younger than himself.

Occasionally something seemed to catch his usually undirected attention. 'The reader can hardly fail to realize the dark Indian night,' wrote one observer of an outdoor evening entertainment, 'the long lines of soft lights rising tier upon tier against the dark background of the trees, the swarthy conjurors with their weird deceits, the barbaric music, the rhythmical swaying of the Nautch girls, the tempestuous frenzy of the kuttak dance – and in the midst of it our soldier and sailor Prince, hardly past his boyhood, in the guise of an eager and animated spectator.'[3]

Of Prince Eddy's intimate diversions during those sultry Indian nights one knows nothing. But one story did filter back to Britain. It concerned his encounter with a young Indian who delivered the laundry to his suite in some maharajah's palace. Whatever the nature of this encounter, it enabled the satirical journal *Truth* to publish an imaginary interview with Prince Eddy about his Indian tour. Although ostensibly poking fun at the Prince's obsession with the laundering and starching of his collar and cuffs, this innocuous-seeming piece of doggerel was rich in double meanings.

Asked what had impressed him most during his Indian tour, Prince Eddy's reply is, 'The man I came across at Shuttadore.' Had this man, asks his interviewer, been a rajah or a pundit or a fakir?

> No, no, it was not one of these
> Who won my heart at Shuttadore!
> No, 'twas a low-caste laundry-man ...
> And this is what impressed me most
> Whilst Hindustan I travelled o'er –
> The skill displayed by Chundra Dass
> The laundry-man of Shuttadore![4]

Until the warrant was issued for the arrest of Lord Arthur Somerset on 12 November 1889, the British public knew very little about the aristocratic involvement in the Cleveland Street case. The trial of the two procurers, the post office employee Henry Newlove and the self-styled Reverend G.D. Veck, had been a rushed, poorly reported affair with no mention made of their upper-class clientele. The fact that Lord Arthur Somerset had fled to France several weeks before the warrant meant that his complicity was known only in certain government and society circles. There had been one or two small, vaguely worded news items but they had been comprehensible only to those in the know.

But on 16 November 1889 all this changed. Under the headline 'The West End Scandals', an obscure Radical journal called the *North London*

Press published a news item about the homosexual brothel case in which the names of the two leading aristocrats were mentioned: one was Lord Arthur Somerset, the other the Earl of Euston, eldest son of the Duke of Grafton. Both men, it reported, had fled the country: Somerset to France and Euston to Peru. The two men had 'been allowed to leave the country, and thus defeat the ends of justice,' the report went on to say, 'because their prosecution would disclose the fact that a far more distinguished and highly placed personage than themselves was inculpated in these disgusting crimes'.[5] That highly placed personage was, of course, Prince Eddy.

The *North London Press*, with a circulation of between four and five thousand, had been in existence for a few months only. It was edited by a twenty-nine-year-old journalist named Ernest Parke. Lithe, energetic, dedicated to his calling, Parke has been described as 'a singular mixture of shrewdness and ideals; an intense Radical, and at the same time a thoroughly practical journalist'.[6] Driven by his passion for a good story and his determination to attack aristocratic privilege, Parke had decided to probe the Cleveland Street affair. He suspected some sort of official conspiracy. Why else should Veck and Newlove have been given such light sentences, and why should Somerset and – as he thought – Euston, have been allowed to escape justice? In his suspicions Parke was joined by those two other great crusading journalists of the period: Henry Labouchere, the member of Parliament who edited *Truth*, and W.T. Stead, the editor of the *Pall Mall Gazette*.

The coupling of Lord Euston's name with that of Lord Arthur Somerset came as a considerable shock to the general public. Henry James Fitzroy, Earl of Euston, now in his early forties, was – as that celebrated authority on sexual matters, Frank Harris, put it – 'the last man in the world to be suspected of abnormal propensities'.[7] Indeed, Euston was generally regarded as one of the most rampantly heterosexual of men. Over six feet tall, well-built, manfully moustached, he had a reputation as a 'stage-door Johnny'. Euston's addiction to chorus girls was so wholehearted that, at the age of twenty-three, he married one: a variety theatre actress named Kate Cook. Unfortunately, and unknown to Euston, the new Lady Euston was already married; but as her commercial traveller husband had, in turn, been already married at the time of his marriage to her, Kate Cook's marriage to Euston was problematic. The couple obtained a divorce. This unhappy experience seems in no way to have blunted Euston's sexual appetite; indeed, it now encompassed, if Parke was to be believed, men as well as women.

The publication of his name in the *North London Press* brought an immediate reaction from Lord Euston. He instructed his solicitor to institute proceedings against Parke for criminal libel. A warrant was issued for Parke's arrest and on 26 November he faced a committal hearing. By then, however, Parke had published another article in the *North London Press* in which his suspicions of a cover-up in the Cleveland Street affair were admirably set out.

'The information affecting Lord Arthur Somerset, the man Hammond, and other persons, distinguished and undistinguished, was in the hands of the authorities at the end of July ...' claimed Parke. But it was not until mid-October, 'in obedience to a hint from a high official at Court, and [after] his resignation of his command and of his office of Assistant Equerry to the Prince of Wales was gazetted', that Somerset disappeared. 'When the warrant against him was issued, he was safe from arrest. In the same way Hammond, the keeper of the den of infamy at Cleveland Street, had been able to put himself beyond the reach of the law. He fled to France, where, at the suggestion of our own Foreign Office, he was expelled as a *mauvais sujet*, and he has fled, it is feared, without any prospect of his being brought to justice.

'The result, therefore, of these extraordinary – these unheard of – delays in fulfilling the forms of law, and protecting the community against nameless crimes, has been that two of the chief offenders have disappeared. But that is not all. Two minor members of this vile conspiracy [Newlove and Veck] were committed for trial and pleaded guilty to the charge at the Old Bailey. Their cases were brought on at the end of the day's proceedings, when few spectators were left and when everybody supposed that the sitting was over. Hurried clandestinely into the dock, these guilty wretches, condemned out of their own mouths, were awarded sentences of four and nine months respectively for offences for which, at a previous Sessions, a minister at Hackney had been condemned to penal servitude for life ...'

'And now', concluded Parke, 'a word as to our own action ... The *North London Press* is now the subject of a criminal libel. It is one small newspaper, fighting wealth, position, the ablest criminal lawyer in London, and the reluctance of those in authority to do their duty ... *If the half of what we know, and are learning from day to day, comes out in a court of law, there has been accumulating under our feet a store of moral dynamite sufficient to wreck the good name of the nation ...*'[8]

What Parke was referring to here, of course, were the allegations of Prince Eddy's involvement. If the Heir Presumptive to the throne were to be revealed as a frequenter of a male brothel he would face, not only a scandal of tremendous proportions but, even more seriously, arrest, trial and the possibility of imprisonment.

At the committal hearing at Bow Street court, Lord Euston conducted himself with admirable aplomb. He scored an immediate advantage by denying Parke's claim that he had fled to Peru to escape justice. He had never been to Peru. In fact, he had not left England at any time during the last eight years.

Although not denying that he had ever been to the house in Cleveland Street, Euston gave the court his account of what he claimed to be his one brief association with it. One night in May or June that year, as he was walking home along Piccadilly, a card was pushed into his hand. On it was written, '*Poses plastiques.* Hammond, 19 Cleveland Street.' (*Poses plastiques* were the Victorian equivalent of strip-tease.) About a week after that, Euston one night decided to visit the Cleveland Street address. His knock was answered by a man who asked him for a sovereign as entrance fee. Euston paid the money and asked when the *poses plastiques* were due to take place.

'There is nothing of that sort here,' answered the man. He then went on to enlighten Euston as to the services offered by the house.

Euston was, he assured the magistrate, appalled. 'You infernal scoundrel,' he exclaimed. 'If you don't let me out I will knock you down.'[9]

He left the house immediately.

The magistrate, considering the libelling of Lord Euston to be a matter of 'very great gravity', directed Ernest Parke to stand trial at the next sessions of the Central Criminal Court.

The trial of Ernest Parke of the *North London Press* for criminally libelling the Earl of Euston opened at the Old Bailey on 15 January 1890 before Mr Justice Hawkins. To know that one was being tried by a judge whose nickname was 'Hanging Hawkins' was not exactly reassuring. The members of the prosecuting and defending counsels were hardly less famous. For the prosecution Sir Charles Russell QC, later to become Lord Chief Justice, was assisted by Mr William Matthews, later Director of Public Prosecutions. For the defence, Mr Frank Lockwood QC, later Solicitor-General, was assisted by Mr Herbert Asquith, afterwards Liberal Prime Minister. It was an impressive line-up.

Lord Euston's counsel opened the case by outlining his client's version of his visit to 19 Cleveland Street, ostensibly to see the advertised *poses plastiques*. He had spent less than five minutes in the house and had stormed out on realizing the true nature of the establishment. Contrary to what Parke had claimed, Lord Euston had not left the country after the flight of Hammond and the arrest of Veck and Newlove; nor had he ever been to Peru. He also denied Parke's written plea of justification in which it was alleged that Lord Euston had had sex in the Cleveland Street house with two men: Jack Saul and Frank Hewitt. Far from having been to bed with them, claimed his counsel, his lordship had never even heard of them.

Parke's counsel then called its six witnesses, the first five of whom were meant to identify Lord Euston as having been the man whom they had frequently seen visiting 19 Cleveland Street. Their performance was farcical. Two of them were barmen, one a coal-merchant, another a railway porter and a fifth a woman who lived opposite and who had seen, she assured the fascinated courtroom, as many as fifty or sixty men visiting the house. All five witnesses were unsophisticated people whose quaint turns of phrase and often unintelligible accents caused considerable amusement.

Their testimony was easily demolished. The first admitted to bad eyesight and an inability to tell one sort of carriage from another. The second disagreed with the first about the gentleman's height, clothes and carriage. The third swore to having seen Lord Euston enter the house on 9 July until he was told that the house had been empty since Hammond's flight on the 5 July. Mrs Morgan, the fourth witness, could not explain why, of all those fifty or sixty men she had seen visiting the house, Lord Euston happened to be the one she could remember. Nor, she was told, did Lord Euston own a blue top-coat with a velvet collar such as she described. The fifth witness admitted to having been told, by the second witness, that the man he had seen leaving the house was Lord Euston: he had never, in fact, seen him until that day in court. None of the witnesses remarked on Lord Euston's exceptional height of six foot four; most seem to have been in the pay of private detectives. All in all, their testimony proved worthless.

The sixth, and final defence witness, was very different. There was nothing unsophisticated or unintelligible about him. This was Jack Saul, the notorious male prostitute and pimp, co-author of *The Sins of the Cities of the Plain*, who claimed to have had sex with Lord Euston at 19 Cleveland Street. By now in his late thirties, with his best years behind him, Saul proved to be a sharp, witty and unashamedly outspoken witness. Throughout his cross-examination, his tone was pert and self-confident.

He was questioned first by Lockwood, for the defence. Saul had known Hammond for ten years. Despite the fact that Hammond had been married and had a son, the two of them earned their livings 'as sodomites'. He had lived in Hammond's Cleveland Street house for about eight weeks in the spring of 1887, and had given Hammond all the money he earned. He often earned as much as £8 a night.

'Do you see any person in this court you have ever seen in Hammond's house in Cleveland Street?' asked Lockwood.

'The gentleman there with the moustache,' answered Saul, pointing to Lord Euston.

'Was that the first time he had been there?'

'Yes, I believe.'

'When was that?'

'Some time in April or May 1887.'

'Where did you meet this person?'

'In Piccadilly, between Albany courtyard and Sackville Street. He laughed at me and I winked at him. He turned sharp into Sackville Street.'

'Who did?' asked the judge.

'The Duke, as we used to call him,' answered Saul.

'Go on,' prompted Lockwood, 'and tell me what happened.'

'The Duke, as we called him, came near me, and asked me where I was going,' explained Saul. 'I said "Home" and he said "What sort is your place?" "Very comfortable," I replied. He said, "Is it very quiet there?" I said yes it was, and then we took a hansom cab there. We got out by the Middlesex Hospital, and I took the gentleman to 19 Cleveland Street, letting him in with my latchkey.

'I was not long in there, in the back parlour or reception room before Hammond came and knocked and asked if we wanted any champagne or drinks of any sort, which he was in the habit of doing.'

This brought forth gales of knowing laughter which the judge immediately silenced. Saul then related what had happened between him and Lord Euston in terms which *The Times* reporter described as unfit for publication. The gist of it was that Lord Euston was 'not an actual sodomite. He likes to play with you and then "spend" on your belly.' The other spending done by Lord Euston that night was to leave a sovereign on the chest of drawers as he went out.

'Did you see Lord Euston at this house again?' continued Lockwood.

'Once, and I did not forget it,' answered Saul. Two others had been present on this occasion: Frank Hewitt, who had since been spirited abroad, and Henry Newlove, who was now in prison. The occasion had been made memorable because of Saul's quarrel with Hammond. He had complained bitterly to Hammond about the number of Post Office employees, boys with perfectly good jobs, who were being allowed to earn extra money in the house while he was obliged to walk the streets. With this Saul tossed his head in what was described as 'a theatrical gesture'.

Sir Charles Russell now rose to cross-examine the witness on behalf of the prosecution.

'Where are you living now?' he asked.

With some very respectable people in Brixton, answered Saul. The man in whose house he was living was known, he added, as 'Violet'.

'When did you first give evidence?'

Saul's answer to this question caused a sensation. 'The first statement I made was at the Criminal Investigation Office to Inspector Abberline.'

This meant that Saul had told the police, many months before, of Lord Euston's visits to Cleveland Street and that no action had been taken against Euston. (Nor, apparently, had the police followed up – or been allowed to follow up – the charges made against Euston by Newlove at the time of his arrest.)

Before he went to Hammond's with Lord Euston in a cab, continued Saul, he had had no idea who he was. 'I picked him up just as I might have picked up any other gentleman,' he explained.

'When did you first learn Lord Euston's name?'

'About a fortnight or three weeks after the first occasion on which Lord Euston visited 19 Cleveland Street.'

'Who told you?'

'A friend of mine in the street.' On being pressed, Saul admitted that the friend's name was Carrington. He was known as 'Lively Poll' and he had a considerable knowledge of the members of the aristocracy.

When he and Lord Euston had parted after their first meeting, continued Saul, Euston had said to him, 'Be sure, if you see me, don't speak to me in the street.' Consequently he had never spoken to him, although he often saw him in Piccadilly and elsewhere.

On being asked by Russell what he had ever done to earn his living, Saul answered, 'Not much.'

'What?' pressed Russell.

'I worked hard at cleaning the houses of the gay people,' he replied. The word 'gay' at this time was used to describe prostitutes: they were often known as 'gay ladies'. He had also done some casual work in two theatres but had not earned much. His earnings, while 'practising criminality in other houses', had been rather better; he had once lived in a house in Nassau Street where 'vicious practices were carried on'.

'Did you live with a woman known as Queen Anne in Church Street, Soho?' asked Russell.

Queen Anne, explained Saul, was a man. Russell asked if this man was in court.

'Yes, sir,' replied Saul. His name was Andrew Grant.

'Did you live with this man Grant?' asked Russell.

'No,' said Saul saucily, 'he lived with me.'

'And were you hunted out by the police?'

'No, they have never interfered,' answered Saul. On the contrary, the police had always behaved very 'kindly' towards him as he walked the streets by night.

Sir Charles Russell was shocked. 'Do you mean they have deliberately shut their eyes to your infamous practices?' he asked.

'They have had to shut their eyes to more than me,' was Saul's wry answer.

On handing Saul a photograph of Lord Euston, Russell asked if he recognized him.

'Yes,' answered Saul. 'You could tell him by his big white teeth and his moustache.'

Lord Euston's behaviour in the witness box was, as it had been during the preliminary hearing, exemplary. He repeated the story of the *poses plastiques*. He denied having visited the house on any other occasion. He had never seen Jack Saul before. While admitting that he knew Lord Arthur Somerset socially, Euston denied having visited him in Boulogne recently. In fact, he had not been out of England for eight years. He had certainly never been to Peru.

This concluded the evidence. The jury having been addressed, Mr Justice Hawkins announced that he would postpone his summing-up until the following morning.

In the course of his two-and-a-half-hour-long summing up, the judge had no difficulty in rejecting the evidence of the first five defence witnesses. This meant that the decision of the jury would rest largely on the testimony of Jack Saul. Describing him as 'a melancholy spectacle' and 'a loathsome object', the judge asked in which of the two men's oaths the jury could place more confidence: the oath of Lord Euston or the oath of this despicable creature. In other words, would they believe the titled gentleman or the low-born male prostitute?

On this point, the jury obviously had very little doubt. They were out for less than three-quarters of an hour. They returned a verdict which found Ernest Parke 'guilty of libel without justification'.[10] The judge sentenced him to twelve months' imprisonment.

The trial of Ernest Parke left several questions unanswered. Why was Lord Euston allowed to appear last, to remain unexamined until all the defence witnesses had given evidence? This gave him every sort of advantage, including an important psychological one.

Although Hammond had been allowed to flee the country, another person who would have been able to identify Lord Euston was the young procurer, Henry Newlove, now in prison. Why was he not called to corroborate Saul's evidence? After all it was Newlove who first told Inspector Abberline that Somerset and Euston were regular visitors to Cleveland Street. Newlove was an unsophisticated boy, who would not have mentioned Lord Euston's name without good reason. In fact, when preparing his client's defence, Parke's solicitor had written to the Home Office requesting that he should be supplied with the depositions of Newlove and the other Post Office boys. This request was refused. But Parke's solicitor was told that he could subpoena the Director of Public Prosecutions for any documents that he might want. These documents would then be brought into court but could only be produced by order of the judge. But Parke's solicitor appears not to have acted on this advice. It was a curious omission. The defence was left to rely on the testimony of Jack Saul alone and, as a male prostitute, his testimony was bound to be suspect.

And why did Inspector Abberline, on being told months before by Saul of Lord Euston's visits to Cleveland Street, not act on this evidence?

Perhaps he wanted to and perhaps he was prevented from doing so by his superiors. Certainly, at the time of Parke's committal hearing at Bow Street, Abberline asked permission of the Police Commissioner to take two of the Post Office boys – Thickbroom and Swinscow – to the proceedings, in the hope that they might be able to identify Lord Euston. The Commissioner passed the request on to the Attorney General. He turned it down. 'We should keep aloof from the present proceedings,' he answered. For what reason?

Nor, apparently, was Saul the only one known to have had sex with Lord Euston. The Earl was a familiar figure in the homosexual underworld. A notorious blackmailer, Robert Clibborn, who was later to blackmail Oscar Wilde, once also milked Lord Euston. Wilde, who was always fascinated by the activities of young criminals, claimed that Clibborn deserved to be awarded the Victoria Cross for the avaricious tenacity with which he blackmailed Lord Euston.

And finally – and most significantly – why was Saul not prosecuted for perjury? If he had lied about Lord Euston's visits to Cleveland Street, if he had indeed 'imputed to Lord Euston heinous crimes revolting to one's notions of all that was decent in human nature', why was he not arrested?[11] Surely, argued Henry Labouchere in an editorial in his newspaper *Truth*, to allow 'a wretch like Saul ... to swear away the honour and good name of a person with impunity, without any action on the part of the Public Prosecutor, is an insult to law and justice'.[12]

It certainly was. And Labouchere was not the only one to think so. On the very day after the appearance of this editorial, the Director of Public Prosecutions wrote to the Attorney General with a request to prosecute Saul. It was refused. The Attorney General's answer was unequivocal. 'No proceedings should at present be instigated against Saul,' he wrote.

Why, one wonders, were the authorities so anxious to keep Saul quiet? As a mere witness in the Parke trial he had been indiscreet enough; were the authorities afraid of what he might say or, worse still, of whose names he might mention, if he were actually required to defend himself?

12. 'I NEVER MENTIONED THE BOY'S NAME'

By the end of 1889 the rumours of the involvement of Prince Eddy in the Cleveland Street affair were reaching their height. It was widely believed that he was about to be brought home from India, either to face trial or to give evidence. The *New York Times* went even further. It was 'obvious to everybody', claimed its London correspondent, 'that there has come to be within the last few days a general conviction that this long-necked, narrow-headed young dullard was mixed up in the scandal, and out of this had sprung a half-whimsical, half-serious notion which one hears propounded now about clubland, that matters will be arranged that he will never return from India.

'The most popular idea is that he will be killed in a tiger hunt, but runaway horses or a fractious elephant might serve as well. What this really mirrors is a public awakening to the fact that this stupid, perverse boy has become a man and has only two highly precious lives between him and the English throne and is an utter blackguard and ruffian.'

Warming to its task, the *New York Times* went on to claim that the revelation that Prince Eddy was 'something besides a harmless simpleton has created a very painful feeling everywhere. Although he looks so strikingly like his mother, it turns out that he gets only his face from the Danish race, and that morally and mentally he combines the worst attributes of those sons of George III, at whose mention history still holds her nose. It is not too early to predict that such a fellow will never be allowed to ascend the British throne; that is as clear as anything can be.'[1]

So widely believed were the rumours about the Prince's enforced return from India to stand trial that an official announcement had to be issued to the press, to the effect that there was no intention of curtailing the Prince's Indian tour.

A further press statement was necessary to deny that the Prince's equerry, Captain George Holford, had been dismissed from his service and was returning home from India. For by now it was being rumoured that Holford had also been implicated in the Cleveland Street affair. 'Let me know whether any warrants are issued and whether others have to go,' wrote the anxious Lord Arthur Somerset to a friend. 'I suppose the story of George Holford was all nonsense, wasn't it?'[2]

On 22 December 1889 a letter, signed by 'A Member of Parliament' was published in the *New York Herald*. Although it might well have been written by a member of Parliament, it was undoubtedly done so at the instigation of those two dedicated royal servants: the Prince of Wales's secretary, Sir Francis Knollys, and his Comptroller, Sir Dighton Probyn. The letter was headlined 'The Policy of Hushing Up'.

'The authorized announcement which has appeared in the papers concerning Prince Albert Victor will not be misrepresented by anyone who is familiar with the kind of talk which has been afloat for several weeks past. Over and over again it has been whispered about that "Prince Eddy" would shortly be recalled from India under circumstances peculiarly painful to himself and his family. It was impossible either to trace these reports to their source or to check them. It may, however, put some slight restraint upon the gossip-mongers to be informed in a semi-official manner that the arrangements in connection with the young Prince's visit to India will not be altered in any way, and that he will return at the time originally fixed, and not before.

'The issue of this notice was, no doubt, the subject of careful consideration beforehand, and it was wise. There are some people who will believe anything, and there is never any telling how far slander may spread. I have heard, though I have not actually seen the paper, that a New York journal recently published an article on certain abominable scandals, with a portrait of Prince Albert Victor in the midst of it. If this is so, a more atrocious or a more dastardly outrage was never perpetrated in the Press.

'Speaking with some knowledge of the charges in question, and of the persons who are really compromised by them, I assert that there is not, and never was, the slightest excuse for mentioning the name of Prince Albert Victor in association with them. A feeling of delicacy can alone have prevented this statement appearing in a form to command universal credence, but now that there are libellers who do not hesitate to assail the young Prince – at a safe distance – it is a mistake for the English Press to maintain absolute silence on the subject. It is much to be wished that the editor or proprietor of the New York paper to which I refer could be reached by the law which he has violated ...'[3]

The unnamed correspondent was protesting too much. A considerably better-informed assessment of Prince Eddy's complicity was to be found in the letters which Lord Arthur Somerset was writing to his great friend, the Honourable Reginald Brett.

Throughout the Cleveland Street scandal, Lord Arthur Somerset had kept in touch with Reginald Brett. At that time, the thirty-seven-year-old Brett, the future 2nd Viscount Esher, was on the threshold of his highly successful career. A cultured, astute and intelligent man, he was already a figure of some importance but his power would reach its apogee during the reign of King Edward VII. In political, diplomatic, military and social matters, Lord Esher was one of the most influential members of the Edwardian court.

But there was another facet to Reginald Brett's character. Although married and the father of four children, he was an active homosexual. The years before his marriage had been marked by a series of passionate or what he called 'rapturous' love affairs with various young men; it was a way of life which his marriage in no way interrupted. In fact Brett not only continued to fall in and out of love with beautiful youths but was also to conceive an unhealthy passion for one of his own sons. He could never remember a single day, he once admitted to a friend, when he was not deeply in love with some young man or other. Five years after the Cleveland Street scandal, he published, anonymously, a white-covered book of verse called *Foam*, in which he glorified 'golden lads'.

So it was not altogether surprising that he and Lord Arthur Somerset should have shared confidences. As well as having sexual tastes in common, the two men moved in the same royal, social and racing circles. When the Cleveland Street affair was first uncovered, it was in Brett that Somerset confided. Always methodical, Brett pasted all the Cleveland Street correspondence – from Somerset and others – into a bound volume which he entitled *The Case of Lord Arthur Somerset*. This volume, which is to be found among Lord Esher's private papers at Churchill College, Cambridge, throws considerable light on Prince Eddy's complicity in the affair.

Somerset's first letters to Brett after his flight to France are concerned with his hopes of making a new life for himself on the Continent. After spending a few days with his brother Lord Henry Somerset in Monaco, Lord Arthur took the Orient Express to Constantinople. Surely Sultan Abdul Hamid II, appropriately known as 'Abdul the Damned', would have no objections to Somerset's sexual preferences. He did not, and Somerset applied for a position in the imperial stables. But he was reckoning without the long arm of the British law. A series of long-standing treaties between the Ottoman Empire and the United Kingdom gave Britain jurisdiction over British subjects living in Turkey. Warned that he could be arrested, Somerset hastily reboarded the Orient Express.

This time he took it as far as Budapest. Perhaps in Hungary, so famous for its horses, he would land a job. But he did not and because people were 'beginning to ask inconvenient questions', Somerset moved on to Vienna.[4] Here, as he explained to Brett, things were worse. Under the common misapprehension that all homosexuals are paedophiles, the Austrian police arranged for him to be trailed by various urchins, singly or in packs, whenever he set foot outside his hotel. When he failed to show the expected interest in their ragamuffin charms (the police, in a choice example of muddled bureaucratic thinking, even dressed one of the boys as a girl) the lads took to shouting insults at him. Fortunately, Somerset understood no German.

From Vienna he went to Paris. In the more tolerant atmosphere of France, Somerset was able to settle down, undisturbed, in a pension in Passy. He was visited here by his sister Blanche, Lady Waterford, who assured Brett that her brother was 'better here than anywhere, and is as nearly happy as one could hope. This is such a snug rabbit hole …'[5]

All through the Cleveland Street scandal, Lady Waterford was very supportive. Some of this may have been due to the fact that she did not actually believe her brother to be guilty. According to one of her friends, Lady Waterford – who had first visited her brother while he was staying in Monaco – had been told by Somerset that 'he was perfectly innocent but that he had been driven into the wilderness in order to screen others who were amongst the highest in the land.'[6]

In no time, this theory had taken root. Although not many shared Lady Waterford's touching belief in her brother's innocence, they were quite ready to believe that Somerset's decision to flee and so avoid a trial had been taken for the noblest of motives: to protect Prince Eddy's name. Lord Arthur Somerset, by keeping silent about the true cause of his exile, was sacrificing himself for the sake of the throne.

True or not, the fact that this theory was being widely discussed was causing considerable anguish in the Prince of Wales's household; they were, as Somerset put it to Brett, 'in a great pother about it at Sandringham'. The Prince of Wales was known to be 'much annoyed at his son's name being coupled with this thing'.[7] Sir Francis Knollys and Sir Dighton Probyn, who seem to have known rather more about it than their royal master, were trying desperately to quash the rumours. In their efforts they were joined by a third royal supporter: this was the Honourable Oliver Montagu.

Montagu, as well as being Somerset's former commanding officer, was an Extra Equerry to the Prince and Princess of Wales. A handsome man, imbued with a strong sense of chivalry, Oliver Montagu had been in love with the Princess of Wales ever since they first met. For year after year the unmarried Montagu devoted himself to the beautiful Princess Alexandra. That their affair remained platonic, there is no question. The Princess of Wales was quite content with his ardent but blameless courtship, while Oliver Montagu asked for nothing more than to be allowed to adore and protect his 'Beloved Lady'.

That protection was seldom more needed than now – when the Princess's favourite child stood in danger of public exposure as a frequenter of a male brothel. Montagu was tireless in his efforts to spare her this shame. Already, together with Knollys and Probyn, he had helped Somerset to slip away to safety ('Oliver Montagu was very kind the day I left and helped me to get away quietly,' reported Somerset to Brett)[8] but he was horrified to find that Somerset's escape was being widely seen for what it in fact was: a means of preventing Prince Eddy's name being dragged through the courts.

Lady Waterford, alarmed to hear that she was being blamed for spreading the rumours about Prince Eddy, wrote to Oliver Montagu to deny that she had done any such thing. His reply was reassuring. 'Believe me,' he wrote, 'no one that I have heard of, and most certainly neither of the parents you allude to [the Prince and Princess of Wales] have ever for one moment suggested ... your having insinuated things about Prince Eddy, though I fear there is no doubt that some female members of your family have done so ...'[9] Oliver Montagu was referring to Isabella, Lady Henry Somerset, and her mother, Lady Somers. As Lord Henry had left his wife in order to go and live with another man, both Lady Henry and her mother were, not unnaturally, obsessed with the evils of homosexuality.

Lady Waterford was likewise anxious to dispel any notion that it was her brother, Lord Arthur, who had taken Prince Eddy to 19 Cleveland Street. 'Please correct any impression that Arthur and *the boy* ever went out together,' she begged Reginald Brett. 'Arthur knows nothing of his movements and was horrified to think he might be supposed to take the Father's [the Prince of Wales's] money and lead the son into mischief of *any* kind.' She was sure, she added, that Prince Eddy was 'as straight as a line'.[10] As Lady Waterford believed her brother to be innocent, one need not put too much faith in her claim that Prince Eddy was as straight as a line. In any case, she was in no position to know: Somerset would certainly not have told her the full truth.

Lord Arthur Somerset was equally anxious to deny that he had introduced Prince Eddy to the Cleveland Street house. It had no more to do with him, he told Brett, 'than the fact that we (Prince Eddy and I) must both perform bodily functions which we cannot do for each other. In the same way we were both accused of going to this place but not together, and different people were supposed to have gone there to meet us.' Somerset went on to deny that it was he who had started the rumour that Lord Euston had taken the Prince to Cleveland Street. 'I have never even mentioned Euston's name,' he protested, 'nor have I ever told *any one* with whom Prince Eddy was supposed to have gone there.'[11]

In his determination to get Somerset to deny publicly the widely believed theory that he was sacrificing himself for Prince Eddy's sake, Oliver Montagu considered visiting him on the Continent. At this Somerset took fright. 'Don't let Oliver or anyone come out to me,' he urged Brett. 'If he starts, let me know and I will move …'[12] Quite clearly, Somerset did not want to be placed in the position of having to admit to Montagu all he knew about Prince Eddy.

An announcement that his solicitor, Arthur Newton, was about to be charged for 'conspiracy to defeat the course of justice' alarmed Somerset still further. 'There was never anything like the virulence of this prosecution,' he wrote. 'I can see that they will end by dragging that name before the public that we all want to avoid.' If Newton were cornered, he continued, 'He will very likely give them a nasty one … they will end by having out in open court exactly what they are all trying to keep quiet.'[13]

Newton, in fact, was doing his bit towards keeping Prince Eddy's name out of court. No more than any of the others involved in the affair did Newton want to be accused of disloyalty towards the throne. In a guarded letter to Brett, he claimed that he had hit upon 'a comparatively simple way' of demonstrating 'the innocence of the person about whom we were speaking yesterday. I mean the person in India.'[14] If Brett would call on him the following day, he would outline his scheme. Whether or not Newton's little intrigue was ever carried out is uncertain.

In the meantime Sir Dighton Probyn was writing to Somerset's mother, the Duchess of Beaufort, in an effort to get her to influence her son. 'Nobody accused your son of having mentioned PAV's name, but his excuse to everybody for having to leave England is that he has been forced to do so to screen another and that his lips are closed. The only conclusion therefore people can draw from this is that he is sacrificing himself to save the young Prince. Who else is there for whom he could make such a sacrifice?'[15]

Instead of visiting Somerset, Oliver Montagu wrote him a strong, or what Somerset called an 'infernal' letter. It was up to Lord Arthur, he urged, to speak up and clear Prince Eddy's name. Was he 'aware of the irreparable harm he was doing by still persisting in his silence as to the real cause of his leaving the country and insinuating that it was for the sakes of others that he had done so ...?'[16]

But that, explained Somerset to Brett, *was* the 'real cause' of his silence. In a discreetly worded but very revealing letter Lord Arthur made his position clear (the italics are the present author's):

'I cannot see what good I could do Prince Eddy if I went into Court. I might do him harm because if I was asked if I had ever heard anything against him – whom from? – has any person mentioned with whom he went there etc? – the questions would be very awkward. *I have never mentioned the boy's name except to Probyn, Montagu and Knollys when they were acting for me and I thought they ought to know. Had they been wise, hearing what I knew and therefore what others knew, they ought to have hushed the matter up, instead of stirring it up as they did, with all the authorities ...*

'What Oliver does not seem to see is that, if I could tell him my reasons for not going into Court, I could not go in. *Nothing will ever make me divulge anything I know even if I were arrested.* But of course if certain people laid themselves out to have me arrested and succeeded, I might possibly lose my temper and annoy them.

'Of course, it has very often, or may I say constantly occurred to me, that it rests with me to clear up this business, but what can I do? A great many people would never speak to me again as it is, *but if I went into Court and told all I knew no one who called himself a man would ever speak to me again.* Hence my infernal position …

'I did what I did then, and still, believe was the best for all concerned. If they don't take care, they will make a hash of the whole thing yet, and then I suppose they will say I did it. At all events you and Newton can bear me witness that I have sat absolutely tight in the matter and have not told even my own father anything.'[17]

Reading this correspondence (some of which, significantly, was destroyed) there can be little doubt that Prince Eddy did visit the Cleveland Street brothel and that the Prince of Wales's entourage was desperate to quash the rumours of his involvement, not because they were false but because they were true.

Goaded by press accusations of unwillingness, and by police complaints of procrastination, the authorities felt compelled to make another move in the Cleveland Street affair. A summons was issued against Lord Arthur Somerset's solicitor, Arthur Newton, and his two assistants, Frederick Taylorson and Adolphe de Gallo, on a charge of perverting the course of justice. In his efforts to protect Somerset and 'other persons', Newton was accused not only of trying to spirit away the ex-waiter Algernon Allies but also of scheming to get three of the telegraph boys out of the country. He had promised each of them £50 down, a new outfit, £1 a week for three years and a passage to Australia where they would be able to start a new life. But as Henry Labouchere put it in his paper *Truth*, 'the proceedings [against Newton and his assistants] look very much to me like a noisy attempt to close the stable door after the steeds have been allowed to issue from the stable.'[18]

Newton was, to say the least, surprised by the summons. As he pointed out to Reginald Brett, with whom he was in constant touch, 'all through the case till that moment the Government had acted with him in endeavouring to minimize the scandal'. At the first of the three Cleveland Street trials — that of Veck and Newlove — Newton had obligingly suggested 'that it was unnecessary to mention names in connection with the case': a suggestion with which the authorities had concurred only too readily. The government, said Newton, 'had acted entirely in unison with him in an endeavour to keep the matter secret'.[19] So why should they be summonsing him now?

Newton need not have worried. Throughout his trial he was to be handled with kid gloves. The government knew – as Somerset knew – that if cornered, Newton could let off a bombshell. Newton was, after all, the first person to have mentioned Prince Eddy's name in connection with the Cleveland Street house: over six months before, at the start of the scandal, he had warned the Director of Public Prosecutions of the Prince's involvement.

The initial hearings into Newton and his assistants over, there was a two-month-long delay while the apprehensive government debated whether or not to continue with the prosecution. During this time the government was remorselessly harried – both in the pages of *Truth* and in the House of Commons – by Labouchere. 'I do not blame Mr Newton,' argued Labouchere; 'so far as I know he only aided Lord Salisbury in defeating justice, but it seems to me that if Mr Newton is prosecuted, Lord Salisbury and several other gentlemen ought also to be prosecuted and charged under the same indictment.'[20]

The trial, presided over by Mr Justice Cave, opened on 16 May 1890 in the Queen's Bench Division in the Law Courts. It was conducted with a suspicious lack of vigour. The charge against Newton's assistant De Gallo had already been dropped. As his other assistant, Taylorson, was claimed to have acted under Newton's instructions, his plea of not guilty was accepted without comment. Sir Charles Russell, who had prosecuted Ernest Parke of the *North London Press* so successfully, now defended Newton with equal expertise. Having been tipped off to the effect that 'a persuasive rather than a hostile attitude towards the authorities would result in the matter not being too deeply gone in to', Russell was at his most emollient.[21] It would not be right, he announced reassuringly, 'even if pertinent to the case', that he should mention the names of the people who had visited the Cleveland Street house. With this the prosecuting counsel – who happened to be no less a figure than Sir Richard Webster, the Attorney General – agreed heartily.

Russell's chief line of defence was that his client was a young man of good character who had been carried away by an excess of zeal. By trying to get various young men out of the country, Newton had merely wanted to protect his clients from possible blackmail. He had certainly not done it to ensure that they would not be able to give evidence in court. With this argument, the prosecuting counsel was only too ready to concur. Of the six counts against him, Newton pleaded not guilty to five but guilty to the general charge of 'perverting the course of justice'. Obligingly, the jury accepted these pleas. Everyone left the court under the impression that Newton would merely be bound over.

Everyone, that is, except the judge. Mr Justice Cave had presided over all this legal egg-dancing in mounting exasperation. When he came to pass sentence, on 20 May, he made his feelings clear. He did not for a moment believe that a mere desire to save his clients from blackmail had been the reason for Newton's attempt to get the boys out of the country. He therefore sentenced him to six weeks' imprisonment.

It was, all things considered, a mild enough sentence. The authorities, relieved that Newton had not carried out his earlier threat of mentioning Prince Eddy's name in court, rewarded him by ensuring that he was not struck off the rolls. Newton did not even suffer, as any solicitor in similar circumstances would have suffered, a period of suspension from practice.

Arthur Newton's subsequent career was highly colourful. For twenty years after his short spell in prison, he enjoyed a successful practice, which included acting for Alfred Taylor, Oscar Wilde's co-defendant, in the Wilde trials of 1895. His career reached its apogee in 1911, with his defence of the notorious wife-poisoner, Dr Crippen. But the Crippen case proved to be his undoing. He was suspended by the Law Society for twelve months for what they considered to be unethical behaviour: the selling of Crippen's 'confession' to a magazine. A year later Newton was charged with obtaining a large sum of money by fraud and false pretences. He was found guilty and sentenced to three years' imprisonment. This time he *was* struck off the rolls.

The Cleveland Street scandal had its climax in a turbulent debate in the House of Commons on 28 February 1890. In an hour-and-a-quarter-long speech Henry Labouchere accused Lord Salisbury's Conservative government of a 'criminal conspiracy to defeat the ends of justice'. Relentlessly, he went through all the suspect aspects of the case: the unimpeded flight of Hammond and the failure to extradite him; the sluggishness in moving against Lord Arthur Somerset; the lack of any examination of the telegraph boys by a magistrate; the rushed trial of Veck and Newlove; the failure to arrest Somerset on his return to England to attend his grandmother's funeral; the railway-station meeting between Lord Salisbury and Sir Dighton Probyn which resulted in the timely flight of Somerset; the reluctance on the part of the authorities to act on police information; and, above all, the curious lack of vigour with which the entire affair had been conducted.

At one point only did Labouchere refer to Prince Eddy – or rather, to 'a gentleman of very high position' – and this was to deny that the Prince was in any way connected with the scandal. But then Labouchere, for all the radicalism of his politics and his readiness to attack such things as royal finances, was not entirely immune to the mystique of monarchy; nor could he possibly have known the truth about Prince Eddy's complicity.

Labouchere was answered in an even longer speech by the Attorney General, Sir Richard Webster. Without actually lying, the Attorney General was able to refute his opponent's accusations by skilful and wordy obfuscation. In short, he made what Labouchere afterwards described as 'the best of a bad case'. The Attorney General's speech was followed by ten minutes of uproar, at the end of which Labouchere was expelled for a week for refusing to withdraw an insulting remark about Lord Salisbury. For two hours more the debate raged on but, in the absence of Labouchere, the battle was as good as lost. What had been, in effect, Labouchere's demand for an enquiry into the handling of the Cleveland Street affair, was beaten by 206 votes to 66.

The matter was concluded a few days later when Lord Salisbury made a personal statement in the House of Lords. He ended his dismissal of Labouchere's accusations with the airy claim that 'the subject is not one that lends itself to extensive treatment, or that commends itself for lengthened debate.'[22]

Had there been a criminal conspiracy to hush up the Cleveland Street scandal? There certainly seems to have been.

A few days after the parliamentary debate, W.H. Smith, Leader of the House of Commons and founder of the famous chain of bookstalls, asked Hamilton Cuffe, Assistant Director of Public Prosecutions, to find out how Labouchere had been able to get hold of so much confidential information for his speech in the House. There had obviously been leaks from police and government circles. Cuffe looked into the matter with great thoroughness. What he discovered would have made Labouchere's case even stronger. Cuffe came to realize that all the procrastination – Labouchere's 'criminal conspiracy' – could be narrowed down to four people, all of them at the very top of the administrative tree. They were the Home Secretary, Henry Matthews; the Attorney General, Sir Richard Webster; the Lord Chancellor, Lord Halsbury; and the Prime Minister, Lord Salisbury. None of these men had acted unlawfully, but an understanding that Lord Salisbury did not want charges pressed against Lord Arthur Somerset affected all their actions.

Why should Lord Salisbury have been so set on shielding Somerset? They were not particularly friendly; nor was there any sort of family connection. A practical politician and a hardened man of the world, the Prime Minister would scarcely have risked his reputation for the sake of Somerset, fellow aristocrat though he may have been. The history of the nineteenth century was not short of publicly disgraced aristocrats; one more would have made no difference. In any case, Somerset *was* disgraced. He might not actually have appeared in court but there were few who did not know that a warrant had been issued for his arrest, and on what charge. He was never able to return to England. For the following thirty-seven years Somerset lived – with a companion named James Andrew Neale – in a villa in Hyères in the South of France. When he died, on 26 May 1926, not even his remains were brought back for burial in the family vault at Badminton.

No, Lord Salisbury must have been acting for reasons of state. The very personification of the ruling class, he regarded his prime duty to be the upholding of its institutions and, above all, its crowning glory – the monarchy. In the course of Queen Victoria's long reign, the throne had developed into a powerful symbol: influential, mystical, sacrosanct. It was up to Lord Salisbury to see that this image was not tarnished. Often, during his premiership, he had felt obliged to give his attention to some relatively minor royal question which, if mishandled, might affect the dignity of the crown.

Six years on, Lord Salisbury was to be involved in a similar piece of duplicity during the official enquiry into the Jameson Raid – that unprovoked invasion of the independent Transvaal by a band of British freebooters. The nickname given to Salisbury's blinkered investigation could well have been given to the Cleveland Street inquest: 'the Lying in State at Westminster'. It was a similar exercise in safeguarding the prestige of the British throne.

Prince Albert Victor, for all his weaknesses, was Heir Presumptive. The Queen was getting old; she had already celebrated the fiftieth anniversary of her accession. The Prince of Wales, who ate, smoked and fornicated too much, was not expected to live into old age. So it was not unlikely that within a decade or so, Prince Eddy would ascend the throne. For a crowned and anointed King-Emperor to be suspected of breaking the law by patronizing a notorious male brothel would be too appalling to contemplate. Whether Lord Salisbury believed that the Prince had visited 19 Cleveland Street was neither here nor there; the Prime Minister's main concern was that the rumour should be quashed; that Somerset, and others, should be prevented from mentioning the Prince's name in open court.

Beyond the patrician figure of Lord Salisbury stood a still more important one: the Prince of Wales. By now he, as well as his circle of advisers – Knollys, Probyn and Montagu – knew even more about the matter than did Salisbury. Scandals, sexual or otherwise, were something which the Prince of Wales had been containing all his adult life. An accomplished diplomat, driven by the supreme monarchical need for self-preservation, the Prince of Wales had handled the matter very adroitly. It was no mean achievement for him and his coterie of polished courtiers to have hushed things up so successfully; to have convinced even a man like Labouchere that there was no substance whatsoever in the rumours about Prince Eddy.

That there had been a conspiracy instigated at the highest levels, there can be very little doubt. Sixty years later, when the writer and politician Harold Nicolson was working on his official life of Prince Eddy's brother, King George V, he was told by the Lord Chief Justice, Lord Goddard, that Prince Eddy 'had been involved in a male brothel scene, and that a solicitor had to commit perjury to clear him'.[23] And while researching in the Royal Archives, Nicolson made a note in his private diary to the effect that there seems to have been a skilful cover-up of the scandal 'to save the name of the Royal Family'.[24] To this day, the present Lord Salisbury is 'not willing to agree' to an examination of the relevant papers.[25]

PART FIVE

DUKE OF CLARENCE

13. 'THE GREATEST POSITION THERE IS'

Not until May 1890, when the last of the three Cleveland Street trials was almost over, did Prince Eddy arrive home from his Indian tour. He had broken his voyage to spend a few days in Egypt, as the guest of the Khedive Tawfik. From there he had sailed on to Athens to visit his Greek relations: George I, King of the Hellenes, was the Princess of Wales's brother. Crown Princess Sophie of Greece, whose wedding Prince Eddy had attended on his way out to India the previous October, wrote to her mother, the German Empress Frederick, to report that 'Eddy leaves tomorrow morning; poor boy he still looks dreadfully yellow and thin! He is such a dear and so good and kind.'[1]

To give some sort of shape to dear, good, kind Prince Eddy's amorphous personality, the royal family decided to take certain steps. The first of these was the bestowing of a new title. On 24 May 1890, the day Queen Victoria turned seventy-one, he was created Duke of Clarence and Avondale and Earl of Athlone. It had been with some reluctance that Queen Victoria had agreed to this bestowal of a dukedom on her grandson. 'I am very sorry Eddy should be lowered to a Duke like any one of the nobility, which a Prince never can be,' she complained to her eldest daughter, the Empress Frederick. 'Nothing is so fine and grand as a Royal Prince ...'[2]

Prince Eddy's brother, Prince George, had other, more significant, objections to the title. So many 'stupid jokes and puns' had apparently been made about 'Albert' and 'Victor'; he could now visualize similar *double entendres* about the activities of 'Clarence' and 'Avondale'. 'Why can't you darling Motherdear', appealed Prince George to Princess Alexandra, 'try and get it altered and let him be called the Duke of Clarence, which is an old English title.'[3]

Prince George's objections were met. From this time on Prince Eddy was usually referred to as the Duke of Clarence. But even this led to criticism. The mischievous Henry Labouchere immediately launched into an attack on the title. 'The only Duke of Clarence who is known to history is the numbskull who was deservedly drowned in a butt of malmsey,' he wrote in *Truth*, 'and, during the present century the title was associated with the aberrations and extravagances for which William IV was unenviably notorious.'[4] What Labouchere was implying, of course, was that Prince Eddy was a numbskull, notorious for his aberrations and extravagances.

Numbskull or not, Prince Eddy was formally introduced, in June that year, into the House of Lords by his father, the Prince of Wales, and his uncle, the Duke of Edinburgh. The colourful ceremony was watched, from the royal gallery, by his adoring mother and sisters. The Prince, who was already a Mason, was also installed, at Reading, as Provincial Grand Master of the Berkshire Freemasons. He was promoted, in quick succession, to honorary colonelships of the 3rd King's Royal Rifle Corps, the 1st Volunteer Battalion of the Queen's Own Cameron Highlanders, the 4th Bombay Infantry and the 4th Bombay Cavalry. If nothing else, this allowed him to sport even more splendidly tailored uniforms.

As, at the age of twenty-six, a royal duke could hardly still be living under his parents' roof, a suite of rooms was prepared for his use in St James's Palace. It was designed to serve as the home in which the Prince could be launched on the next stage of his career; for by now the family had decided that marriage was the only solution to the problem of Prince Eddy. Both to give his life some sense of purpose and, more important, to lay the ghost of the Cleveland Street scandal, Prince Eddy must find a wife or, more accurately, must have a wife found for him.

Marlborough House expected no resistance from the Prince on the subject. 'If he is properly managed,' wrote Sir Francis Knollys with brutal frankness, 'I do not anticipate any real opposition on Prince Eddy's part.'[5] Indeed, it would never have occurred to the pliable Prince to go against his family's wishes. He was also conscious enough of his royal birth and obligations, of the dynastic imperatives, to realize that he would have to marry sooner or later. That there might be any choice in the matter would never have occurred to him. Whatever his sexual preferences, Prince Eddy was to prove quite capable of contemplating marriage and, indeed, of professing himself to be in love with a woman. In fact, once the subject had been raised, the young man astonished his family by the volatility with which he seemed to be tumbling in and out of love.

The royal family's first choice of a suitable bride was, inevitably, one of his many royal cousins; 'for of course', as Queen Victoria put it in a letter to her grandson, 'any Lady in Society *would never* do'.[6] Even before he had been despatched to India, Prince Eddy had been manoeuvred in the direction of Princess Alix of Hesse, the sixth child of Queen Victoria's daughter, the late Princess Alice, and of her husband Louis IV, whose cumbersome title was Grand Duke of Hesse and by the Rhine. Dutifully, Prince Eddy proposed marriage. But Princess Alix – or 'Alicky' as she was known in the family – who was a serious-minded young woman, was having none of him. Rumours of Prince Eddy's complicity in the Cleveland Street scandal, which were at their height at the time that Princess Alix was considering his proposal, may well have reached the Grand Ducal Palace in Darmstadt. Courts are notorious whispering galleries. The situation would not have been unfamiliar to Princess Alix: her own brother Ernest, who was generally described as 'artistic', was apparently homosexual. 'No boy was safe,' the wife of Grand Duke Ernest was to complain in later years. 'From the stable lads to the kitchen help, he slept quite openly with them all.'[7]

On his return from India in May 1890, Prince Eddy was greeted by Princess Alix's refusal of his proposal. 'I fear all hopes of Alicky's marrying Eddy are at an end,' wrote Queen Victoria to the Empress Frederick. 'She has written to tell him how it pains her to pain him, but she cannot marry him, much as she likes him as a Cousin, that she knows she would not be happy with him and that he would not be happy with her and that he must *not* think of her ... she says that if she is *forced* she will do it, but that she would be unhappy, and he too.

'This', continued the Queen, 'shows great strength of character as all her family and all of us wish it, and she refuses the greatest position there is.'[8]

But not quite resigned to Princess Alix's refusal, Queen Victoria made one last effort. 'Is there *no* hope about E?' she asked one of Princess Alix's sisters. 'She should be made to reflect seriously on the folly of throwing away the chance of a very good Husband, kind, affectionate and steady ...'[9] Only a doting grandmother could ever have referred to Prince Eddy as 'steady'.

Having turned down this opportunity of becoming a future Queen Empress of Great Britain, Princess Alix married Tsar Nicholas II and by becoming Empress of All the Russias was to be murdered, in a blood-stained cellar in Ekaterinburg, in 1918.

To his sentimental mother, Prince Eddy duly professed himself heartbroken at Princess Alix's 'cruelty'. But as he could not have known her very well and could not even have set eyes on her during the seven months that he was in India, his desolation should not be taken too seriously.

Queen Victoria's second choice was another of the Prince's German cousins: Princess Margaret of Prussia, the youngest daughter of the wid-owed Empress Frederick. Although 'Cousin Mossy' was not 'regularly pretty', wrote the Queen to Prince Eddy on 19 May 1890, a fortnight after Princess Alix's rejection, 'she has a very pretty figure, is very ami-able and half English with great love for England which you will find in very few, if any others'.[10]

Although Prince Eddy would no doubt have married Cousin Mossy if pushed, the objection to this particular match came from the Princess of Wales. She liked the girl well enough but the fact that she was a Prussian, the sister of Kaiser Wilhelm II, put her completely out of the running. Princess Alexandra's hatred of Prussia – dating back to the Prusso-Danish War a quarter of a century before – remained vehement. 'As you know ...' wrote Sir Francis Knollys to the Queen's private secretary, 'I am a strong advocate for Princess Margaret and I wish the Princess [of Wales] would see these things differently ...'[11]

It was at this stage that Prince Eddy alarmed everyone by suddenly becoming involved with the most unsuitable of candidates: Princess Hélène d'Orléans.

Princess Hélène d'Orléans was the nineteen-year-old daughter of the Comte de Paris, Pretender to the French throne. Banished from Republican France in 1886, the Orléans family had settled in England. They were, of course, staunchly Roman Catholic. This made Princess Hélène doubly unsuitable as a consort for a future King of England: on both political and religious grounds, the thing was impossible.

As far as Prince Eddy was concerned, the affair with Princess Hélène was hardly a case of love at first sight. It was left to his two unmarried sisters, Princess Victoria and Princess Maud, to tell him that Princess Hélène was fond of him. 'I did not realize this at first although the girls constantly told me she liked me,' he admitted to his brother, Prince George. 'I saw Hélène several times at Sheen [Sheen Lodge, Richmond, was the home of his married sister Princess Louise, Duchess of Fife] and naturally thought her everything that is nice in a girl, and she had become very pretty which I saw at once and also gradually perceived that she really liked me ... I naturally got to like, or rather to love her, by the manner she showed her affection for me.'[12]

Prince Eddy's somewhat lukewarm attitude was more than offset by the ardour of Princess Hélène. Right from the start, apparently, she was the driving force in this curious and controversial romance. For one thing, she seems to have been genuinely in love with Prince Eddy. To this nineteen-year-old girl, the elegantly dressed, well-mannered and warm-hearted young man was a figure of considerable allure; he had the sort of sleepy charm that some women find irresistible. To Queen Victoria, the Princess afterwards admitted, 'I loved him so much and perhaps I was rash, but I couldn't help myself, I loved him so much. He was so good.'[13] To hear Prince Eddy described as 'good' might have amused the likes of Sir Francis Knollys and Sir Dighton Probyn but, in the sense that he was kindly and considerate, Prince Eddy *was* good. 'No man', wrote one observer, 'was ever more beloved by his immediate relations. His servants and dependants adored him and his friends and companions were devoted to him.'[14]

But Princess Hélène d'Orléans was fuelled by another passion: an ambition to become Queen of England. Already she was showing signs of that force of character that was to distinguish her when, in later years as the wife of the Italian Duke of Aosta, she outstripped even her husband in her active support for Mussolini's fascist regime. 'The Duce himself', wrote one admiring diplomat's wife at the time, 'lends a willing and attentive ear to her advice on many subjects of importance.'[15] That she and her husband would have made a more brilliant reigning couple than her husband's cousin, little King Victor Emmanuel III and Queen Elena, the Duchess of Aosta never doubted. These burgeoning aspirations made Princess Hélène more than ever determined to marry the Heir Presumptive to the British throne.

It did not take long for rumours of this marital manoeuvering to reach the ears of Queen Victoria. Fondly imagining that her grandson had been heartbroken by his rejection at the hands of Princess Alix of Hesse, the Queen was astonished to hear that – within a week of this rejection – Prince Eddy was becoming romantically involved with Princess Hélène.

'I can't believe this,' she wrote to the Prince, 'for you know that I told you (as I did your Parents who agreed with me) that such a marriage is utterly *impossible*. None of our family can marry a Catholic without losing all their rights and I am sure that she will never change her religion, and to change her religion merely to marry is a thing much to be deprecated and which would have the worst effect possible and be most unpopular, besides which *you* could not marry the daughter of the Pretender to the French Throne. Politically in this way it would also be impossible.

'That being the case you should avoid meeting her as much as possible as it would only lead to make you unhappy if you formed an attachment for her.'[16]

But ranged against the Queen was Prince Eddy's immediate family. The Prince of Wales was only too thankful to see his wayward son showing an interest in marriage at all, while Princess Alexandra and her three daughters were actively encouraging the match. These four sentimental, childlike women thrilled to the romance of the situation: they could perfectly understand why Princess Hélène should have fallen in love with the 'adorable' Eddy. In Princess Alexandra's eyes, the Princess had the added attraction of not being German. Beside this advantage all the disadvantages simply melted away. Egged on by this doting cabal, the impressionable Prince Eddy was only too ready to oblige them by paying court to Princess Hélène. He could not, however, have paid her very serious attention for throughout the summer during which the romance was supposed to be blossoming, the Prince was with his regiment in York. And even their occasional meetings would have been chaperoned.

Chief provider of the settings for these fleeting encounters was Prince Eddy's eldest sister, the shy and awkward Princess Louise, Duchess of Fife. In August 1890 the scene moved from Sheen Lodge which lay so conveniently close to the home of the Comte de Paris at Twickenham, to the Fifes' Scottish seat, Mar Lodge, near Balmoral. The Comte and Comtesse de Paris, with their daughter, were invited to stay at Mar Lodge. Also invited were the Princess of Wales and Prince Eddy, who was by then on one of his extended autumn leaves of absence from military duties. The Prince of Wales was not present; nothing would induce him to forgo his customary cure at Homburg. While the Comtesse de Paris, who habitually wore tweeds and smoked a pipe and cigars, was quite happy to join the men on their shooting and stalking expeditions, the Princess of Wales concentrated on Princess Hélène. She persuaded her to promise to change her religion and to marry Prince Eddy. Unbeknown to her parents, the Princess agreed.

The first of the many hurdles over, the second, and far more formidable one, had to be tackled: Queen Victoria's approval must somehow be obtained. Princess Alexandra, appreciating that the old Queen was far more sentimental than was generally appreciated, decided that the young couple must appeal to her directly. Arranging for a picnic lunch to sustain them on their journey, she sent them off by carriage to Balmoral. Her plan succeeded brilliantly. 'You can imagine what a thing to go through and I did not at all relish the idea ...' admitted Prince Eddy in a letter to his brother Prince George, 'I naturally expected Grandmama would be furious at the idea, and say it was quite impossible etc. But instead of that she was very nice about it and promised to help us as much as possible, which she is now doing ... I believe what pleased her most was my taking Hélène into her, and saying we had arranged it entirely without consulting our parents first. This as you know is not quite true but she believed it all ...'[17]

There was now let loose a flood of letters, reports, memoranda and *aides-mémoire* involving the Queen, the Prince of Wales, the Prime Minister, their private secretaries and assorted members of the government. How practical, or advisable, would it be for a future monarch to marry the daughter of the Pretender to the French throne who had renounced her true religion and turned Protestant? It was Arthur Balfour, minister in attendance at Balmoral that season, who first reported to the Prime Minister, his uncle Lord Salisbury — who had only just emerged from the morass of the Cleveland Street scandal — on this new royal dilemma.

'The Queen', explained Balfour in his characteristically sardonic fashion, 'is much touched by the personal appeal to *herself*. With admirable dexterity (this surely cannot be the *young man's* idea) they came hand in hand straight to her, and implored her to smooth out not merely the political difficulties, but the family difficulties also. In making her their confidante, they have made her their ally. She would have been in a much less melting mood if the approaches had been conducted in due form through the parents. But the Sovereign has been touched through the Grandmother.' The Queen, who was no fool, quickly appreciated that Princess Hélène was 'a clever woman ... who will be the making of her husband'.[18]

He foresaw, continued Balfour, 'a great deal of trouble over it all, but it is impossible not to see the humorous side of the business. Will it be believed that neither the Queen, nor the young Prince, nor Princess Hélène, see anything which is not romantic, interesting, touching and praiseworthy in the young lady giving up a religion, to which *she still professes devoted attachment*, in order to marry the man on whom she says she has set her heart! They are moved even to tears by the magnitude of the sacrifice, without it, apparently, occurring to them that at best it is the sacrifice of religion for love, while at the worst it is the sacrifice of religion for a throne – a singular inversion of the ordinary views on martyrdom ...'

The Queen felt sure that 'the combination of romance and conversion – the brand plucked from the burning', would make the match acceptable to everyone other than the Roman Catholics; 'and the wrath of the R.C.s', continued Balfour, 'she contemplates with something like satisfaction'.[19]

Lord Salisbury treated the matter less flippantly. In a ponderous memorandum to the Queen, he pointed out the many disadvantages of the match. 'It may profoundly affect the feelings of the people towards the throne, and of foreign countries towards England,' he warned. The British did not like the French. Might they not regard the Princess's conversion to Protestantism as a supremely self-serving act? And might she not, in later life, fall back under Roman Catholic influences? Then what about the French? Surely the Republicans would resent the Comte de Paris becoming the father-in-law of a future King of England? And would the Royalists and Catholics not resent the Princess's change of religion?

To the Prince of Wales's suggestion that Princess Hélène be allowed to remain a Roman Catholic provided she gave an understanding that the children would be brought up in the Anglican Church, Lord Salisbury was dismissive. Even to contemplate any such idea would be to rouse the anger of the middle and lower classes, he said.

In the end, it all depended on the Comte de Paris. Without his consent, the Princess could not change her religion. And this he adamantly refused to give. Nor did the Pope, whom the desperate Princess rushed to consult in Rome, prove any more accommodating. Faced with this insurmountable obstacle, the affair had to end. The relationship was broken off.

The bitter-sweet story of Prince Eddy and Princess Hélène has gone down as one of history's great royal romances. This seems to be borne out by the fact that on the Prince's elaborate tomb in the Albert Chapel at Windsor there lies, to this day, a bead wreath with the single word 'Hélène' on it. The Prince of Wales reported his son as being 'quite wretched'[20] at the break-up of the affair, and Queen Victoria felt sure that he would not recover from the blow for many years. But those who – with good reason – understood Prince Eddy better, viewed the business more cynically. 'He declares that he will never marry anyone else,' reported Sir Francis Knollys to Sir Henry Ponsonby, 'which I believe People have said before in similar cases.'[21] And Ponsonby himself, meeting the Prince accidentally at Marlborough House immediately after the break-up, reported that 'His Royal Highness did not appear depressed but talked away in a most lively manner.'[22]

But positive proof that Prince Eddy's emotions were not all that seriously engaged is to be found in a series of curious letters which, at the very time that he was believed to be passionately in love with Princess Hélène, he was writing to someone else.

Prince Eddy was one of those men who is happiest with a female confidante. His closest companions were undoubtedly his mother and sisters; they could be relied upon to give him that uncritical adoration and reassurance which his self-doubting nature always needed. It is in the light of this taste for feminine companionship that one must read his letters to Lady Sybil St Clair Erskine, the nineteen-year-old daughter of the 4th Earl of Rosslyn. Lord Rosslyn was the half-brother of the Prince of Wales's current mistress, Lady Brooke. For artlessness, for muddle-headedness, as examples of a complete misunderstanding of the true nature of love – and all written at a time when the Prince was supposed to be besotted by Princess Hélène d'Orléans – these letters can hardly be surpassed.

'I thought it was impossible a short time ago to [love] more than one person at the same time,' he wrote in the summer of 1891, 'and I believe according to things in general it should be so, but I feel that exceptions will happen at times. I can explain it easier to you when next we meet, than by writing. I only hope and trust that this charming creature which has so fascinated me, is not merely playing with my feelings ... I can't believe she would after what she has already said, and asked me to say ... If one could only transplant oneself now and then, and then all of a sudden appear before the person one most wishes to see how delightful that would be. I am sure that if it were only possible, the world would be a great deal happier than it is. Don't you think so?'

'I wonder if you really love me a little?' he wrote a week later. 'I ought not to ask such a silly question I suppose but still I should be very pleased if you did just a little bit ... It is very hot today and I feel very languid and not up to doing much ...'

Would she, by the way, always be sure to destroy the coat of arms and signature on his letters? 'You can't be too careful what you do in these days, when hardly anybody is to be trusted.'[23]

Needless to say, the lady did nothing of the sort.

Throughout the time that Prince Eddy was conducting his simultaneous love affairs with Princess Hélène and Lady Sybil St Clair Erskine, he was involved in a third relationship: with a young doctor named Alfred Fripp.

In July 1890, Prince Eddy was taking a break from his never very exacting military duties with the 10th Hussars, then headquartered at York, by spending a few weeks at the Royal Hotel in nearby Scarborough. While he was there he fell ill with what has been described as 'a sharpish attack of fever'.[24] As the Prince's usual doctor, Dr Jallard, was on leave, he was attended by Jallard's locum, the newly qualified, twenty-four-year-old Alfred Fripp. For the following three weeks, Fripp was in daily attendance on his royal patient.

The two young men had met before. Alfred Fripp was related to, and a godson of, Prince Eddy's old tutor, Canon Dalton. While

Dalton had been at Cambridge with the Prince, the tutor had twice been visited by his godson, then nineteen years of age and about to enter medical school. Fripp, like Prince Eddy's Cambridge mentor, Jim Stephen, was one of those notable Victorian scholar-sportsmen. Described as a 'broad-shouldered young giant', he had captained the Cricket XI at Merchant Taylors' School and was to captain the Rugby XV at Guy's Hospital. He was also a powerful swimmer and oarsman. To his sporting and scholastic achievements, young Fripp brought an open and affable manner: 'his cheerfulness', wrote one companion, 'was ever a most marked characteristic.' That Prince Eddy, in his gauche Cambridge period, should be attracted to this charming young giant was only to be expected. 'Dined and spent the evening in HRH's room – tête-à-tête for two hours with him,' noted Fripp in his diary during his second visit to Cambridge.[25]

Now, six years later, the two young men were again thrown together. If anything, the passing years had improved Alfred Fripp's looks and personality. The recently qualified doctor was, says one observer, 'tall, robust, tanned, with an infectious smile, a ready laugh, and a great fund of common sense. His whole manner suggested confidence, his voice and smile brought hope ...'[26] Understandably, Prince Eddy professed himself to be 'delighted to be in his hands'.[27]

The delight was mutual. It was not every day that a young locum, accustomed to slaving in the out-patients department of a crowded London hospital, found himself in sole charge of the Heir Presumptive to the throne. Fripp's letters home reflect his barely concealed satisfaction. 'HRH seems to take kindly to me,' he wrote. 'We get on very well together, but my ingenuity is sorely taxed to exhibit the right mixture of firmness and politeness. You would be amused to see Colonel This and the Hon. That dancing around and asking me the most minute directions – what time is he to take his meals; then the menu for each meal is submitted for me. I have to have long talks with each, and then again with HRH who pours out all his little woes and always makes me smoke in his room. He smokes himself until he is stupid. I have knocked him down to three cigarettes and one cigar a day ...

'Don't mention HRH's illness outside our house as the Prince of Wales particularly wants it not to get into the papers. He is afraid the public will get the impression that his son is a chronic invalid.'[28]

By the second week of August 1890, Prince Eddy had recovered and was able to set off, as arranged, for Scotland where he was to spend the autumn, first with his sister, the Duchess of Fife, at Mar Lodge; and then with the Prince and Princess of Wales, at Abergeldie, near Balmoral. He was seen off at the station by Alfred Fripp. This by no means, however, meant the end of their association, for so taken with Fripp was Prince Eddy that he had invited him to Scotland. Just as soon as Dr Jallard returned from leave, three days later, Fripp travelled north to spend what he afterwards described as 'those wonderful weeks'.[29] The friendship, as Fripp's biographer puts it, 'had begun in earnest'.[30]

Because Alfred Fripp's visit coincided with that of the Comte and Comtesse de Paris and their daughter to Mar Lodge that August, he was accommodated at the Fife Arms Hotel until they left. But once the French royal family had gone, Fripp moved into Mar Lodge. Here the two friends spent most of the time in each other's company: going for long walks over the heathery hillsides, playing lawn tennis, attending the Highland Games at Braemar. When Prince Eddy shot his first stag, he made the customary presentation of the head to Fripp. Obliged to pay a four-day-long official visit to Wales, Prince Eddy insisted that Fripp accompany him. Throughout the crowded programme of speech-making, foundation stone-laying, tree-planting and bridge-opening, the young doctor acted as the Prince's equerry.

As so often before, the gentle Prince Eddy was bringing out the protective instincts in this big, genial, self-assured young man. But Fripp's concern for his royal friend was not entirely disinterested. Alfred Fripp was an ambitious person and time and again he mentions his hopes of this royal friendship opening up doors, in both a social and a professional sense. Already, apparently, this unusual relationship between the relatively humbly-born doctor and the Heir Presumptive was causing puzzlement and resentment among Fripp's colleagues.

The sensible Fripp, who never allowed himself to be overawed by the unaccustomed grandeur of his new milieu, had an amusing anecdote to tell about the parsimony of his host, the coarse-mannered but immensely rich Duke of Fife. With almost every day spent in the slaughter of game, the larders at Mar Lodge were crammed with venison, far more than the household could possibly cope with. 'Send some of it to Fripp's nurses at Guy's,' suggested the ever considerate Prince Eddy. On being asked by the Duke of Fife how much venison should be sent, Fripp explained that there were four separate messes for the nursing staff, to say nothing of the rest of the staff and the servants. After a great deal of discussion, it was decided that, of the over fifty haunches in the larders, six should be sent to the hospital. A servant was duly summoned and instructed to despatch the six haunches. But as he was leaving the room, the Duke followed him. 'John,' Fripp heard Fife whisper to the man, '*three* will do.' And then, just as the servant was about to close the door, the Duke gave another whispered command. 'Oh, John,' he said, '*one* will do.'

The story had a sequel. Two days later, when Fripp was seated beside the visiting Princess Alexandra at luncheon, a telegram was handed to him. Politely, without opening it, he put it in his pocket. But the Princess insisted that he read it. As Fripp seemed amused by its contents, she asked to see the telegram herself. It had been sent by the matron of Guy's Hospital and read, 'Venison returned as carriage not paid.'[31]

At the end of September Fripp accompanied Prince Eddy to Abergeldie, Scottish home of the Prince and Princess of Wales. 'This is a charming place,' he wrote to his parents, 'a genuine old Scotch castle with gates and portcullis and turrets and battlements and the River Dee tumbling just under the walls and the salmon jumping merrily ...'[32] Life at Abergeldie was both more formal and more extravagant than it had been at Mar Lodge. In one of his ecstatic letters home, the young man gives a picture of a typical evening at the castle.

'Presently enter the Princess of Wales and Princess Victoria. All bow very low – though perhaps you were all smoking together in the garden an hour ago. Then enter the Prince of Wales, low bow again – the Duke of Clarence always last. The two princes wear full dress kilts, the ladies much dressed, jewels etc. Mr Cross (the House Steward, old, respectable, plain evening-dress) announces dinner. Dinner very good, good cook, splendidly served, but of inordinate length. Many red-coated, monstrous, overfed men. Mr Cross bosses the wine, which is very good. There is one other functionary in plain clothes, the head page, all the others in royal scarlet.

'Conversation general and lively and loud, so that the Princess may hear. Prince tells many anecdotes, has a marvellous memory and active brain. A grand host, polite to everyone. Princess charming. When she does not like a dish she says it is "German" and laughs. She explains that she hates the Germans. We do not sit long with the fruit. Then time for two cigarettes before joining the ladies ... talking till about 12. Ladies to bed. All the men to the Equerries' Room. Smoking, letter-writing, talking, whiskey or any conceivable drink you like.'[33]

One morning, while Fripp was in his bath, the valet whom Prince Eddy had assigned as his personal servant came to tell him that the Queen had arrived and had asked for him to be presented to her. Scrambling into his clothes he hurried downstairs and was ushered into the presence of the remarkably tiny old lady in black. Accustomed to bellowing to Princess Alexandra, the giant Fripp automatically raised his voice to the Queen.

'I am not deaf,' said Queen Victoria sharply.

That established, the two 'chatted for a long time, chiefly about water-colour art and about the Duke of Clarence's health'.[34]

In spite of the stories about Prince Eddy's 'dissipations', of which one imagines Queen Victoria did not know the precise nature, she remained very fond of her grandson. His good points were those which she especially prized: politeness, attentiveness, tranquillity. With her, he was always on his best behaviour. Although an ardent theatregoer (a passion which he shared with his new friend, Alfred Fripp) the Prince never complained about the 'tiresome theatricals' – those amateur productions – which the Queen obliged her family to sit through. 'It is extraordinary how pleased Grandmama is with such small things,' he wrote to Prince George in February 1891, 'for she is quite childish in some ways about them. It was the same thing with the *tableaux* in Scotland this autumn. But I suppose it is because she has no other amusement, that she takes such interest and pleasure in these performances.'[35]

'There!' the Queen would exclaim at some obvious twist in the plot of one of these amateurishly acted productions, 'you didn't expect *that* did you?'[36]

In the Queen's Journal for that autumn of 1890 there is a charming vignette of an evening at Balmoral. 'After dinner', she noted, 'the other ladies and gentlemen joined us in the Drawing Room and we pushed the furniture back and had a nice little impromptu dance, Curtis's band being so *entraînant*. We had a quadrille, in which I danced with Eddy!! It did quite well, then followed some waltzes and polkas.'[37]

She had loved Prince Eddy, the heartbroken old Queen said after his death, 'like a son'; and his devotion to her 'was as great as that of a son'.[38]

Young Dr Fripp was again presented to the Queen the following summer, when he attended a garden party at Marlborough House. For his friendship with Prince Eddy had outlasted – if perhaps on a less intense level – 'those wonderful weeks' spent together in Scotland. Back in London the two young men would lunch or dine together, go for long walks through the gaslit streets or the leafy parks, visit the theatre or take Turkish baths. The Marlborough House garden party was made what Fripp calls 'even more memorable' by the fact that Prince Eddy drew him into the house to give him a souvenir of their friendship: it was 'a black pearl pin' which he cherished for the rest of his life.[39]

The fact that Queen Victoria had questioned Alfred Fripp about her grandson's health is significant. For although the Prince had apparently been cured of that 'sharpish attack of fever' at Scarborough, his family remained concerned. The Prince had never been robust (he already suffered from, among other things, gout) and his illness at Scarborough had caused considerable alarm. Royal illnesses tend to be kept secret; it would never do for the public to discover that the Heir Presumptive was anything other than strong and healthy. This is why Fripp had warned his parents not to mention Prince Eddy's indisposition.

But, inevitably, word leaked out. Alfred Fripp had hardly arrived in Scotland before the correspondent of a London newspaper reported that 'There is a young doctor at the Fife Arms, named Fripp, who goes over to Mar Lodge once or twice a day ostensibly to play lawn tennis with Prince Albert Victor. The real fact, however, is that he is here at the instance of a well-known Court Surgeon, and is in constant attendance on HRH who, driving through to Sir James Mackenzie's funeral, certainly looked very ill.'[40]

This was not strictly true. Fripp had been invited to Scotland as a friend and not a doctor; there was no shortage of doctors in attendance on the royal family. Nevertheless, the Prince's relations were ready to make use of the friendship to check up on his condition. From Homburg, in August 1890, the Prince of Wales wrote to Sir Dighton Probyn, who had travelled up from Sandringham to Scarborough to see the ailing Prince Eddy. 'So you had a long conversation with Mr Fripp about my son,' wrote the Prince, 'and I am glad he told you his candid opinion about his health, which I regret to hear is not satisfactory, and the future will have to be considered very carefully ... I want you to write and tell Dr Fripp to ask to have an interview with the Princess, and tell her candidly what he has said you, so that she may know how matters are, which are far more serious than she has any idea of.'[41]

Probyn promptly wrote to Fripp, by now with Prince Eddy at Mar Lodge, quoting the Prince of Wales's letter. 'I am sure', added Probyn, 'it is best that the Parents should know exactly what you think about their son. Hide nothing from the Princess. The young Prince may be improving. I hope he is, but what we want, and you, I am sure, as much as anybody, is a thorough and permanent restoration to health, no mere tinkering up for a few years, but a lasting cure. The gout and *every other ailment must be completely eradicated* from his system, and until that is done, the young Prince must be prepared to submit to any system of dieting or what he may think discomfort ordered by his medical advisers.'[42]

When finally, at Abergeldie, the Prince of Wales and Fripp met face to face, the Prince lost no time in tackling the doctor about his son's health. 'He knew all about Prince Eddy and his illness and progress,' reported Fripp to his parents, 'but he extracted a detailed account from me, questioned me on every point, said he was very pleased with the way the Prince had got on and with the good control I had over him ...'[43]

But for what ailment, exactly, had Fripp been treating his patient during those three weeks at the Royal Hotel, Scarborough? What had been the nature of that 'sharpish attack of fever'? Probyn's underlining of the phrase *'every other ailment must be completely eradicated'* gives one clue. A prescription found among Fripp's papers after his death gives another: Prince Eddy was suffering from a gonorrhoeal infection. Whether this had been contracted from vaginal or anal sex there is no indication.

14. THE DEATH AND THE LEGEND

His series of matrimonial flurries over, Prince Eddy resumed his unsatisfactory way of life: his half-hearted military career and those public duties for which he showed neither taste nor talent. 'I would chuck it all up for five thousand a year,' he once admitted to a Cambridge friend.[1] He also resumed – or rather, continued – his far more pleasurable activities: his sexual adventuring. Indeed, so outrageous, so reckless was the Prince's behaviour that, by the summer of 1891, the Prince of Wales decided that his son must again be sent out of the country. That July the Prince of Wales wrote to Queen Victoria to say that he thought Prince Eddy should be despatched on a prolonged tour of the colonies. Not mentioning his real reason for wanting to get his son out of England, the Prince referred grandiloquently to Prince Eddy being taught to 'take an interest and appreciate the importance which our great Colonies are in connection with the great Empire over which you rule'.[2]

Queen Victoria was not impressed. Although she agreed that Prince Eddy should travel, she could not agree that it should be to the colonies. Continental Europe was where he should be sent. 'He ought to be able to take his place amongst all the European Princes and *how can he*, if he knows nothing of European courts and countries?' she argued. Both he and his brother George, although charming boys, were far too English; their only visits had been to English-speaking dependencies. 'These colonies offer no opportunities for the cultivation of art or of any historical interest whatever ... You know yourself, who are so fond of going abroad, how it enlarges one's views and rubs off that angular insular view of things which is not good for a Prince.'[3]

To this eminently sensible letter, the Prince of Wales had to admit that 'the real reason why we thought visits to certain colonies were desirable was because the voyages would be longer.'[4] It is difficult, he went on to say, 'to explain to you the reasons why we do not consider it desirable for him to make lengthened stays in foreign capitals'.[5]

But the Queen knew – or imagined she knew – exactly what these reasons were. There were just as many 'designing pretty women in the colonies' as anywhere else, she argued; Prince Eddy, she repeated, would acquire more polish by visiting the courts of Europe.[6]

As usual the Prime Minister, the long-suffering Lord Salisbury, was drawn into the argument. The Prince of Wales, wrote Sir Francis Knollys to Lord Salisbury's private secretary, 'dare not tell [the Queen] his real reason for sending Prince Eddy away, which is intended as a *punishment*, and as a means of keeping him out of harm's way; and I am afraid that neither of those objects would be attained by simply travelling about Europe.'[7]

But why was it so important for Prince Eddy to be kept away from the capitals of Europe? And what was he being punished *for*? Surely not for womanizing? In the society in which the Prince moved, there would have been nothing unusual or shocking about a young unmarried man consorting with prostitutes, mistresses or even married women. Such behaviour would have been considered perfectly acceptable, even expected, in royal and aristocratic circles. The Prince of Wales was hardly priggish about such matters; nor was he in any position to criticize. His own behaviour, during this period, was anything but circumspect. In June 1891, he was obliged to give evidence in the famous Baccarat Case: the libel action brought by a guest at a house party against a group of fellow guests – the Prince of Wales chief amongst them – who had accused him of cheating at baccarat. The trial, unmasking what to the public looked like a sybaritic and dissolute way of life, caused a sensation. Queen Victoria was appalled. 'I feel it a terrible humiliation and so do all the people,' she wrote to the Empress Frederick. 'It is very painful and must do his prestige great harm.'[8]

The Prince of Wales's continuing love affair with Daisy Brooke (his 'own adored little Daisy wife') led, in turn, to yet another public humiliation. A pamphlet entitled *Lady River*, which everyone knew meant Lady Brooke, in which Daisy Brooke's various scandalous activities, including her affair with the Prince of Wales, were exposed, was widely distributed in aristocratic circles. A hostess had only to announce a public reading from the pamphlet for her drawing-room to be crowded out. Once again, the personal intervention of Lord Salisbury was needed before the matter could be satisfactorily cleared up.

One can appreciate why the Princess of Wales who, although able to cope with her husband's many infidelities in private, hated being exposed to public humiliation, decided to prolong her stay abroad that autumn. Instead of returning from Denmark to celebrate her husband's fiftieth birthday on 9 November 1891, she went to visit her sister Dagmar, the Tsaritsa Marie Feodorovna, in Russia. Her gesture did not go unnoticed.

Prince Eddy's dissipations must have been in some way exceptional for the Prince of Wales – so racked by his own scandals – to consider sending him away. If Prince Eddy's transgressions were indeed homosexual, he would have had every opportunity for committing them in London. One knows from his few surviving letters that he often met friends from his Cambridge days, particularly his greatest friend Henry Wilson, for little dinners *à deux* in clubs or restaurants. Wilson, who played host to that assortment of young men ('who had', as another member of the circle put it, 'no particular intellectual gifts but did possess certain very definite qualities which were necessary to gain his friendship') at his 'chummery' in Chiswick Mall, would have been in a very good position to shepherd the Prince through London's homosexual underworld. After a good dinner and possibly a balloon of brandy too many, Prince Eddy and a companion would have been able to stroll, unrecognized, along Piccadilly and into Hyde Park where, in the darkness under the great trees, they could have sampled whatever sexual activities were being offered by soliciting guardsmen. Or they could have taken a hansom cab to one of the many *maisons de passe* or even made their way to the Hundred Guineas Club in time for the nightly lights-out after which every conceivable and entirely incognito variety of sexual gratification was on offer.

Only if Prince Eddy were enjoying such reckless and illegal adventures, can one understand why his father was so anxious to keep him out of the courts and capitals of Europe. There were, as Queen Victoria had pointed out, just as many 'designing pretty women in the colonies' but there would not have been, at that time, any active homosexual coteries there. The capitals of Europe, on the other hand, all had well-established homosexual underworlds. In cities like Paris, Berlin, St Petersburg, Vienna and Rome there was a great deal of homosexual activity; it was particularly widespread in all levels of the German and Russian military. There were said to be more soldier prostitutes in the Russian army than in any other. These poorly paid, largely peasant conscripts from the far reaches of the Russian Empire were only too ready to earn a little extra money by buggering or being fellated by some rich, idle, aristocratic fop. How else could they possibly save up enough to get married?

In the end – as Queen Victoria strongly disapproved of the colonial idea and the Prince of Wales felt that a tour of Europe's capitals would be too risky – the problem of Prince Eddy was approached in the conventional fashion. Once again, it was decided that the answer lay in a suitable marriage. 'A good sensible wife with some considerable character is what he needs most,' wrote the despairing Prince of Wales to Queen Victoria, 'but where is she to be found?'[9]

She was to be found in the person of Princess May of Teck.

Princess May was the only daughter of the four children of the Duke and Duchess of Teck. The Tecks were members, albeit fringe members, of the British royal family. The Duke of Teck was the son, by a morganatic marriage, of Duke Alexander of Wurttemberg, while the Duchess of Teck was Queen Victoria's first cousin: like the Queen, the Duchess of Teck (born Princess Mary Adelaide of Cambridge) was a granddaughter of King George III. The Tecks were a somewhat unorthodox couple. The Duke was moody, irascible and obsessed by the fact that, as his mother had not been born royal, there was a morganatic 'taint' in his blood. The Duchess was extravagant, effusive and enormously fat. Two factors overshadowed their lives: a lack of money and a lack, because of the Duke's parentage, of a clearly defined royal status. These factors were seriously affecting the chances of their only daughter, Princess May, making a good marriage. She was regarded as too royal for a non-royal marriage and not royal enough for an important royal match. In the spring of 1891 she turned twenty-four; this was considered late for a princess to be unmarried.

Princess May appears to have inherited none of her parents' failings. On the contrary, life with her cantankerous father and capricious mother had brought out all the stability of her own nature: she was even-tempered and unemotional. Her manner was reserved, even shy, but when one penetrated this façade, she revealed considerable depth of character, surprising self-confidence and a fund of common sense. She was also very good-looking with an excellent figure and a dignified bearing. When set against these solid virtues, the royal family decided that her somewhat equivocal status could be overlooked. For, quite unbeknown to herself or Prince Eddy, Princess May was now chosen as the young man's future wife and, ultimately, Britain's Queen.

In October 1891, Princess May was summoned to Balmoral. Her mother was not invited: Queen Victoria always found the company of the ebullient Duchess of Teck far too exhausting. During the ten days that the Princess spent at Balmoral she impressed the Queen considerably. 'I think she is a superior girl – quiet and reserved *till* you know her well ...' she reported to the Empress Frederick. 'She is the reverse of *oberflächlich* [superficial]. She has no frivolous tastes, has been very carefully brought up and is well informed and always occupied.'[10] Princess May was, she later said, 'a *solid* girl, which we want'.[11]

Whether this was what Prince Eddy wanted was, it seems, neither here nor there. Although the young man was once heard to say that he did not like Princess May very much, Sir Francis Knollys assured Sir Henry Ponsonby that he did not 'anticipate any real opposition on Prince Eddy's part'; if he 'is told he *must* do it – that it is for the good of the country, etc, etc,' then he would. But did Sir Henry suppose that Princess May 'will make any resistance'?[12]

Princess May would not. No more than any other princess did she ever expect to marry for love; marriage was simply regarded as part of the royal vocation. And Princess May was imbued with a particularly strong sense of royal obligation. Brought up to revere the monarchy, to believe that it was one's solemn duty to support it, it would never have occurred to her to turn down this opportunity of serving it in so spectacular a fashion. For although shy, Princess May had 'a profound conviction of her own capacities';[13] she never doubted that she would be able to sustain her new role. And, with her relatively modest background, the prospect of becoming Queen of England was a heady one. At a stroke those years of comparative obscurity and poverty would be wiped out. Even without her parents' enthusiastic encouragement, Princess May was prepared to marry Prince Eddy. An added incentive was that, although she did not know him very well, she rather liked him. Whatever his faults, there was nothing repulsive about Prince Eddy.

As Knollys had predicted, the young man raised no objections. 'You may, I think, make your mind quite easy about Eddy ...' wrote the Prince of Wales to Queen Victoria on 3 December 1891, 'he has made up his mind to propose to May.'[14]

The proposal took place that very evening. In the course of a ball at Luton Hoo, home of the Danish Minister at the Court of St James's, Prince Eddy led Princess May into an overfurnished little boudoir and asked her to marry him. 'Of course', noted the Princess in her diary that evening, 'I said yes.'[15] So elated, in fact, was Princess May by the proposal that, later that evening, forgetting her habitual reserve, she lifted her skirts a fraction and, in full view of her fellow female guests, danced about the room.

Two days later, after the couple had had their photographs taken, Prince Eddy left Luton Hoo for London and Windsor, to make an official announcement of his engagement to his parents and to seek the sanction of Queen Victoria. The Queen professed herself delighted and, in a letter thanking the Archbishop of Canterbury for his congratulations, blithely assured him that 'the young people will set an example of a steady, quiet life which, alas, is not the fashion these days.'[16]

In her letter to Princess May, Queen Victoria sounded a very necessary note of caution. 'Marriage is the *most* important step which can be taken and should not be looked upon lightly or as *all roses*,' she warned. 'The trials of life in fact *begin* with marriage ...'[17] Wisely, she advised a short engagement. She realized that the better Princess May came to know Prince Eddy, the more aware she would become of his curious personality. Accordingly, the wedding date was set for 27 February 1892, just over two and a half months after the announcement of the engagement.

But even this, apparently, was not soon enough. Within days of the announcement, Princess May was having second thoughts. They were not about her own abilities but about the desirability of being married to Prince Eddy. Matters were not helped by the Prince of Wales always asking her to 'keep Eddy up to the mark', 'see that Eddy does this, May' or 'May, please do see that Eddy does that'. In mounting alarm the Princess appealed to her mother. 'Do you think I can *really* take this on, Mama?' she once asked. The Duchess of Teck's answer was characteristically robust. 'Of course you can, May.' Had she herself not 'taken on' the notoriously difficult Duke of Teck?[18]

Prince Eddy's attitude to the business is difficult to gauge. His letter of thanks to his aunt, Princess Louise and her husband, the sexually ambivalent Marquess of Lorne, was hardly that of an ardent, recently affianced young man. 'I wonder if you were surprised when you saw that I was engaged?' he wrote. 'I daresay you were, for I must say I made up my mind rather suddenly, which I think however was the best thing after all, and it is really time that I thought of getting married, if I ever am to be. Anyway, it is now settled at last, and I think I have done well in my choice, for I feel certain May will make an excellent wife, and you may be certain that I shall do my best to make her a good husband ...' He signed himself 'your affectionate old nephew Eddy'.[19]

There was nothing tepid about the Duchess of Teck's attitude. She was ecstatic. 'Aunt May Teck will be in the 7th heaven,' wrote the Empress Frederick to one of her daughters; 'for years and years it has been her ardent wish, and she has thought of nothing else. What a marriage, and what a position for her daughter!'[20]

At White Lodge, the Tecks' home in Richmond Park, the elephantine Duchess was indeed in 'the 7th heaven'. While admitting to a close friend that Prince Eddy was 'naturally timid' and prone to underestimate his abilities, the Duchess closed her mind to the other possible disadvantages of the match. A worldly and well-informed woman, she would almost certainly have heard the rumours of – if nothing else – Prince Eddy's alleged involvement in the Cleveland Street scandal. She would have regarded any such involvement as most Victorians would have regarded it: sex between men was simply another manifestation of male lust, a sign of a jaded sexual appetite. Marriage would soon put a stop to that nonsense and, if it did not, it would be one of the prices to be paid for a brilliant match.

Through rooms awash with letters, telegrams, fabrics, flowers and the profusion of her daughter's trousseau, the Duchess of Teck moved in a whirl of pleasurable activity. 'I am so happy', she once exclaimed, 'that I am afraid.'[21]

On 4 January 1892, almost exactly a month after Prince Eddy had proposed, he accompanied the rest of his family from London to Sandringham where his twenty-eighth birthday was to be celebrated, on 8 January. With the party travelled Princess May and her parents. The sprawling Sandringham House, never the warmest of places in winter, made a particularly inappropriate setting for a house party decimated by illness: Prince Eddy's brother, Prince George, was recovering from a dangerous attack of typhoid fever; five members of the household, including the Prince's sister, Princess Victoria, and his equerry, Captain Holford, had fallen victim to the influenza epidemic that was sweeping the country; the Princess of Wales and Princess May had heavy colds. The entire party were taking doses of quinine, as a precautionary measure.

On the day before his birthday, Prince Eddy felt unwell while out shooting. He was persuaded to go back to the house where Prince George took his temperature and sent him up to bed. Prince Eddy's bedroom, where the drama of the next few days was to be played out, was a surprisingly small one for the man who was destined to be King of England: by spreading out his arm as he lay in bed, the Prince could touch the mantelpiece on the opposite wall. On the following day – Prince Eddy's birthday – it was realized that he, too, had influenza. In spite of this, he managed to make his way downstairs to look at his presents. But he was unable to attend the birthday dinner that evening and so missed the typical Sandringham after-dinner entertainment provided by a ventriloquist and a banjo player. 'Poor Eddy got influenza, cannot dine, so tiresome,' telegraphed Princess Alexandra airily to Queen Victoria.[22]

On 9 January Prince George insisted that Dr Laking, Physician-in-Ordinary to the Prince of Wales, be sent for to assist the local medical attendant, Dr Manby. Laking diagnosed incipient pneumonia as well as influenza and telegraphed for the specialist, Dr Broadbent. Prince Eddy had never been very strong and, during the following six days, his condition gradually deteriorated. Sometimes he lay quite still while his devoted mother, who almost never left his side, fanned his face and wiped his brow; at other times he railed deliriously, shouting about his regiment, his brother officers and Lord Salisbury. As the doctors had insisted that only his parents be allowed into the sickroom, the rest of the family, including Princess May and her parents, crowded into the little sitting-room next door. But on 13 January, when it was clear that he was dying, his brother and sisters, and Princess May, were given permission to come into the room.

'All we could hear were the sounds of terrible agony in his throat and chest and our own sobs,' said Princess Alexandra afterwards. For seven long, harrowing hours the watchers sat by the bedside until, at half-past nine on the morning of 14 January 1892, he began murmuring, over and over again, 'Who is that? Who is that?'[23] A few minutes later, he died.

The Prince and Princess of Wales were desolate. Oliver Montagu, Princess Alexandra's faithful admirer, who had done so much to keep Prince Eddy's name out of the Cleveland Street scandal, a mere two years before, came hurrying to Sandringham. 'The Prince broke down terribly at our first meeting,' he reported to a friend, 'as did also the poor Princess, but they got calmer after and took me to see the poor boy three different times before I left again. He looked quite peaceful and calm.'[24]

For a while, their shared sorrow brought husband and wife closer together. On a booklet containing the sermon preached at Sandringham Church on the Sunday after Prince Eddy's funeral, the Prince of Wales wrote the inscription, 'To my dearest wife, in remembrance of our beloved Eddy, who was taken from us. "He is not dead but sleepeth." From her devoted but heart-broken husband, Bertie.'[25]

Once Prince Eddy's body had been put in its coffin and removed to Sandringham Church, the little room in which he had died was preserved as a shrine to his memory. A Union flag was draped over the bed and on his dressing-table were laid out, just as he had left them, his wristwatch, brushes, comb and soap dish. For many years afterwards, a fire was kept burning in the grate. On to the royal family's pew in Sandringham Church was affixed a little brass plate which read, 'This place was occupied for 28 years by my darling Eddy, next to his ever loving and sorrowing mother.'[26]

The Princess of Wales had wanted her son to be buried at her beloved Sandringham and Queen Victoria was inclined to grant her wish but the Prince of Wales, conscious of his son's status as the Heir Presumptive, insisted that he be given an official funeral in St George's Chapel at Windsor. On the morning of 20 January the coffin was taken on a gun-carriage from Sandringham Church to Wolverton station and from there by train to Windsor. Even on this solemn occasion things did not go smoothly for poor Prince Eddy. The hurriedly printed invitation cards gave the time of the funeral as 3 o'clock in the morning and had to be altered by hand to 'afternoon'. And, at the end of the service, the Prince's aunts, Princesses Helena, Louise and Beatrice, whom the Princess of Wales had not wanted to attend, found themselves unable to open the door of their pew. Nothing would convince them that it had merely jammed; they felt sure that they had been purposely locked in.

Perhaps the most poignant moment during the funeral service came when the Duke of Teck handed the Prince of Wales a replica of Princess May's bridal bouquet of orange blossom which was then laid on the coffin. Not unnaturally, in the mind of the general public, the most vivid image was that of the heartbroken bride-to-be standing beside the coffin of her beloved prince, their dreams of marital bliss cruelly shattered by fate. Queen Victoria's appreciation of the situation was more realistic. 'May never really loved poor Eddy,' she commented briskly.[27]

One would have thought, from the tone of the sermons and obituaries, that Prince Eddy had been a saint. Fulsome tributes were paid to his manliness, his devotion to duty, even to his high moral standards. But one or two proved less obsequious. The *Illustrated London News* admitted that 'he had no great intellectual gifts; he was not a scholar; he was not a conversationalist.' He did, however, show 'a very strong affection for his home and his mother'.[28] The editorial in *Reynolds Newspaper* was harsher. 'For the poor young man who has just died', it declared, 'we have nothing but pity. Weak physically, not strong mentally, having seemingly no interest whatever in life, there was a certain element of the tragic in that curious and cruel constitution of Society which placed him in a position for which he had no aptitude and no love ...'

There was little doubt, continued the editorial, that the Prince would have abdicated his rights to the throne 'had he not been restrained by his relatives and by those who find it to their advantage to pretend that a monarchy is the ideal form of government.

'Nothing can stay the advancing march of democracy. The extinction of the English monarchial system is a mere question of time. It may end with the Queen or her possible successor. A good deal will depend on the character of the Heir Presumptive to the throne ...'[29]

If *Reynolds Newspaper* was wrong about some things, it was right about a great deal depending on the new Heir Presumptive, Prince George. Fortunately for the monarchy, his character was very different from that of his late brother. It was difficult to escape the notion that the greatest contribution Prince Eddy made to the throne was in dying.

Although the twenty-six-year-old Prince George was only a few degrees more intelligent, articulate and imaginative than his late brother, he was an altogether more suitable candidate. Those years in the Navy had encouraged his particular strengths: his diligence, his conscientiousness, his dependability. Of Prince Eddy's apathy and waywardness, Prince George had no trace. And, in inheriting his brother's position, Prince George also inherited his fiancée. After a decent interval, Prince George became engaged to Princess May; they were married eighteen months after Prince Eddy's death. According to Dr Manby, who attended Prince Eddy during his last days, Prince George and Princess May began falling in love at the very time that Prince Eddy lay dying. 'When attending the Duke of Clarence in his bedroom that fatal time,' claimed Dr Manby's daughter many years later, 'he could see, out of the window, Princess May and Prince George pacing the gardens hand in hand.'[30] The allegation is difficult to believe. Would two such reticent people, at that heart-rending time, have allowed themselves to be seen – not only by Dr Manby but by the entire company, including the Prince and Princess of Wales – in such a compromising position? Their shared concern for the dying Prince Eddy may well have drawn the couple together but the engagement of Princess May to Prince George seems to have been no more of a love match than her previous engagement had been. On the other hand, the two of them suited each other very well. They shared, among other things, an iron sense of duty. In later years, as King George V and Queen Mary, they developed into a dedicated and impressive royal couple.

Except by his immediate family, Prince Eddy was quickly forgotten. Any chance of his being remembered, or at least more fully understood, was foiled by the deliberate destruction of all important documentation concerning his life. In his will, Prince Eddy's father, King Edward VII, directed that all his own private and personal correspondence, including letters to, from and concerning the members of his family, should be destroyed. Already the King's sister, Princess Beatrice, had burned, or censored by transcription, large portions of Queen Victoria's diary. This act of vandalism was augmented by Edward VII's destruction of many of Queen Victoria's private letters concerning her family. When Queen Alexandra died in 1925, her instructions that all her private papers should be likewise burned were only too faithfully carried out by her confidante and friend, Charlotte Knollys, sister of that great repository of royal secrets, Sir Francis, afterwards Lord Knollys. In this wholesale conflagration, all but the most innocuous papers concerning Prince Eddy were lost; his file, as blandly expressed by the Royal Archives, 'has not survived'.

In most biographies of Queen Victoria and her family, Prince Eddy featured as an ill-defined figure. He was usually presented as a dissipated simpleton, as a slow-witted but otherwise conventional young rake. He was often described in terms of cliché: one writer claimed that he lived for 'wine, women and song', another that he had 'an eye for a prettily turned ankle', a third that he 'could hear the rustle of a pair of silk knickers four rooms away'. Any possibility that he might have been homosexual was either not mentioned or dismissed out of hand. The concept, apparently, was too ghastly to contemplate. The fact that the Prince professed himself to be in love with Princess Hélène d'Orléans and Lady Sybil St Claire Erskine was naïvely regarded as proof that he could not possibly have had sex with men. The idea that, homosexual or not, he might have visited the male brothel in Cleveland Street, in the same way that the reputedly heterosexual Lord Euston visited it, was dismissed as nonsensical.

But as the years went by, and his contemporaries gradually died off, so did the balance tip the other way. Theories about Prince Eddy's private life became progressively more outlandish. The thinly veiled claim, made by Dr T.E.A. Stowell in 1970, that he had been Jack the Ripper, unleashed a torrent of ill-informed speculation. Stories of his involvement in the Ripper murders, his secret marriage, his rampant homosexuality were suddenly presented as fact and widely believed. The most bizarre concerned his death. In spite of all written evidence to the contrary, it was claimed that he did not die of pneumonia. One theory was that he had been poisoned. In order that the succession pass to his more suitable brother and so shore up a collapsing dynasty, Prince Eddy had to be eliminated. Why else, it was argued, had his fingernails turned so suspiciously blue as he lay dying? Others claimed that he had been killed by increasingly heavy doses of morphine; that he had, in short, been put to permanent sleep. Several insist that he had syphilis and that he had died, totally insane, from syphilitic softening of the brain. For the last three years of his life, ever since the Ripper murders, he had been kept under strict medical control, in a permanently drugged state.

Frank Spiering, author of *Prince Jack: the True Story of Jack the Ripper*, alleges that the Prince did not die at Sandringham at all. He claims that Dr Stowell was assured by the head gardener at Sandringham that Prince Eddy had not died during the long period that he had been working in the gardens of the house. More than one biographer asserts that the Prince had died, a virtual prisoner, in a sanatorium or lunatic asylum in the south of England.

Then there is the theory that he did not die in 1892 at all but lived on – as a recluse – for many decades. Exactly why, or how, a vast body of people ranging from Queen Victoria to the humblest servant successfully kept the matter quiet is never made clear. One account has him living on the Osborne estate, quite mad, until 1930. In *The Ripper and the Royals* that ineffable pair, Joseph Sickert and Melvyn Fairclough, present the wildest theory of all. It is that Prince Eddy's death in 1892 was faked and that he was held captive for the following forty years.

By November 1891, they tell us, the Prince of Wales, after consultation with those Masonic conspirators who had been responsible for the Jack the Ripper murders, had decided that Prince Eddy must be removed from the line of succession. For one thing, his brother Prince George would make a more suitable King; for another, Prince Eddy's accession to the throne would almost certainly uncover the truth about his secret marriage to the Roman Catholic, Annie Crook. So his death must be faked and he imprisoned. With this in mind, the Prince of Wales despatched his son to Balmoral late in November 1891. He was to remain there until such time as his fake death could be organized and his future place of imprisonment decided upon.

But this, apparently, did not satisfy the mastermind behind the whole Masonic conspiracy, Lord Randolph Churchill. The faking of Prince Eddy's death would not solve the problem: the Prince must actually die. Lord Randolph thereupon sent two henchmen to Balmoral, ostensibly to deliver furniture but in reality to do away with Prince Eddy. Their gruesome task was made considerably easier by the fact that they happened to come across the Prince poised on a particularly precipitous rocky outcrop from which he was – quite alone – busily painting a Highland landscape. All they had to do was to push him over. Having done the deed, they hurried back to London. But the Prince had not been killed. Either he was discovered by a member of the staff or else he managed to make his own way back to the castle. If his body had not been broken, however, his spirit had. From that time on, the terrified Prince Eddy was ready to comply with any plans for his 'disappearance'.

Sickert and Fairclough – in common with those writers who claim that the Prince's last months were spent in a lunatic asylum – blithely ignore the fact that it was during this very period that Prince Eddy was at his most visible. Far from being hidden at Balmoral or confined to a sanatorium in the south of England, he was involved in all the public appearances that followed his engagement to Princess May of Teck on 3 December 1891. There was hardly a day between the announcement of his engagement and his final visit to Sandringham exactly a month later on which Prince Eddy was not attending some private or public function.

Undeterred by such considerations, Sickert and Fairclough – with information allegedly provided by the ubiquitous Inspector Abberline – move on to disclose Prince Eddy's place of captivity. As busy Balmoral was clearly out of the question, the royal family had to look elsewhere. They struck a bargain with yet another of those high-ranking Freemasons, this time the 13th Earl of Strathmore. If the Earl would agree to hide Prince Eddy in his remote Scottish home, Glamis Castle, they would grant his family a unique honour: one of his female descendants would be allowed to marry a future King of England. To this the delighted Earl of Strathmore agreed. Prince Eddy was handed over. The royal family kept its promise. Some thirty years later the youngest daughter of the 14th Earl of Strathmore, Lady Elizabeth Bowes-Lyon, was married to the future King George VI. Fairclough gamely overcomes the awkwardness of the fact that, at the time of the marriage, the bridegroom was not regarded as the future King, by claiming that his elder brother, Edward, Prince of Wales, had no intention of ever ascending the throne. Edward VIII's love affair with Mrs Wallis Warfield Simpson was merely the means by which he was able to implement his long-held determination to abdicate.

Prince Eddy's place of imprisonment secured, his death, at Sandringham on 14 January 1892, was duly faked. In fact, says Melvyn Fairclough, the Prince was not even at Sandringham that day: he was, as he had been since November, at Balmoral. Whether or not a real body was put into the coffin, the author does not say. A wing of Glamis Castle, already famous for one monster – a hairy, egg-shaped creature who apparently lived for over a century – now became the home of a much less frightening captive. For over forty years, until his death in 1933, Prince Eddy remained at Glamis. His days were spent painting landscapes. As proof of this theory, Joseph Sickert reproduces a photograph of a man, palette in one hand and paintbrush in the other, sitting beside an easel. His strongest reason for believing this to be a photograph of Prince Eddy is because the sitter happens to be sporting a lot of cuff; Prince Eddy, Fairclough reminds us triumphantly, was always known as 'Collar and Cuffs'. The two men ignore the uncomfortable evidence that Prince Eddy, whose hair was seriously thinning by the time of his death, is here pictured, in his late forties, with a full head of lustrous silver hair.

How this massive deception of the faked death and forty-year-long imprisonment – involving the royal family, the royal households, the royal doctors, the Bowes-Lyon family and the staffs at Sandringham House, Balmoral Castle and Glamis Castle – could possibly have been kept secret, is not revealed. Fiction, in this case, is a great deal stranger than fact.

Yet when all these fanciful stories about the life and death of Prince Eddy have been discounted, one is still left with an enigma. He remains an odd, mysterious figure. That dandified prince with his buoyant moustache and hooded eyes exudes a strangely unfathomable aura. That he was lethargic, diffident and vacuous is well attested but about his more intimate life there is an intriguing air of mystery. Possibly bisexual, probably homosexual, almost certainly implicated in the Cleveland Street scandal, Prince Eddy remains a supreme conundrum of the late Victorian era.

$\mathcal{E}$PILOGUE
THE WARRIOR'S TOMB

Of all the monuments and statues, effigies and bas-reliefs to the dead kings, queens, princes and princesses that crowd St George's Chapel at Windsor, none is more flamboyant than the tomb of Prince Albert Victor, Duke of Clarence and Avondale. The least known amongst them, Prince Eddy has been honoured with the most impressive memorial. As an example of the misrepresentation necessary to enhance and glorify the often puny royal image, it could hardly be bettered. The tomb is the work of the leading sculptor of the *fin de siècle*, Sir Alfred Gilbert. Conceived soon after the Prince's death in 1892, it was not completed until 1926. Although Gilbert's statue of Eros in Piccadilly Circus is probably his best-known work, the Duke of Clarence's tomb is undoubtedly his masterpiece.

Situated in the heart of the Albert Memorial Chapel, the Victorian annex to St George's Chapel, the monument is an example of that most voluptuous of styles, *L'Art Nouveau*. Quite unintentionally, the sinuous lines and seductive fluidity exactly capture the spirit of the secret world in which the Prince is said to have moved: the world of the Yellow Book, the Green Carnation, the Gilded Lily, the Mauve Decade. It is a masterly tribute to the Age of Decadence.

There is, however, no hint of decadence in the actual effigy of the dead Prince. The recumbent marble figure, depicted in Hussar uniform and stretched out on a swirling cloak, is one of high Victorian medi-evalism. It is the effigy of a brave and blameless knight. Prince Eddy is presented as the royal family, with its instinct for self-preservation, would have wanted him to be presented. The prince born to be king lies like some sleeping warrior: noble, honourable and unsullied, the *beau idéal* of virtuous manhood.

NOTES

The files of the Director of Public Prosecutions at the Public Record Office, Chancery Lane, contain the official papers on the Cleveland Street Case, comprising police reports and statements, correspondence, legal opinions, transcripts of court proceedings, indictments, sworn informations and newspaper cuttings. These papers are filed in seven boxes, numbered DPP/95/1–7. The Home Office reports on the case are housed in the Public Record Office, Kew, in two boxes: HO 144/477/X24427 and X24427a. The correspondence of the 2nd Viscount Esher on the Cleveland Street affair is bound up in a volume labelled 'The Case of Lord Arthur Somerset' and is kept among the Esher Papers in the Archives Centre, Churchill College, Cambridge. These letters, with relevant dates, are referred to below under the heading CLAS.

PROLOGUE: THE MYSTERY PRINCE
1. Longford, *Victoria R. I.*, p. 512.
2. *The Times*, 10 Nov. 1970.
3. Ibid., 4 Nov. 1970.
4. Ibid., 9 Nov. 1970.
5. Ibid., 14 Nov. 1970.
6. Queen's Librarian to the author.

CHAPTER ONE: 'THE LAD THAT'S LETTERED GPO'

1. Pope-Hennessy, *Queen Mary*, p. 124.
2. d'Arch Smith, *Love in Earnest*, p. 29.
3. Nicholson, *Garland*, p. 27.
4. Beardsley, *Letters*, p. 58.
5. HO 144/477/X24427.
6. *Vanity Fair*, 19 Nov. 1887.
7. Davenport-Hines, *Sex*, p. 79.
8. Hibbert, *Edward VII*, p. 73.
9. Croft-Cooke, *Feasting*, p. 51.
10. Hyde, *Other Love*, p. 129.
11. Bell, *Davidson*, pp. 114–15.
12. Hyde, *Cleveland Street*, p. 15.
13. O'Brien, *Memories*, p. 6.
14. Hyde, *Cleveland Street*, p. 17.

CHAPTER TWO: 'APPLES OF SODOM'

1. Croft-Cooke, *Feasting*, p. 236.
2. Magnus, *Kitchener*, p. 235.
3. Weeks, *Coming Out*, p. 41.
4. Symonds, *Letters*, p. 808.
5. Croft-Cooke, *Feasting*, p. 135.
6. Weeks, *Coming Out*, pp. 40–1.
7. Croft-Cooke, *Feasting*, p. 157.
8. Ibid., p. 125.
9. Ibid., p. 173.
10. Hyde, *Oscar Wilde*, p. 217.
11. Davenport-Hines, *Sex*, p. 47.
12. Hyde, *Other Love*, pp. 205–6.
13. Saul, *Sins*, Vol. I, pp. 92–6.
14. Ibid., Vol. II, p. 40.
15. Mayne, *Intersexes*, p. 220.
16. David Trent to the author.

17. Saul, *Sins*, Vol. I, p. 87.
18. Ibid.
19. Ibid., p. 89.
20. Leeves, *Diary*, p. 101.
21. Ibid., p. 108.
22. Ibid., p. 103.
23. Ibid., p. 109.
24. Hyde, *Other Love*, p. 94.
25. Ellmann, *Oscar Wilde*, p. 258.
26. Mayne, *Intersexes*, p. 427.
27. Saul, *Sins*, Vol. II, pp. 53–5.
28. Ibid.
29. Ibid., p. 56.
30. Ibid.
31. Ibid., Vol. I, pp. 8–19.
32. Ibid., p. 38.
33. Ibid., Vol. II, p. 34.
34. Ibid., p. 37.
35. Ibid., Vol. I, p. 96.
36. DPP 1/95/1.

CHAPTER THREE: MOTHERDEAR'S BOY
1. Victoria, *Dearest Mamma*, p. 236.
2. Ibid., p. 30.
3. Ibid., p. 43.
4. Battiscombe, *Alexandra*, p. 70.
5. Victoria, *Dearest Mamma*, p. 236.
6. Ibid., p. 212.
7. Ibid., p. 226.
8. Ibid., p. 278.
9. Ibid., p. 285.
10. Ibid., p. 287.
11. Battiscombe, *Alexandra*, p. 62.
12. Victoria, *Dearest Mamma*, p. 289.

13. Ibid., p. 306.
14. Greville, *Leaves*, Vol. 4, p. 186.
15. Ibid., p. 187.
16. Victoria, *Dearest Mamma*, p. 288.
17. Victoria, *Your Dear Letter*, p. 17.
18. Nicolson, *George V*, p. 4.
19. Battiscombe, *Alexandra*, p. 85.
20. Ibid., p. 121.
21. Cohen, *de Rothschild*, p. 140.
22. Ibid., p. 139.
23. Battiscombe, *Alexandra*, p. 123.
24. Pope-Hennessy, *Queen Mary*, p. 56.
25. Battiscombe, *Alexandra*, p. 122.
26. Vincent, *Duke of Clarence*, p. 25.
27. Arthur, *George V*, p. 31.
28. Battiscombe, *Alexandra*, p. 122.
29. Bullock, *Prince Edward*, p. 47.
30. Cust, *Edward VII*, p. 33.

CHAPTER FOUR: 'A CAREFULLY BROUGHT-UP BOY'
1. Pimlott, *Hugh Dalton*, p. 77.
2. Carpenter, *Days and Dreams*, p. 77.
3. Pimlott, *Hugh Dalton*, p. 71.
4. d'Arch Smith, *Love in Earnest*, p. 192.
5. Gore, *George V*, pp. 58–9.
6. Vincent, *Duke of Clarence*, p. 55.
7. Pimlott, *Hugh Dalton*, p. 70.
8. Ibid., p. 71.
9. Nicolson, *George V*, p. 39.
10. Ibid., pp. 41–2.
11. Benson, *Edward VII*, p. 21.
12. Anstruther, *Browning*, p. 40.
13. Ibid., p. 192.
14. Weeks, *Coming Out*, p. 25.

15. Battiscombe, *Alexandra*, p. 140.
16. Ibid., p. 141.
17. Nicolson, *George V*, p. 41.
18. Battiscombe, *Alexandra*, p. 153.
19. Magnus, *Edward VII*, p. 158.
20. Rose, *George V*, p. 8.
21. *The Lancet*, 27 Aug. 1993.
22. Nicolson, *George V*, pp. 45–6.
23. Langtry, *Days I Knew*, p. 81.
24. *Cape Argus*, 16 Feb. 1881.
25. Dalton, *Voyage*, pp. 551–2.
26. Nicolson, *George V*, p. 55.
27. Magnus, *Edward VII*, p. 169.
28. Nicolson, *George V*, p. 50.
29. Ibid., p. 51.
30. Magnus, *Edward VII*, p. 170.
31. Mayne, *Intersexes*, p. 186.
32. Nicolson, *George V*, p. 58.
33. Ibid., p. 50.
34. Ibid., p. 61.

CHAPTER FIVE: THE STUDENT PRINCE

1. Gore, *George V*, p. 48.
2. Battiscombe, *Alexandra*, p. 163.
3. Ibid., p. 162.
4. Nicolson, *George V*, p. 65.
5. Battiscombe, *Alexandra*, p. 139.
6. Pope-Hennessy, *Queen Mary*, p. 52.
7. Asquith, *Memories*, p. 238.
8. Cust, *Edward VII*, p. 33.
9. Marie of Romania, *Story*, Vol. I, p. 43.
10. Bullock, '*Ich Dien*', p. 44.
11. Battiscombe, *Alexandra*, pp. 163–4.

12. Vincent, *Duke of Clarence*, p. 135.
13. Ibid., p. 137.
14. Ibid., p. 21.
15. Ibid., p. 138.
16. Magnus, *Edward VII*, p. 178.
17. *Granta*, Feb. 1891.
18. Harrison, *Clarence*, p. 164.
19. Vincent, *Duke of Clarence*, p. 145.
20. Ibid., p. 144.
21. Ibid., p. 147.
22. Ibid., p. 145.
23. Anon. ('X'), *Myself*, p. 36.
24. Vincent, *Duke of Clarence*, pp. 152–4.
25. Ibid., p. 157.
26. Anon. ('X'), *Myself*, p. 37.
27. Weeks, *Coming Out*, p. 51.
28. Asquith, *Life and Letters*, 26 Feb. 1897.
29. Howells, *Legacy*, pp. 169, 172.
30. Newsome, *Excursions*, p. 24.
31. Newsome, *Edge of Paradise*, p. 230.
32. Ellmann, *Oscar Wilde*, p. 52.
33. Croft-Cooke, *Feasting*, p. 115.
34. Anstruther, *Browning*, pp. 117–18.
35. Croft-Cooke, *Feasting*, p. 116.
36. Anon. ('X'), *Myself*, p. 37.
37. Anstruther, *Browning*, p. 118.
38. Anon. ('X'), *Myself*, p. 377.
39. MacCarthy, *Portraits*, Browning, p. 172.
40. Anon. ('X'), *Myself*, p. 37.
41. *Punch*, 23 Nov. 1883.
42. Victoria, *Letters*, 2nd Series, Vol. III, p. 592.
43. Vincent, *Duke of Clarence*, p. 163.
44. St Aubyn, *Edward VII*, p. 104.

45. Rose, *George V*, p. 21.
46. Magnus, *Edward VII*, p. 189.
47. Battiscombe, *Alexandra*, p. 168.
48. *Illustrated London News*, 23 Jan. 1892.
49. Vincent, *Duke of Clarence*, pp. 184–5.

CHAPTER SIX: THE CHOCOLATE SOLDIER

1. Pease, *Elections*, p. 84.
2. Vincent, *Duke of Clarence*, p. 188.
3. St Aubyn, *Royal George*, p. 299.
4. Vincent, *Duke of Clarence*, pp. 104–5.
5. St Aubyn, *Royal George*, p. 299.
6. Pope-Hennessy, *Queen Mary*, p. 192.
7. St Aubyn, *Royal George*, p. 239.
8. St Aubyn, *Edward VII*, p. 104.
9. Vincent, *Duke of Clarence*, pp. 19, 20.
10. Pope-Hennessy, *Queen Mary*, p. 193.
11. Pimlott, *Hugh Dalton*, p. 4.
12. Ibid., p. 66.
13. Vincent, *Duke of Clarence*, p. 178.
14. Ibid., p. 184.
15. Bullock, *Prince Edward*, p. 53.
16. Pope-Hennessy, *Queen Mary*, p. 193.
17. St Aubyn, *Royal George*, p. 299.
18. Pope-Hennessy, *Queen Mary*, p. 193.
19. Bullock, *Prince Edward*, p. 53.
20. Pope-Hennessy, *Queen Mary*, p. 191.
21. Fairclough, *Ripper*, p. 17.
22. Ibid., pp. 1–14.
23. Ibid., pp. 101–2.
24. Ibid., p. 3.
25. Ibid., p. 1.
26. Ibid., p. 241.
27. Ibid., p. 119.

CHAPTER SEVEN: ROYAL JACK

1. Rumbelow, *Jack the Ripper*, p. 83.
2. Ibid., pp. 108–9.
3. Ibid., p. 113.
4. Ibid., p. 293.
5. Stowell, *Criminologist*, Nov. 1970.
6. Rumbelow, *Jack the Ripper*, p. 140.
7. Spiering, *Prince Jack*, Foreword.
8. Harris, *Jack the Ripper*, p. 126.
9. Rumbelow, *Jack the Ripper*, pp. 218–19.
10. Ibid.
11. Spiering, *Prince Jack, passim.*
12. Rumbelow, *Jack the Ripper*, p. 219.
13. Ibid.

CHAPTER EIGHT: RIPPING FOR THE PRINCE

1. Bell, *Virginia Woolf*, p. 36.
2. Harrison, *Clarence*, p. 181.
3. Ibid., p. 176.
4. Fairclough, *Ripper*, p. 14.
5. Ibid., p. 8.
6. Ibid., p. 56.
7. Ibid., p. 92.
8. Ibid., p. 88.
9. Ibid., p. 74.
10. Ibid., p. 154.
11. Ibid., p. 236.
12. Ibid., p. 160.
13. Ibid., p. 221.
14. Sitwell, *Essences*, p. 190.
15. Howells, *Legacy*, p. 127.
16. Ibid., pp. 172–3.
17. Ibid., p. 197.
18. Vincent, *Duke of Clarence*, p. 198.

19. Rumbelow, *Jack the Ripper*, p. 19.
20. Howells, *Legacy*, p. 143.
21. Ibid., p. 198.

CHAPTER NINE: KINGS AND QUEENS

1. Magnus, *Edward VII*, p. 219; Battiscombe, *Alexandra*, p. 180.
2. Lees-Milne, *Nicolson*, Vol. II, p. 230.
3. Harrison, *Clarence*, p. 217.
4. Nicolson, *George V*, p. 39; Vincent, *Duke of Clarence*, p. 178.
5. Vincent, *Duke of Clarence*, p. 267.
6. *The Times*, 15 Jan. 1892.
7. Ibid.
8. Crowley, *World's Tragedy*, p. xxvii.
9. Battiscombe, *Alexandra*, p. 185.
10. Bailey, *Homosexuality*, p. 100.
11. Freeman, *William Rufus*, p. 159.
12. Norton, *Mother Clap's*, p. 21.
13. Ibid., p. 22.
14. Burnet, *History*, p. 78.
15. Zee, *William and Mary*, p. 423.
16. Ibid.
17. St Aubyn, *Queen Victoria*, p. 498.
18. Weeks, *Coming Out*, p. 38.
19. Peile, *Candied Peel*, p. 82.
20. Newsome, *Edge of Paradise*, p. 327.
21. *The Times*, 15 Jan. 1892.
22. Sheppard, *Cambridge*, pp. 160–1.
23. St Aubyn, *Edward VII*, p. 105.

CHAPTER TEN: 'MY LORD GOMORRAH'

1. Hyde, *Cleveland Street*, p. 43.
2. *Pall Mall Gazette*, 30 Mar. 1889.
3. DPP 1/95/1.
4. DPP 1/95/4.

5. DPP 1/95/1.
6. *New York Herald*, 22 Dec. 1889.
7. DPP 1/95/4.
8. CLAS, 18 Sept. 1889.
9. DPP 1/95/1.
10. Ibid.
11. CLAS, 20 Sept. 1889.
12. DPP 1/95/5.
13. *North London Press*, 14 Dec. 1889.
14. Hyde, *Cleveland Street*, p. 90.
15. DPP 1/95/1.
16. DPP 1/95/2.
17. Ibid.
18. St Aubyn, *Edward VII*, p. 105.
19. CLAS, 24 Oct. 1889.
20. DPP 1/95/1.
21. Hyde, *Cleveland Street*, pp. 96–7.
22. HO 144/477/X24427.
23. CLAS, 27 Feb. 1890.

CHAPTER ELEVEN: 'THE WHOLE TERRIBLE AFFAIR'

1. *New York Times*, 10 Nov. 1889.
2. Vincent, *Duke of Clarence*, p. 222.
3. Ibid., pp. 233–7.
4. *Truth*, 25 Dec. 1890.
5. *North London Press*, 16 Nov. 1889.
6. O'Connor, *Memoirs*, p. 83.
7. Harris, *Life and Loves*, p. 369.
8. *North London Press*, 23 Nov. 1889.
9. DPP 1/95/4.
10. Ibid.
11. Ibid.
12. *Truth*, 30 Jan. 1890.

CHAPTER TWELVE: 'I NEVER MENTIONED THE BOY'S NAME'

1. *New York Times*, 17 Nov. 1889.
2. CLAS, 9 Nov. 1889.
3. *New York Herald*, 22 Dec. 1889.
4. CLAS, 28 Nov. 1889.
5. Ibid., 20 Mar. 1890.
6. Ibid., 6 Dec. 1889.
7. Ibid., 10 Dec. 1889.
8. Ibid., 21 Oct. 1889.
9. Ibid., 27 Dec. 1889.
10. Ibid., 31 Dec. 1889.
11. Ibid., 10 Dec. 1889.
12. Ibid., 27 Dec. 1889.
13. Ibid., 23 Dec. 1889.
14. Ibid., 13 Dec. 1889.
15. Ibid., 29 Dec. 1889.
16. Ibid., 10 Dec. 1889.
17. Ibid.
18. *Truth*, 2 Jan. 1890.
19. CLAS, 22 Dec. 1889.
20. *Truth*, 2 Jan. 1890.
21. CLAS, 12 May 1890.
22. DPP 1/95/6.
23. Lees-Milne, *Harold Nicolson*, p. 231.
24. Pimlott, *Hugh Dalton*, p. 77.
25. Hatfield Archivist to the author.

CHAPTER THIRTEEN: 'THE GREATEST POSITION THERE IS'

1. Pope-Hennessy, *Queen Mary*, p. 190.
2. Ibid., p. 194.
3. Ibid.
4. *Truth*, 25 May 1890.
5. Pope-Hennessy, *Queen Mary*, p. 189.

6. Ibid., p. 197.
7. Elsberry, *Marie of Romania*, p. 62.
8. Pope-Hennessy, *Queen Mary*, p. 196.
9. Hough, *Louis and Victoria*, p. 149.
10. Pope-Hennessy, *Queen Mary*, p. 197.
11. St Aubyn, *Edward VII*, p. 106.
12. Pope-Hennessy, *Queen Mary*, p. 197.
13. Ibid., p. 199.
14. *The Times*, 16 Jan. 1892.
15. Waddington, *Letters*, p. 274.
16. Pope-Hennessy, *Queen Mary*, pp. 196–7.
17. Ibid., p. 198.
18. Young, *Balfour*, pp. 122–3.
19. Ibid.
20. Magnus, *Edward VII*, p. 221.
21. St Aubyn, *Edward VII*, p. 109.
22. Pope-Hennessy, *Queen Mary*, p. 199.
23. Ibid., p. 200.
24. Roberts, *Fripp*, p. 58.
25. Ibid., p. 27.
26. Ibid., p. 36.
27. Ibid., p. 32.
28. Ibid., p. 33.
29. Ibid., p. 29.
30. Ibid., p. 33.
31. Ibid., p. 39.
32. Ibid., p. 40.
33. Ibid., pp. 48–9.
34. Ibid., p. 47.
35. Pope-Hennessy, *Queen Mary*, p. 206.
36. St Aubyn, *Edward VII*, p. 499.
37. Victoria, *Letters*, 11 Oct. 1890.
38. Bullock, *Prince Edward*, p. 14.

39. Roberts, *Fripp*, p. 57.
40. Ibid., p. 58.
41. Ibid., p. 58.
42. Ibid., p. 59.
43. Ibid., p. 39.

CHAPTER FOURTEEN: THE DEATH AND THE LEGEND
1. *Reynolds Newspaper*, 24 Jan. 1892.
2. Pope-Hennessy, *Queen Mary*, p. 194.
3. Ibid., p. 195.
4. Ibid., p. 193.
5. Ibid., p. 195.
6. Magnus, *Edward VII*, p. 238.
7. Ibid.
8. Ibid., p. 228.
9. Ibid., p. 238.
10. Pope-Hennessy, *Queen Mary*, pp. 207–8.
11. Ibid., p. 214.
12. Magnus, *Edward VII*, p. 239.
13. Pope-Hennessy, *Queen Mary*, p. 211.
14. Ibid., p. 209.
15. Ibid., p. 210.
16. Benson, *As We Were*, p. 194.
17. Pope-Hennessy, *Queen Mary*, p. 215.
18. Ibid., p. 222.
19. Longford, *Darling Loosy*, p. 239.
20. Victoria, *Empress Writes*, p. 212.
21. Waddington, *Letters*, p. 33.
22. Pope-Hennessy, *Queen Mary*, p. 222.
23. Battiscombe, *Alexandra*, pp. 189–90.
24. Hyde, *Cleveland Street*, p. 244.
25. Battiscombe, *Alexandra*, p. 191.

26. Anon., *Notebooks*, p. 212.

27. Pope-Hennessy, *Queen Mary*, p. 227.

28. *Illustrated London News*, 23 Jan. 1892.

29. *Reynolds Newspaper*, 24 Jan. 1892.

30. Pope-Hennessy, *Lonely Business*, p. 226.

Made in the USA
Monee, IL
20 July 2020